US Foreign Policy and Democracy Promotion revises our understanding of the origin
of this great American preoccupation—think Teddy Roosevelt, not Woodrow
Wilson—and recasts conventional wisdom on figures like Harry Truman and Ronald
Reagan. It's an indispensable addition to the literature on democracy promotion.

James Traub, author of The Freedom Agenda: Why America Must
Spread Democracy (Just Not the Way George Bush Did),
Farrar, Straus and Giroux, 2008

For the past century, democracy promotion has been an important aspect of
American foreign policy. This excellent volume shows how specific presidents
from Teddy Roosevelt and Woodrow Wilson to George W. Bush and Barack
Obama have wrestled with this often hotly contested issue. It will be a vital edition
for anyone interested in American foreign policy.

Joseph S. Nye, Harvard University and author of The Future of Power

An extremely refreshing perspective on a subject of long-standing concern ...
American democracy promotion strategies. With a dazzling array of leading scholars
from across the disciplines ... this volume does something that so many others have
failed to: place at the centre of its analysis of US foreign policy the holder of the
world's most powerful office: the President of the United States ... strongly
recommended.

*Professor Inderjeet Parmar, Chair, British International Studies
Association and City University London*

A lot of ink has been spilled on the subject of US democracy promotion, but I am
aware of no other study that tackles it as Cox, Bouchet and Lynch have done here:
by deploying a top notch posse of scholars to examine the phenomenon from the
perspective of every American president from Theodore Roosevelt to Barack
Obama. Framed brilliantly by Tony Smith's sweeping theoretical and historical
introduction, the subsequent chapters yield many novel insights, from TR's surprising contributions to American democracy promotion to Obama's curious
ambivalence. This excellent collection proves how much can be learned about an
important phenomenon simply by examining how leaders have grappled with it in
a variety of challenging contexts.

*William C. Wohlforth, Daniel Webster Professor of Government,
Dartmouth College, USA*

Democracy promotion as an instrument of US foreign policy is a topic which has
generated a prolific literature. But this collection is unique. First because it takes
the subject from its historical roots and covers a huge period of time starting with
Theodore Roosevelt and finishing with Barack Obama. Secondly, because it insists
on something which is quite rare in the whole literature: the practicalities of
democracy promotion and not simply its discourse. Democracy promotion on the
ground is at the core of this original endeavour. The result is impressive. It gives a
very illuminating interpretation on the continuity of us foreign policy in this
domain and confirm the persistent obstacles it faces in spite of some non negligible

achievements, when US interests and values match local expectations. A must read book for students and scholars interested in us foreign policy and more generally on the interaction between values and interests, between principles drawn in Washington and stubborn realities on the ground.

Zaki Laïdi, Director of Research, Sciences PO, France

This is an impressive and valuable book. Instead of the usual polemics about the United States as paragon or hypocrite, this book provides solid analysis of the scope and limits of US democracy promotion. It does so with both historical sweep and contemporary focus, and lines of argument significant for both the scholarly and policy communities. And it holds together well, much more effectively integrated than edited volumes often are.

Bruce W. Jentleson, Duke University, USA

A comprehensive and critical assessment of the complex relationship between American foreign policy and the promotion of democracy around the world. These prominent contributors examine the role of US presidents in promoting democracy, as well as conceptual and institutional questions. A must reading for students, scholars, and policymakers interested in understanding the making of American foreign in the last seven decades and the role of the liberal idea in advancing world order.

Fawaz A. Gerges, Professor of International Relations and director of the
Middle East Centre at the London School of Economics and author of
Obama and the Middle East: The End of America's Moment?

US FOREIGN POLICY AND DEMOCRACY PROMOTION

The promotion of democracy by the United States became highly controversial during the presidency of George W. Bush. The wars in Iraq and Afghanistan were widely perceived as failed attempts at enforced democratization, sufficient that Barack Obama has felt compelled to downplay the rhetoric of democracy and freedom in his foreign policy.

This collection seeks to establish whether a democracy promotion tradition exists, or ever existed, in American foreign policy, and how far Obama and his predecessors conformed to or repudiated it. For more than a century at least, American presidents have been driven by deep historical and ideological forces to conceive US foreign policy in part through the lens of democracy promotion. Debating how far democratic aspirations have been realized in actual foreign policies, this book draws together concise studies from many of the leading academic experts in the field to evaluate whether or not these efforts were successful in promoting democratization abroad. They clash over whether democracy promotion is an appropriate goal of US foreign policy and whether the United States has gained anything from it.

Offering an important contribution to the field, this work is essential reading for all students and scholars of US foreign policy, American politics and international relations.

Michael Cox is Professor of International Relations at the London School of Economics (LSE), where he is Co-Director of LSE IDEAS. He is co-editor of the London School of Economics CWSC journal, *Cold War History*, and editor of the journal *International Politics*.

Timothy J. Lynch is Associate Professor in American Politics at the University of Melbourne.

Nicolas Bouchet is Deputy Editor for Research at Chatham House.

Routledge Studies in US Foreign Policy

Edited by:

INDERJEET PARMAR, CITY UNIVERSITY AND JOHN DUMBRELL,
UNIVERSITY OF DURHAM

This new series sets out to publish high-quality works by leading and emerging scholars critically engaging with American foreign policy. The series welcomes a variety of approaches to the subject and draws on scholarship from international relations, security studies, international political economy, foreign policy analysis and contemporary international history.

Subjects covered include the role of administrations and institutions, the media, think-tanks, ideologues and intellectuals, elites, transnational corporations, public opinion, and pressure groups in shaping foreign policy, American relations with individual nations, with global regions and global institutions and the United States's evolving strategic and military policies.

The series aims to provide a range of books – from individual research monographs and edited collections to textbooks and supplemental reading for scholars, researchers, policy analysts and students.

US FOREIGN POLICY AND DEMOCRACY PROMOTION

From Theodore Roosevelt to Barack Obama

Edited by
Michael Cox, Timothy J. Lynch
and Nicolas Bouchet

 Routledge
Taylor & Francis Group

LONDON AND NEW YORK

First published 2013
by Routledge
2 Park Square, Milton Park, Abingdon, Oxon OX14 4RN

Simultaneously published in the USA and Canada
by Routledge
711 Third Avenue, New York, NY 10017

Routledge is an imprint of the Taylor & Francis Group, an informa business

British Library Cataloguing in Publication Data
A catalogue record for this book is available from the British Library

Library of Congress Cataloging in Publication Data
US foreign policy and democracy promotion / edited by Michael Cox, Timothy
J. Lynch and Nicolas Bouchet.
pages ; cm. -- (Routledge studies in US foreign policy)
Includes bibliographical references and index.
1. New democracies. 2. Democratization--International cooperation. 3. United
States--Foreign relations--20th century. 4. United States--Foreign relations--21st
century. I. Cox, Michael, 1947- II. Lynch, Timothy J., 1969-
III. Bouchet, Nicolas.
JC423.U797 2013
327.1'1--dc23
2012039646

ISBN: 978-0-415-67979-4 (hbk)
ISBN: 978-0-415-67980-0 (pbk)
ISBN: 978-0-203-55037-3 (ebk)

Typeset in Bembo
by Integra Software Services Pvt. Ltd, Pondicherry, India

Printed and bound in Great Britain by MPG Printgroup

CONTENTS

CONTRIBUTORS

Nicolas Bouchet received a Ph.D. in international relations from the University of London for research into the use of democracy promotion as an instrument of foreign policy during the Clinton presidency, and is Deputy Editor for Research at Chatham House. He is the author of 'Barack Obama's Democracy Promotion at Midterm', *The International Journal of Human Rights* (May 2011) and 'The Democracy Tradition in US Foreign Policy and the Obama presidency', *International Affairs* (January 2013), as well as articles on democracy promotion for *The Guardian* and *The World Today*.

Thomas Carothers is vice president for studies at the Carnegie Endowment for International Peace and director of the Endowment's Democracy and Rule of Law Program. Widely recognized as one of the leading international authorities on democracy promotion, he has worked on democracy assistance projects for many public and private organizations and has carried out extensive field research on democracy-related issues. He is the author or editor of more than ten books and reports on democracy and rule of law promotion, including 'Democracy Policy under Obama: Revitalization or Retreat?' (Carnegie, 2012) and 'U.S. Democracy Promotion During and After Bush' (Carnegie, 2007) as well as many articles in prominent journals and newspapers. He is a graduate of Harvard Law School, the London School of Economics and Harvard College.

Michael Cox holds a Chair in International Relations at the London School of Economics where he is also Co-Director of the fourth world-ranked university foreign policy think-tank – IDEAS. Professor Cox has held several senior positions in the profession including the Chair of the European Consortium for Political Research (ECPR). He is the editor of *International Politics*. He is also the author and editor of over 25 books including *American Democracy Promotion* (2000); *E.H.Carr: The Twenty Years' Crisis* (2001); *Global 1989: Continuity and Change in World Politics* (2010), *Soft Power and US Foreign Policy* (2010) and the highly successful textbook, *US Foreign Policy* (2nd edition, 2012). He is currently working on a four-volume study on the International Relations of the Cold War for Sage Publications.

John Dumbrell holds degrees from the Universities of Cambridge and Keele. He specializes in American political history and is the author of *The Carter Presidency: A Re-evaluation* (1995). He is currently Professor of Government at Durham University. His most recent books are: *President Lyndon Johnson and Soviet Communism* (2004); *A Special Relationship: Anglo-American Relations from the Cold War to Iraq* (2006); *Clinton's Foreign Policy: Between the Bushes* (2009); and *Rethinking the Vietnam War* (2012). He is a contributor to the forthcoming *Companion to Presidents Ford and Carter* (ed. Scott Kaufman) (Wiley-Blackwell).

Martin H. Folly is senior lecturer in international history in the Isambard Centre for Historical Research at Brunel University, London. He is the author of *Churchill, Whitehall and the Soviet Union, 1940–45* (Palgrave, 2000), *The United States in World War II* (Edinburgh University Press, 2002), *The Palgrave Concise Historical Atlas of the Second World War* (Palgrave, 2005) and the *Historical Dictionary of United States Diplomacy from World War I Through World War II* (Scarecrow, 2010). He has published articles on the negotiation of the North Atlantic Treaty and essays on Averell Harriman and Lord Inverchapel, ambassadors in London and Washington, DC during the 1940s.

Timothy J. Lynch is Associate Professor in American Politics and Director of the Graduate School of Humanities and Social Sciences at the University of Melbourne, Australia. He is the author of *Turf War: The Clinton Administration and Northern Ireland* (Ashgate, 2004) and, with Robert Singh, of *After Bush: The Case for Continuity in American Foreign Policy* (Cambridge, 2008). He is the Editor-in-Chief of the new *Oxford Encyclopedia of American Military and Diplomatic History* (2013) and author of the forthcoming *Cambridge Essential History of Post-Cold War US Foreign Policy*. A Fulbright scholar, he holds a Ph.D. in political science from Boston College, Massachusetts.

Tony McCulloch is Senior Fellow in North American studies at the UCL Institute of the Americas where he teaches American foreign policy and leads the Canadian Studies programme. He was previously Head of History and American Studies at Canterbury Christ Church University. He has published widely on American and Canadian politics and foreign policy, especially in the era of FDR, and is currently completing a book entitled *Tacit Alliance: Franklin Roosevelt and the Anglo–American 'special relationship' (1933–1940)* for Edinburgh University Press, to be published in 2014.

Henry R. Nau is Professor of Political Science and International Affairs at the Elliott School of International Affairs, The George Washington University and National Fellow at the Hoover Institution (2011–12). He holds a BS degree in Economics, Politics and Science from the Massachusetts Institute of Technology, and MA and Ph.D. degrees from The Johns Hopkins University School of Advanced International Studies (SAIS). His published works include *Conservative Internationalism: Armed Diplomacy Under Jefferson, Polk, Truman and Reagan* (Princeton University Press, forthcoming), *Perspectives on International Relations: Power, Institutions, and Ideas* (3rd edition, CQ Press, 2011); *At Home Abroad: Identity and Power in American Foreign Policy* (Cornell University Press, 2002); *The Myth of America's Decline: Leading the World Economy into the 1990s* (Oxford University Press, 1990); 'The Jigsaw Puzzle and the Chess Board: The Making and Unmaking of Foreign Policy in the Age of Obama,' *Commentary*, May 2012; 'Ideas have Consequences: The Cold War and Today', *International Politics*, July 2011; Obama's Foreign Policy: The swing away from Bush', *Policy Review*, April/May 2010; and 'Conservative Internationalism: From Jefferson to Reagan', *Policy Review*, August/ September 2008.

Adam Quinn is Lecturer in International Relations at the University of Birmingham. From 2008–12 he was convenor of the American Foreign Policy Group of the British International Studies Association. Previous publications related to the theme of this book include *US Foreign Policy in Context: National Ideology from the Founders to the Bush Doctrine* (Routledge, 2010); 'The Deal: The Balance of Power, Military Strength and Liberal Internationalism in the Bush National Security Strategy', *International Studies Perspectives*, 9:1, February 2008; and (with Michael Cox) 'For Better, For Worse: How America's Foreign Policy became Wedded to Liberal Universalism', *Global Society*, 21:4.

Jon Roper is Professor of American Studies at Swansea University. He has published widely on presidential leadership and American democratic ideas. His books include *The American Presidents: Heroic Leadership from Kennedy to Clinton* (2000) and *Democracy and its Critics* (2012), recently republished in the Routledge Revivals series.

Tony Smith is the Jackson Professor of Political Science at Tufts University. He is a member of the Council on Foreign Relations and a senior fellow at the Center for European Studies, Harvard University. In 2012, Princeton University Press published an expanded version of *America's Mission: The United States and the Worldwide Struggle for Democracy*. He is currently at work on the birth of the idea of global democracy promotion in American history in the two centuries prior to the birth of Woodrow Wilson in 1856.

John A. Thompson is Emeritus Reader in American History in the University of Cambridge and an Emeritus Fellow of St Catharine's College, Cambridge. His publications include *Reformers and War: American Progressive Publicists and the First World War* (Cambridge University Press, 1987), *Woodrow Wilson* (Longman, 2002) and many articles on the history of American foreign policy. He is currently working on a book entitled *A Sense of Power: The Roots of America's Global Role*, due to be published by Cornell University Press. Focusing on the first half of the twentieth century, the book seeks to answer the question of why the United States came to play such an extensive and active role in world politics.

FOREWORD

The issues discussed in this book are by no means new. Indeed, the relationship between American grand strategy, democracy promotion and international security has been debated with great intensity ever since the unexpected collapse of Soviet power between 1989 and 1991. Yet as any student knows, this fascinating and controversial topic was initiated long before the demise of Soviet power, and was undertaken as much by political theorists in the Kantian tradition like Michael Doyle as it was by scholars solely concerned with the study of American foreign policy. In fact, as Tony Smith – one of the contributors to this book – pointed out some years ago, democracy was not very much studied by those interested in the United States' historic role in world affairs – either because it did not fit easily into the dominant realist canon of the time or because critics of American foreign policy (of which there were undoubtedly several) could not quite bring themselves to concede that anything the United States did abroad could have added to the sum of human happiness. Thankfully, the debate has moved on since then, taken forward in the first instance by a generation of political scientists interested to test the validity of the democratic peace theory, and then developed further by a number of other writers – including the current author – who were keen to explore the complex and often surprising ways in which the 'liberal leviathan', as I have defined the United States, understood the relationship between the construction of world order and the promotion of liberal and liberal democratic values.

In this most welcome addition to an already extensive literature the editors have attempted to do something rather novel; namely, look at the issue of democracy promotion not as some theoretical problem but rather through the prism of the foreign policy practices of succeeding American presidents – beginning with Theodore Roosevelt and concluding with Barack Obama. And in the process they have managed to illustrate what many of us have always known to be true: that individuals matter in history, and that perhaps no individuals matter more in the conduct of American foreign policy than the president himself. This is not the whole story of course. No man after all is an island, and no president operates within a vacuum. Still, by reinstating the most powerful man in the world into the narrative about American democracy promotion, this excellent book makes a distinctive contribution to a debate that shows no sign of vanishing off the political agenda any time soon.

Professor G. John Ikenberry
Albert G. Milbank Professor of Politics and International Affairs
Princeton University

INTRODUCTION

Presidents, American democracy promotion and world order

Michael Cox, Timothy J. Lynch and Nicolas Bouchet

The relationship between American foreign policy and the promotion of democracy around the world has never been a simple one. Indeed, if one were to believe what was once written by the overwhelming majority of students of American grand strategy, democracy was never, ever, a major American foreign policy aim. Rather its mission was either to expand its power while denying it was doing so, promote its economic interests (hardly the same thing as extending freedom to others), or maintaining something broadly understood as the balance of power: stability by any other name. For many years in fact authors as ideologically diverse as Hans J. Morgenthau and Noam Chomsky, Kenneth Waltz and William Appleman Williams could write, and sometimes write with great verve, about the international role of the imperial republic without even contemplating the possibility that the promotion of democracy mattered at all. And one could readily understand why – especially during that *longue durée* known as the Cold War. The conflict with the Soviet Union may have been fought under the banner of defending or extending the 'free world'. But in the pursuit of this entirely laudable goal, Washington more often than not found itself supporting regimes that were anything but free, most notably in what soon came to be known as the Third World. Perhaps one should not have been surprised by this. As has been argued elsewhere, the habit of backing right-wing autocracies was a long established one in the American foreign policy tradition, and certainly preceded the rise of the USSR. Justified on different grounds from protecting 'moderate' elites from irrational mobs, through to that old imperial favourite that only 'civilized' people (invariably ones with white skins) were mature enough to run their own affairs, the United States' record on democracy promotion was not always the positive one some later claimed it to be.[1]

Yet as Tony Smith was to argue in one of the most challenging books written on American foreign policy – significantly a few years after the Cold War had come to an end – trying to understand American foreign policy through the twentieth century without reference to American democracy was almost impossible.[2] As one of his many admirers noted at the time, Smith's book – *America's Mission* – showed that liberal internationalism was not just a cultural quirk of unsophisticated Americans, or some veneer stuck on to obscure the United States' more nefarious intentions, but was, rather, central to the way Americans thought about themselves and their role in the wider world. Indeed, according to Francis Fukuyama, this understudied dimension of American thinking had significantly contributed to the creation of a liberal world order after the Second World War.[3] Marginalized for too long in a debate dominated by realists and radicals who could only think of foreign policy in terms of either power or profit (or both) Smith's focus on what he saw as the US's underlying purpose reinstated something that had for too long been missing from the discussion.

But the end of the Cold War did more than just make Smith's book seem timely. It also opened up a wider space for the first serious debate about the role of democracy promotion in American foreign policy. There were several fairly obvious reasons for this, perhaps the most important being that the collapse of authoritarianism in former communist countries in Europe was not just a stand-alone event, but was, in fact, the third such 'wave' that was slowly, but surely, making the world a much more democratic place.[4] This not only raised the important question as to why this was happening, and indeed what part the United States had played in bringing this about. It also had massive implications for global security. After all, if it was agreed that the democracy represented the future and was fast laying the foundations for a more peaceful and prosperous world, then it followed that the United States ought to be doing even more in promoting the democratic ideal.[5] The argument was not an entirely new one of course. It had been discussed in the pages of scholarly journals for some time, at least ever since the liberal political theorist Michael Doyle first suggested that there was indeed a liberal tradition that had much to say to American policy-makers.[6] But it was only in the 1990s that the discussion moved from the classroom to the corridors of American power. Indeed, by the middle of the decade, one could not attend a major international relations conference or policy briefing in the United States without hearing yet another discourse on the pros (and sometimes the cons too) of the democratic peace theory and what this meant for the United States.[7]

The 1990s thus saw the emergence of democracy promotion from under the rubble left behind by the dark days of the Cold War.[8] With a liberal president now in the White House advised by some very influential people who insisted that the idea of a democratic peace was as close to being a 'law' as any known theorem in international affairs, it very much looked as if a new foreign policy dawn was about to break.[9] But nothing, as we know, lasts forever, and even if Bill Clinton remained hugely popular at home (and even more so abroad) the Democrats still managed to lose the White House in 2000. However, even though they may have lost politically, they had at least left a marker. Indeed, having at first rejected Clinton's liberal humanitarianism in the name of a higher form of realism, George W. Bush after 9/11 was virtually compelled to do a 180-degree turn. Now the only way of combating the global threat posed by radical Islam – at least according to Bush – was not by pursuing a classical realist strategy by working closely with established elites in the Middle East, but rather by allowing the pure waters of democracy to cleanse the Augean stables that had become the breeding ground for extremist ideologies. Taking inspiration from lessons drawn from the end of the Cold War (and, without embarrassment, from a whole range of liberal theories too) President Bush very quickly became a convert to the idea that freedom held the key that would unlock the door in a region whose dysfunctional character not only threatened to destabilize a part of the world controlling much of the world economy's oil, but might even destroy the world itself. Whether all of his advisers became converts to the democratic cause remains a moot point. Some would even insist that Bush only discovered this particular argument after he had failed to discover weapons of mass destruction in Iraq. Still, if any 'doctrine' attaches itself to his name it is that very American one that insists that the United States is not like other countries and has a very special mission – and that mission has always been, and is bound to remain, the liberation of others from the bonds of tyranny.[10]

Much has been written about the controversial years coinciding with the Bush presidency. But however controversial his policies may have been, there is at least agreement about one thing: that by associating his intervention in Iraq with the idea of democracy promotion it did great damage to the idea. In fact, by linking democracy promotion with what many now came to regard as a deeply flawed foreign policy design, democracy promotion now almost became a dirty word. This however was not the only problem it was confronting. The other challenge arose because of developments in Asia. Here the economic rise of authoritarian China posed an even bigger conundrum perhaps. Admittedly, no other state in the world was seeking to emulate China; and its soft power appeal was limited to say the least. Still, its very success coming as it did when the democratic capitalist West was now in deep economic trouble did not augur well.[11] As a former Clinton official noted not long after the great financial crash of 2008, if China continued to surge ahead while the Western economies floundered, this could easily constitute one of the greatest geopolitical setbacks for the United States since the end of the Second World War.[12]

The almost professorial Barack Obama was very well aware of these various issues. He was even more sensitive to the fact that the United States was in deep trouble more generally, and that changes would have to be made to its foreign policy that would, he hoped, help restore the United States' standing in the world while helping it deal more directly with its own economic problems at home. It is too soon to make any fair-minded judgement about Barack Obama's historic record. But it is not too soon to make an assessment of his foreign policy outlook when he first came into office. Liberal he may well have been, but adventurous abroad he was not. Indeed, if Obama had any inclination at all it was not to go forth and slay undemocratic dragons. Rather, it was to bring the United States' ambitions more closely into line with what he saw as its diminishing capabilities. This was not only likely to lead to a more modest foreign policy. It was bound to compel the United States to seek *rapprochement* with those states (often undemocratic in character) that could help it shore up world order in an era of uncertainty. Obama's foreign policy language even seemed to reflect this shift. Bush had talked of well-defined friends and clearly targeted enemies; of an undemocratic 'them' and a 'democratic' us; and of course, of some states being 'evil' and others 'good'. Obama engaged in no such moralizing. Quite the opposite. In fact, whereas Bush had seen the world in terms of allies and enemies, Obama now referred increasingly to a range of new 'partners' that could just as easily include China and Russia as it could the United States' more established friends in Europe. The wheel appeared to have come full circle: the realists looked like they were back in power. Forcible regime change and confrontation with states that denied freedom to their own people had been consigned into that proverbial dustbin of history.[13]

Surprise as they say is the stuff of real history; and in the same way that Bush was quite literally ambushed by 9/11, so too was Obama by the upheavals in the Arab world that have since gone under the somewhat simple-minded heading of the 'Arab Spring'. And dealing with this challenge has proved just as difficult.[14] Initially, the Obama team clearly did not know how to respond to a movement that within months had destroyed the old political order in a good part of the Middle East. However, Obama was nothing if not a fast learner. He may not have shared the rhetorical fervour of a Bush. Indeed, he had earlier insisted that his approach to the world in general, and the Middle East in particular, would be closer to that of George Bush Sr rather than Bush Jr. But under pressure at home to do something, and faced with a torrent of events in Tunisia, Egypt and Libya, one thing became increasingly clear: if the United States did not align itself with forces for political change – even forces it had earlier opposed like the Muslim Brotherhood in Egypt – it would in the end be the political loser.[15] In this way the Arab spring helped reform and reshape Obama's foreign policy.

It is in the midst of these turbulent times that we have decided to launch this particular volume, hoping of course that it will make its own contribution to the ongoing debate on democracy promotion. It tries to do so in at least three very important ways: first, by basing its conclusions on original historical research; second, by showing that American leaders have for decades (and not just recently) faced difficult choices when it comes to balancing American core interests with its underlying values; and, finally, by pointing to the fairly self-evident fact that American presidents matter a great deal when it comes to determining the country's foreign policy. Several of the chapters were first presented at a 2010 conference on 'US Presidents and Democracy Promotion' organized by Timothy J. Lynch and Nicolas Bouchet at the Institute for the Study of the Americas in the University of London, a substantial inspiration for which was one of the current editor's previous books on democracy promotion.[16] Naturally enough, this book does not claim to be exhaustive. There are for instance no chapters on the Republican presidencies of Dwight Eisenhower, Richard Nixon and George H.W. Bush. Nor have we bothered with too much theory. Still, we very much hope this study will continue, or possibly even initiate, a new debate – one that seriously addresses the issue of democracy promotion, not as if it were some moral beauty contest but as one part of a strategic puzzle that might help us understand the dilemmas that have confronted (and will continue to confront) American policy-makers as they attempt to navigate their way past the rapids, the sandbanks and the rocks that make up that potentially treacherous stretch of water prosaically referred to by academics (like us) as the international system.

It is perhaps appropriate that one of the major figures in this debate – Tony Smith – opens the book with a typically wide-ranging contribution. Smith disentangles the roots of the liberal theory that has driven American democracy promotion, laying out the interplay of ideas of economic interdependence, multilateral institutions, American leadership and, above all, democratic peace. He traces the evolution of the 'liberal internationalist agenda for American foreign policy' through a 'pre-classical' stage dating back to the American revolution, a 'classical' stage starting with the Spanish–American War of 1898, a post-Second World War 'hegemonic' stage and finally a 'progressive imperialism' ushered in by George W. Bush. But as he goes on to show, the Wilsonian tradition may not be able to bear any more heavy lifting. Indeed, what he terms 'the liberal internationalist framework for policy that had done so much to establish America's pre-eminence in world affairs between 1945 and 2001' has, ironically, been contributing 'to its decline' since. In this very important sense perhaps, history may not have come to an end but it may well have turned a very important corner.

Woodrow Wilson is usually considered the founding father of American democracy promotion. But as Adam Quinn argues in his fascinating chapter, even if Theodore Roosevelt can hardly be regarded as an 'evangelist' for democracy, he was nonetheless influenced by some of the same ideas that contributed to Wilson's vision of a new world order. As he puts it, 'Roosevelt remains a significant figure if we seek to understand the emergence of the United States as an assertive global power actively embracing value-laden intervention in the internal affairs of other nations'. Starting with his 'reinvigoration' of the Monroe Doctrine, Quinn shows how Roosevelt contributed significantly to democracy promotion by expanding the horizons of American foreign policy in a way that moved from 'exemplarism' to involvement in the domestic affairs of other countries. Criticized by some for his imperialist outlook, it was only by crossing the Westphalian line of non-interference that Roosevelt laid the foundation for much of what followed in American foreign policy during the twentieth century.

Woodrow Wilson of course holds pride of place in the historical debate about American democracy promotion. But as John Thompson shows in his distinct contribution, Wilson's attitude towards democracy and democracy promotion was never as clear-cut as some of his own rhetoric sometimes seemed to suggest. Wilson may have often used the language of freedom; and clearly he believed democracy to be the superior form of government. But when he deployed the idea he frequently did so more to justify his policies to the American people rather than allowing democracy to define American interests. Moreover, as Thompson goes on to show, Wilson's experience during and just after the First World War reveals that his commitment to democracy as a source of a peaceful world order was never total. Others have pointed to Wilson's known views on race and how these shaped his beliefs about who was, and who was not, ready for democracy. But Thompson makes a different, but equally important, point; namely, that when Wilson talked in his typically eloquent way about democracy, he did not call for the promotion of democracy everywhere – far from it – but rather for a world in which pre-existing democratic polities would remain secure and safe against the many threats they faced following the calamity that was the First World War.

According to many writers Wilson stands as a monument to a failed idealism that was soon overtaken by something much less edifying when American foreign policy floundered – or so the standard narrative goes – between the basest form of dollar diplomacy as practised in the 1920s and an isolationist indifference to the political suffering of others as many claim became the American default position in the 1930s. Certainly, the strong post-war reaction to its earlier participation in the First World War, followed in turn by the collapse of the American economy after 1929, made the inter-war years especially lack-lustre ones when it came to the conduct of American foreign policy. Even that hero of American liberalism, Franklin D. Roosevelt, did not buck the trend, attacking the League of Nations in one infamous statement and showing apparent indifference to the rise of the dictators through a good part of the 1930s. Yet as Tony McCulloch reveals in his intellectually robust defence of Roosevelt, this was by no means the whole story. Indeed, in a careful dissection of the 32nd president's many speeches he reveals a very different Roosevelt: one who from 1936 onwards made it quite clear that the world was facing its greatest international test ever, and that in this struggle the United States stood four square on the side of the European democracies against the aggressive appetites of the dictators. He cast the Second World War in much the same terms. This was no power struggle he insisted but a contest fought by the 'United Nations' for a new world in which freedom from want, and from political persecution, would, one day, become the global norm. Of course, Roosevelt was realist enough to understand the nature of power; and to realize too that the post-war world would involve the United States working with countries like the USSR who did not share the United States' beliefs (something for which he was later roundly condemned by his many Republican enemies). But as McCulloch shows, this four-time president continues to stand as an important historic link in the liberal chain connecting original Wilsonianism with those who after 1947 faced a new world and a new adversary in the shape of the Soviet Union.

Dealing with the problems generated by the rise of Soviet communism fell to Harry Truman, the man from Independence, Missouri – who by his own admission seemed ill-equipped to lead the United States at one of the most difficult and dangerous moments in its international history. Much criticized by an earlier generation of liberals who viewed Truman as having abandoned the Rooseveltian tradition, Truman now stands among the 'greats' or at least 'near greats' in terms of his reputation. But as Mark Folly shows in his nuanced contribution, Truman left behind a mixed legacy in terms of the promotion of democracy. On the one hand, as Folly demonstrates with great skill, Truman committed the United States firmly to the principle that it had a vital interest in the fate of democracy abroad. On the other hand, because his policies were shaped by 'a crude and flawed definition of democracy', not to mention an exaggerated understanding of the Soviet threat, this inevitably led him to make his peace with a series of non-democratic regimes around the world. In this way, Truman set the United States on a course that privileged 'order and stability' over freedom, and 'economic prosperity linked to American free enterprise' over and above the 'application of concepts of political or social liberty', and by so doing compromised America's core values. Therein perhaps lay the great tragedy of American diplomacy.

Truman's successor, Dwight D. Eisenhower, shared many if not most of Truman's views about the wider world. This did not make him a dunce or a reactionary as some once claimed. He had for instance a rather more balanced view of the Soviet Union than his immediate Democratic predecessor; and he was perfectly well aware that the era of European colonial rule was fast coming to an end. Still, during his eight years in office, there is little evidence to show that he ever seriously believed it was in the American national interest to promote democracy to countries in the world which, in his view, were probably not culturally or economically ready for it anyway. Indeed, it is significant that the one large Third World country at the time that did come close to practising democracy – namely India – seemed to be viewed with either indifference or condescension in his White House.[17] The election of a very different kind of president in 1960 thus appeared to herald a new political dawn. And in some ways it did as Jon Roper reveals in his fine chapter. Kennedy may have been a staunch anti-communist; however, this did not prevent him sympathizing with nationalist movements in the developing world while seeking to channel that powerful political impulse 'towards democracy rather than communism'. His short presidency indeed saw the development of an approach to achieve this by means of modernization and nation-building policies underwritten by the Alliance for Progress and the newly formed Agency for International Development. Lyndon Johnson, Roper continues, was equally convinced of democratization's value in containing communism and Soviet influence in the developing world. But, as the United States became mired down in Vietnam, it became clear that trying to encourage modernization while at the same time fighting a counter-insurgency was unlikely to advance the cause of democracy in developing countries. Ultimately, American democracy promotion efforts failed not because its leaders were cynical realists, but rather because the barriers to transplanting American values in countries wracked by poverty, run by often reactionary elites, and animated by anti-imperialism, simply proved too much.

In terms of democracy promotion the Nixon–Kissinger years were undoubtedly bleak ones. Both men had fairly clear views about the world in which power mattered more than ideas, and where the great powers in particular mattered more than the rest. Sharing neither Kennedy's liberal outlook nor his sympathy for the political aspirations of the Third World, they brought to the job an almost nineteenth-century worldview in which the idea of democracy hardly figured at all. Indeed, if countries in the Third World freely chose a political path that did not chime with the global interests of the United States, then so much the worse for that ill-fated country. As Kissinger famously observed of one very important Latin American country at the time – Chile – if its people were irresponsible enough to vote in a Marxist government, then they had better beware the consequences. Even the idea of human rights received short shrift from Kissinger. He hardly ever raised it with the Russians in his extended discussions over what he saw as the much weightier issue of arms control. There is no evidence that he raised it with the Chinese. And in his discussions with the increasingly large number of Latin American dictators, he always seemed more concerned to protect them from congressional criticism than making the case for human rights. Indeed, in one interview, he reassured General Augusto Pinochet that the various attacks levelled against him were inspired by either ill-advised liberals back in Washington or those on the wider international left who were instinctively hostile to a Chilean government that Kissinger firmly believed had stopped Chile going communist under Salvador Allende.[18]

There was much relief in certain circles, therefore, when Jimmy Carter took over in the White House vowing to place human rights at the heart of a new American foreign policy. In his lucid chapter, John Dumbrell carefully maps out Carter's efforts to operationalize and entrench human rights in the decision-making process. These, however, had mixed results. In fact, as Dumbrell shows so well, Carter's pursuit of human rights was far more selective in practice than his public statements appeared to imply. In fact, human rights as a principle was closely connected in the mind of certain key advisers, such as Zbigniew Brzezinski, as yet another crucial weapon in the Cold War. Nonetheless, Carter's policies clearly did have some positive impact in Latin America and South Africa. They may also have provided an important launch pad for democracy promotion efforts by his various successors. And who knows? They may have also done much (as Zbigniew Brzezinski hoped they might) to weaken Soviet power in eastern Europe too.[19]

If Dumbrell finds much to praise in the oft-criticized foreign policy of the Carter administration, Henry Nau finds perhaps even more in the record of Ronald Reagan.[20] According to Nau, Reagan was perhaps the first American president who viewed the world, American security and the ongoing struggle with the Soviet Union, as a competition of ideas in which the freedom embodied by the United States could and would trump its competitors. Of course, as others have pointed out, Reagan did not always stand on the side of the democratic angels, as his policies in Central America and Afghanistan demonstrated. Nor is there much to indicate that he asked embarrassing political questions in his important discussions with the House of Saud as he solicited their economic support in waging his ongoing 'war' against global communism. Nonetheless, in what he saw as the major struggle of the time, what in the end was at stake (and a reason why the United States would in the end win) were two different ways of life. Furthermore, as Nau shows, Reagan did not just feel America was an example for others to follow: it was crucial that it helped foster the conditions favourable to freedom elsewhere

Reagan

by assisting the spread of democracy through the creation of such bodies as the National Endowment for Democracy, as well as by applying diplomatic and economic pressure on those non-democratic states who continued to oppose the United States. By so doing, Reagan left an important legacy, one which successors would be able to build upon in a new world hopefully free of the terrors associated with the Cold War.

The two-term Reagan was followed in turn by the one-term Republican president George Herbert Walker Bush. Experienced in foreign policy in ways that Reagan had not been when he assumed office, the Bush legacy (insofar as we can speak of one) was, and remains, a deeply ambiguous one. At one level he displayed great diplomatic skill when it came to negotiating the end of the Cold War in Europe; and it was on his watch – though not necessarily because of his policies – that democracy got its first outing in countries such as Poland and Hungary. On the other hand, there was always something deeply cautious and realist – some might argue wise – about Bush's approach to international affairs. Only reluctantly did he decide to go to war with Iraq. Then, having defeated Saddam Hussein's armies in 1991, he did not go on and liberate Iraq itself. He was even more careful when it came to dealing with Mikhail Gorbachev as the communist leader tried desperately to hold together the old Soviet Union. Reform was one thing he argued, but it was not up to the United States to encourage a rush towards democratic self-determination if this fostered disorder in a part of the world where there were thousands of nuclear weapons. Stability was not necessarily a good thing in itself. But the disintegration of a mighty empire (like the fall of many empires before) would achieve nothing if it led to political chaos and economic decline.

In Bill Clinton's bid to win the White House, he was highly critical of what he claimed was Bush's overly cautious approach to political change, a caution that had even seen the Bush team reassuring the Chinese leadership after Tiananmen Square that Washington would not seek to exploit the outrage for its own political advantage. In Nicolas Bouchet's chapter, he carefully explores the Clinton record, pointing out that even if Clinton did not put into practice everything he preached, he did at least embrace the concept of democratic enlargement with an enthusiasm that had very rarely been displayed by American leaders before him. While conservative critics and realists alike attacked him for failing to understand the limits of such a strategy, he nonetheless remains an important figure in the field – almost certainly the first not to draw a neat line between trying to act liberally abroad and advancing the American national interest. And to this end (and like Reagan before him) he made real progress in trying to make democracy promotion a more central part of American foreign policy. But like all reforming presidents before him, he could not, in the end, deliver on all of his promises, both in terms of the promotion of democracy itself or in convincing all Americans that this should become an integral component of American grand strategy. Thus, when he left office in 2000, his legacy was by no means assured.

The foreign policy of the new, incoming Bush administration, was initially defined in terms of an almost instinctive opposition to everything that had gone

before under the much despised liberal, Clinton. For this reason Bush was at first
highly critical (or at least immensely sceptical) of Clinton's emphasis on democracy
promotion and the associated idea that the United States should be engaged in
nation-building. But as Tim Lynch shows in his fine chapter, 9/11 changed all
that. Inspired by Republican icon Ronald Reagan, and informed now by the idea
that in the war against the new totalitarians, freedom and democracy were major
weapons, the Bush team (some cynically and some genuinely) came round to the
view that in the great battles that lay ahead the United States had to stand for an
ideal, one that in the words of Bush would extend the 'reach of freedom' and by
so doing help secure the United States. As others have pointed out, the new Bush
doctrine was as divisive in terms of how it has been interpreted as it has proved
difficult to measure in terms of its actual impact. But as Lynch goes on to show,
even if highly imperfect in its implementation and problematic in terms of its
results, Bush did at least change the terms of the debate in the Middle East,
showing that there was in fact another political alternative to the autocracies
that had so misruled the region for so long. Indeed, it may even be that the
American-engineered demise of regimes in Kabul and Baghdad played their own
role – however indirectly – in fostering the kind of environment that later made
the Arab Spring of 2011 possible.

The book closes with Thomas Carothers' systematic evaluation of Barack
Obama's attempts to recalibrate American policy after both the optimism of the
Clinton years and the controversies associated with the policies of George W. Bush.
Obama, as we have already suggested, faced a difficult set of choices – difficult in
particular for a leader of a Democratic Party which, though keen to attack Bush's
handling of foreign policy, had to be careful in not rejecting the idea of democracy
promotion *tout court*. As one observer noted a year before Obama even became
president, because of Bush, the Democrats now had a 'democracy problem'.[21]
Carothers examines what he sees as the success of Obama in disassociating the idea
of democracy with what had transpired under Bush but without abandoning the
'freedom agenda' altogether. This was a very fine line to walk, as Carothers
demonstrates. Indeed, in his speeches both before and during the Arab Spring,
Obama sometimes sounded as if he was saying two quite contradictory things in
the same speech. Democracy, of course, he insisted, remained the best system of
government. However, 'no system of government', he argued in Cairo in 2009,
should be 'imposed by one nation' on another. Not only did this smack of
imperialism; there was every chance that such a policy would fail.[22] Nor one suspects
has Obama abandoned his caution – even now, more than two years into the Arab
Spring. Indeed, it still looks as if he will require a lot of persuading before arriving
at the conclusion that America's promotion of democracy throughout the region –
as opposed to certain countries – is the miracle medicine that will cure all of the
Middle East's many ills.

What then of the future? How will the United States confront the world during
the rest of the twenty-first century? To say it is 'too soon to tell' would be banal.
However, as we enter the second decade of the new century – one likely to be a

little less 'American' than the last one – we can at least take comfort from the fact that even if utopia is impossible the demand for greater political participation and human rights from peoples around the world remains a constant one. And so long as it does, the United States will forever be compelled to 'promote' its values, sometimes enthusiastically, sometimes not. Whether it will always do so wisely or well remains to be seen. But on the basis of the historic record so far, there are still (cautious) grounds for optimism. Nothing is set in stone; nor is it ever likely to be in an uncertain world where the American people are regularly called upon every four years to choose a new, or possibly the same, man to run American foreign policy. If nothing else this book, we hope, demonstrates at least one thing: that whoever occupies the White House matters, and thus, by implication, how ordinary Americans cast their vote is perhaps just as important in shaping America's future as the advice he (and eventually she) will be receiving from his or her assembled experts. If American democracy promotion is important, and is to remain so, it will only be because America remains a vibrant democracy itself. ‑Self reinforcing behaviour

Notes

1 David F. Schmitz, *Thanks God They're on Our Side: The United States and Right-Wing Dictatorships 1921–1965* (Chapel Hill, University of North Carolina Press, 1999).
2 Tony Smith, *America's Mission: The United States and the Worldwide Struggle for Democracy in the Twentieth Century* (New Jersey, Princeton University Press, 1994).
3 See Francis Fukuyama's review of Tony Smith's book in *The New Republic* (http://press.princeton.edu/titles/9696.html).
4 Samuel Huntington, *The Third Wave: Democratization in the Late Twentieth Century* (University of Oklahoma Press, 1991).
5 Bruce Russett, *Grasping the Democratic Peace: Principles for a Post-Cold War World* (New Jersey, Princeton University Press, 1993).
6 See Michael W. Doyle, 'Liberalism and World Politics', *The American Political Science Review*, Vol. 80, No. 4, December 1986, and 'Kant, Liberal Legacies and Foreign Affairs', parts I and II, *Philosophy and Public Affairs*, Vol. 12, Nos. 3 and 4, 1983.
7 John Owen summed the up mood well: 'The theory [of democratic peace] which originated in the work of the eighteenth-century philosopher Immanuel Kant and was refined in the 1970s and 1980s by several researchers working independently, has, since the 1990s, been one of the hottest research areas in international relations'. See his 'Iraq and the Democratic Peace', *Foreign Affairs*, November/December 2005.
8 Douglas Brinkley, 'Democratic Enlargement: The Clinton Doctrine', *Foreign Policy*, Spring, No. 106, 1997.
9 See Michael Cox, *US Foreign Policy After the Cold War: Superpower Without a Mission?* (London, Chatham House and Pinter, 1995).
10 Adam Quinn, *US Foreign Policy in Context: National Ideology from the Founders to the Bush Doctrine* (London and New York, Routledge, 2010).
11 Stefan Halper, *The Beijing Consensus: How China's Authoritarian Model Will Dominate the Twenty-First Century* (New York, Basic Books, 2010).
12 Roger Altman, 'The Great Crash 2008: A Geopolitical Setback for the West', *Foreign Affairs*, January–February 2009.
13 On Obama's foreign policy see David E. Sanger, *Confront and Conceal: Obama's Secret Wars and Surprising Use of American Power* (New York, Crown Books, 2012) and James Mann, *The Obamians: The Struggle Inside the White House to Redefine American Power* (New York, Viking Books, 2012).

14 Fawaz Gerges, *Obama and the Middle East* (Basingstoke, Palgrave Macmillan, 2012).
15 See Ryan Lizza, 'The Consequentialist: How the Arab Spring Remade Obama's foreign policy', *The New Yorker*, 2 May 2011, http://www.newyorker.com/reporting/2011/05/02/110502fa_fact_lizza
16 Michael Cox, G. John Ikenberry and Takashi Inoguchi eds; *American Democracy Promotion: Impulses, Strategies, and Impacts* (Oxford, Oxford University Press, 2000).
17 Jean Edward Smith, *Eisenhower in War and Peace* (New York, Random House, 2012).
18 See Christopher Hitchens, *The Trial of Henry Kissinger* (London, Verso Books, 2001).
19 There is now an extensive literature on the relationship between the liberal human rights campaign and the end of the Cold War. For one of the more recent studies, see Sarah B. Snyder, *Human Rights Activism and the End of the Cold War: A Transnational History of the Helsinki Network* (Cambridge: Cambridge University Press, 2011).
20 On Carter's reputational rise since the end of the Cold War, see Douglas Brinkley, 'The Rising Stock of Jimmy Carter: A Revisiting Perspective of our 39th President', *Diplomatic History*, Fall, Vol. 20, No. 4, 1996.
21 See Ronald D. Asmus, 'The Democrat's Democracy Problem', *Washington Post*, 17 June 2007.
22 See the useful and, as yet, unpublished paper on Obama's dilemmas by Anthony N. Celso, 'Obama and the Arab Spring', delivered at the Western Political Science Association meeting, 22–24 March 2012, http://wpsa.research.pdx.edu/meet/2012/celsopaper.pdf

1

DEMOCRACY PROMOTION FROM WILSON TO OBAMA

Tony Smith

Charting the tortured course of American democracy promotion from its origins as a consciously assembled set of concepts to guide foreign policy set out by Woodrow Wilson in 1913 to its incarnation in the hands of Barack Obama a century later presents a host of problems. Fortunately, there is at least limited agreement on the distinct elements essential to a 'liberal internationalist', or (in the American context) 'Wilsonian', approach to world affairs. There is also general agreement on how liberalism differs from other approaches to the study of international relations such as realism or Marxism. Where the concepts that constitute liberal internationalism come under dispute, however, lies in efforts to explain how these elemental forces interact with one another to create an identity in theoretical terms that is convincingly unified. Turning to the historical record offers only limited help to sort out the contradictions among those who claim to understand the logic of liberal theory. Given the variety of policies pursued over the past century by four generations of leaders in very varied circumstances under the name of Wilsonianism, how does one recognize an essential character to liberalism and so have firmer footing to appreciate its strengths and weaknesses?

The argument of this chapter is that the prime mover of liberal theory is the ability of democratic peoples and governments to maintain an enduring peace among themselves based on their character as individuals, groups and political units. Other elements that are part of the liberal agenda – economic interdependence, multilateral institutions and American leadership – synergistically complement democracy as constituent elements of the project, but in theoretical terms their contribution is secondary to the key role played by the spirit and institutions of peoples living in constitutional democracies. We then turn from theory to history, examining various stages in the evolution of the liberal internationalist agenda for American foreign policy, showing how in different hands, confronted with varied circumstances, democracy promotion has nonetheless been formulated in a way that has been the chief preoccupation of Washington when it has been acting in a liberal mode, so that practice has remained true to the theory. This chapter's aim is to show a unity of theory and practice that gives the liberal project a self-understanding that today it often appears to lack.

The Wilsonian vision in theory

Unlike Marxism, which benefited from a unified worldview thanks to its origins with a single individual, and unlike realism, whose terms are contested within a relatively tight intellectual discourse, different interpreters of the liberal internationalist or Wilsonian framework for American foreign policy divide the concepts that make it up in various ways that to the uninitiated may seem bewildering. Some even find up to eight distinct aspects of liberalism, each calling for analysis in its own terms. We would submit, however, that these differences are minor and can be reconciled without too much debate by positing four separate yet interconnected concepts as basic to this way of thought: (1) cooperation among democratic governments; (2) linked in economic openness; (3) through well-structured multilateral institutions; and (4) under a United States that willingly assumed the responsibilities of leadership.[1] The ultimate ambition of these elements when combined is the surest hallmark of Wilsonianism: the belief (often derided as 'moralistic' or 'idealistic') that together, and if expanded far enough, they have the capacity to create a world order of enduring peace, and in the process, as Wilson put it, 'to make the world safe for democracy'.

Based on something of a consensus as to what defines liberalism, we can perhaps also agree that these defining characteristics of the argument make it distinctively different from other leading Western paradigms of analysis such as realism, Marxism or constructivism (which would include feminism). Unlike the realists, liberals insist that 'regime-type matters'; that is, that democratic peoples and states are different in fundamental ways from peoples living under authoritarian rule or imbued with authoritarian cultures. Unlike Marxists, liberals insist that capitalism is not a basic reason for conflict but can be an important force for peace, while Leninism is inherently incompatible with freedom and so with the ennoblement of thought and purpose that makes democratic peoples able to live in peace with one another. Unlike constructivists, liberals maintain that ideas and values must be grounded in democratically functioning institutions both domestically and internationally; a homogeneity of values and ideas alone (which constructivism centres on), even if achievable (which is unlikely), is far from adequate for keeping the world from war.[2]

Yet one should not mistake a general agreement that might be reached as to what concepts constitute a liberal internationalist approach to world affairs and what makes it distinctive from other approaches as meaning that sharp disagreements do not exist on other counts. The most hotly debated questions concern how the constituent elements of liberalism join to one another in a common project. Some give pride of place in the dynamic forces leading to peace to the integrative powers of capitalism; others favour multilateralism as the engine of increased state cooperation, and still others (and this essay is an example) stress the character of democratic cultures and governments as the most basic ingredient in the mix that leads to the emergence of an increasingly pacific world order.

But let us not overstate the dimensions of the dispute. Thanks to a major study published by political scientists Bruce Russett and John Oneal in 2001, a persuasive account is available demonstrating how the three forces of democracy, economic openness and multilateralism might be integrated with each other in a 'virtuous circle' giving rise to peace. Russett and Oneal used an impressive range of empirical measures to establish democratic government as the most important variable in their trinity of practices that make up liberalism. Despite this accomplishment, their study is not exempt from criticism, for it omits at its peril the importance of American leadership in creating, protecting and promoting a Wilsonian world order. The result is to depict a liberal order as one held together by magnetic internal forces of attraction, completely disregarding the indispensable role played by a hegemonic actor, whose conduct is basic to perpetuating a 'pacific union' or 'zone of democratic peace'. Not only is the United States given no role whatsoever in their study; the importance of a hegemonic power is explicitly discounted.[3]

To envision the set of integrated concepts that typify liberalism more graphically, imagine a four-sided diamond, each point of which represents one of the elemental features of liberal internationalism.[4] Each facet has its own distinctive quality, yet each relates to the other three in ways that are not only mutually reinforcing but actually work to mix the characteristic features of each element into compounds that are equally distinctive. For instance, consider the role of multilateralism. In a politically plural world presupposed by the character of democratic nations linked through pacts of self-defence and through ties of economic interdependence, rules-based international regimes capable of authoritative determinations as to the rights and obligations of member countries are an imperative need. Multilateralism (to the point of what is sometimes called a 'pooling of sovereignties') is thus the necessary product of a particular political and economic structure of a liberal world order; yet at the same time international regimes contribute directly to the perpetuation of an order of plural democracies and economic openness. Multilateralism is thus both cause and effect of political pluralism and market integration – especially in the domain of international law – so that while it needs to maintain its independent identity as a distinct aspect of liberalism for analytical purposes, in practice it melds its character into hybrid features with other concepts. In a parallel manner, each of these four elements retains its unique character or existence for analytical purposes, yet the four integrate with each other as one in what should be understood as creating an effective unity that is greater than the sum of its parts. Moreover, the promise of this unity is peace, which no aspect alone can promise convincingly to deliver, and whose possibility of realization is the prime tenet of liberalism's secular faith.

When such an admixture is achieved in practice – when theory is embodied in values, interests, institutions and policies that endure over time – the result that liberalism posits is a 'pacific union' or a 'zone of democratic peace' (to use phrases with wide currency in the 1990s). Today, the European Union is the leading historical example of the freedom and peace that liberal practices may bring (although others have looked at American–Canadian relations or at the cooperation apparent in Mercosur, founded in 1991, or at relations among the members of the Association of Southeast Asian Nations, founded in 1967). The brilliance given by the facets of the diamond of synergistically related forces arises from the radiance of its promise – Immanuel Kant's 'perpetual peace' (which George W. Bush frequently referred to as 'permanent peace'), the conviction, in turn, that allowed Woodrow Wilson to believe not only that 'the world must be made safe for democracy' but that it could be so were the guiding ideas of liberal internationalism embodied in affairs of state.

Where debate truly begins in earnest is over the relative importance to attribute to these various aspects of the Wilsonian project. Some see the dynamic power of corporate global capitalism as having a role that drives all else before it. One may either condemn or salute this process of world economic integration. Those who condemn it see liberalism as camouflaging with words like 'democracy', 'freedom', 'prosperity' and 'American leadership', culminating in 'an enduring peace' that in reality is a self-interested, predatory global economic system that enriches the few, keeps weak 'democratic' states beholden to corporate influence, which in due course will feed conflict domestically, regionally and globally in a manner that may well sap the strength of the United States.[5] Today questions surrounding the rise of China remind us of Lenin's phrase that 'the capitalists will sell us the rope by which we will hang them'. By contrast, liberals who endorse a leading role for economic openness and integration stress the prosperity and the pacifying interdependence such arrangements encourage. They can point to the experience of the European Union (born in important measure as a result of the Marshall Plan and the character of the American occupation of Germany) as a demonstration of the proposition that prosperity gives strength to the middle class (perhaps the most potent social force favouring a democratic culture and government) while interdependence increases the harmonization and sharing of sovereignty that over time can reduce, perhaps even eradicate, the differences in interest and perception that give rise to conflict.

The 'Washington Consensus' born in the 1980s holding that privatization, deregulation and openness would result in an increasingly globalized economy maintained that multilateralism, democracy and peace would all be reinforced by such liberal practices. In this respect, Washington's leadership in creating the Bretton Woods System in 1944, compounded by the effort to promote European economic integration through the Marshall Plan in 1947, were preludes to efforts decades later to promote such schemes as the North American Free Trade Agreement (NAFTA, which became effective in 1994) and the creation of the World Trade Organization (WTO) in 1995.[6] What critics and partisans of this process might agree on is the leading role played by free-market capitalism in how the various features of a Wilsonian order reinforce one another. American leadership, democratic government and multilateralism are all at the service of international capital, the driving force of the liberal agenda.

Other theorists hold that multilateralism is the key variable in the Wilsonian project. Wilson himself saw collective security embodied in the League of Nations as the greatest accomplishment his presidency might achieve to secure the peace of the world.[7] Although he originally conceived of the League as dominated by democratic peoples, he ultimately had to abandon this ambition, faced with the demands of the British, the Japanese and others that whatever the quality of states that applied for membership in the League, should they agree to be bound by a commitment to work for disarmament and abide by the collective arbitration of differences (backed up by the threat of common action against governments that threatened the unprincipled use of force that would break the peace) then they might become members of the organization. From this perspective, membership in multilateral institutions mitigates the concerns of what social scientists today call 'the security dilemma' and so check the anarchy of international relations, one of the causes of war. Moreover, the League might serve as a training ground for rules-based behaviour on the part of participating governments (a rudimentary form of constitutionalism). But the hope that Wilson most relied on was the role that a democratic United States would play in leading the League. As he put it in his famous address to the Senate on 10 July 1919, the country's role was clear, its responsibility enormous:

> [At the Peace Conference] it was universally recognized that America had entered the war to promote no private or peculiar interest of her own but only as the champion of rights which she was glad to share with free men and lovers of justice everywhere. We had formulated the principles upon which the settlement was to be made […] We were welcomed as disinterested friends […] The united power of free nations must put a stop to aggression, and the world must be given peace […] The League of Nations was […] the only hope for mankind […] Shall we or any other free people hesitate to accept this great duty? Dare we reject it and break the heart of the world? […] The stage is set, the destiny disclosed. It has come about by no plan of our conceiving, but by the hand of God who led us into this way. We cannot turn back. We can only go forward, with lifted eyes and freshened spirit, to follow the vision. It was of this that we dreamed at our birth. America shall in truth show the way. The light streams upon the path ahead and nowhere else.

Those who maintain the importance of multilateralism, economic openness or American leadership as leading features of the liberal project are persuasive that these features of Wilsonianism carry significant weight in the liberal project. Yet it would seem that both from a theoretical point of view and from an analysis of the thinking of Wilson and most of his successors, the most dynamic feature of the liberalism has always been the creation of a community of democratic states, whose prospects for peace will be immeasurably enhanced through successful efforts at worldwide democracy promotion. Economic openness, multilateralism and American leadership all have critical roles to play, to be sure, but the primacy of the spread of democratic government trumps all other forces on the liberal agenda, and this for reasons that can be argued theoretically and demonstrated in case studies.

The reason that democracy has always been the key variable in the forces that have distinguished liberalism is that it creates the kind of peoples and institutions that alone can make the other facets of Wilsonianism function in harmony with one another as they should. (Put in the terminology of modern political science, democratic government is more of an 'independent variable' whereas the other features of liberalism have more the characteristics of 'dependent variables'.) Take the leadership role of the United States in the liberal agenda. For Wilson, the raw power of the United States made it a candidate for leadership. But the origin of this power lay in important measure in the United States' democratic nature, which rendered it morally and efficiently superior to those people and institutions that were authoritarian in character. Moreover, its leadership could be counted on to act in terms of the common interest of world peace. In line with Enlightenment thinking, especially as embodied in the organizational practices of Reformed Protestantism in the United States, men and women of reason and conscience were capable of a degree of honesty, disinterestedness, trustworthiness and honour that made government based on the consent of the governed not only possible but more effective than any other form of government known to history. In terms used today, governments that were transparent and accountable, based on an informed and engaged citizenry acting in terms of 'covenanted' or constitutional agreements, were capable of rising above self-interested passions and entering into accord with other similarly constituted peoples for the sake of the general good, a common peace. The same virtues that made mutual understanding and cooperation domestically transferred on the world stage as well. Whatever the degree of reciprocity involved in the synergistic interaction among the various forces that make up the force of liberalism, the character and practices of democratic peoples and governments thus emerge as the most critical factor to the proper functioning of the whole.[8]

Still, we must be careful not to exaggerate the idealism of Wilson's beliefs. He was well aware that democracy faced internal challenges. Individuals could come to different positions on important matters despite the use of reason and an appeal to conscience. Conflict was inherent in the human condition. One of the primary achievements of Wilson's Presbyterian Church was the understanding the congregations had that, though they held certain beliefs deeply, their convictions might be subject to change or even be mistaken, and accordingly that though others might disagree with them, these others had a right to their freedom of conscience and should be addressed with deference and restraint, even if the disagreements were fundamental. A respect for the moral integrity of those who were different and a desire to cooperate despite differences was thus an aspect of the 'covenanting' that was basic to Wilson's religious convictions. When seen within the context of mutual respect differences need not lead to war.

Wilson was also aware of the doctrine of original sin – that it was in the nature of humans to be self-serving at the expense of others, to be self-aggrandizing, even to be capable of formulating projects of domination based on protestations of emancipation and freedom. As a result, the democratic enterprise would necessarily not run smoothly. In his own time, Wilson was critical of predatory capitalism both at home and as an international force. He came to the presidency as a Progressive inveighing against the greed, cruelty and anti-democratic characteristics of the monopoly capitalism of his era. Subsequently he criticized the efforts of American banks to exercise control over China and some parts of Latin America in a way that infringed on the sovereignty of states and their ability to move in progressive directions that would make them increasingly likely to become constitutional democracies.[9] Yet another challenge that might undermine democracy was the threat of demagogic rule based on a leader's charismatic ability to mobilize popular energies in a way that undermined constitutional rule. Wilson realized that democracy could 'degenerate'.[10]

As a young man, Wilson engaged in the study of democracy in order to make American citizens more self-aware of their responsibilities and so improve the quality of public life. His undertaking was all the more critical because, as he insisted, democracy carried within it problems that an unenlightened people could fail to deal with correctly and so undermine in their ignorance and passion. Yet should a democratic people and political system of an enlightened sort become the dominant form of regime type in world affairs then all else would be possible. Accordingly, when Wilson called for increased economic interdependence between the United States and Latin America in his Mobile Address of 27 October 1913, he made it clear that ties based on capitalism red in tooth and claw were not the mechanism he hoped to see bind together the Western hemisphere but instead economic links that contributed to the prosperity of all in a way that favoured an equitable distribution of gain consonant with the encouragement of a democratic citizenry and government. His liberal internationalism thus endorsed only a qualified form of economic globalism favourable to democratic development.

Similarly, Wilson's notion of multilateralism was qualified. It was not international organizations of themselves that he counted on to promote the cause of peace, but institutions dominated by democratic peoples who alone were capable of being trustworthy and disinterested in the sense of committing themselves to serving their own interests only as the general interest was secured. Hence the resistance Wilson put up at the Paris peace negotiations in the first months of 1919 to the idea that the League of Nations might admit governments not based on the consent of the governed (much as he originally hoped that mandates created by the League be governed in such a way the peoples under international control be introduced to democracy). Eventually he recognized the futility of maintaining his position and recognized that even authoritarian governments might see the merits of collective security sought through the League. Moreover, membership in such rules-based organizations might prove to be training grounds in constitutionalism for authoritarian states. However, his trump was his conviction that thanks to its democratic character, the United States (supported by close democratic allies) could provide the 'disinterested' leadership such organizations needed for the period in which an increasing number of transitions to democratic rule might be effected.[11]

In short, whether he considered the free market, Open Door aspect of his foreign policy package, or its call for multilateral institutions for the sake of conflict resolution and collective security, or why the United States had been selected by history (or by Providence, as he sometimes put it) to be the vanguard country in the search for peace, Wilson presupposed the influence of democratically constituted individuals, citizenries and states on his vision of a liberal world order, and trusted to the leadership of the United States to provide the public goods needed to make such a system function effectively. Free markets and international organizations might well reinforce democratizing trends, to be sure – a reciprocal interaction was intrinsic to liberal thinking – but the paramount driving force for world peace had to be democracy embodied in individuals, collectivities and governments. Only these virtues could give to economic interdependence and multilateral organizations their *gravitas*, and give American leadership in world affairs the mandate of heaven, without which the United States would only repeat the self-aggrandizing behaviour of other great powers and hopes for world peace would again be destroyed, and this by a war Wilson understood could be even worse than the conflagration of 1914–18.[12]

Four stages of liberal internationalism in practice

If we turn from theory to the historical record, the paramount position of democracy in the liberal agenda is also evident. What we would call 'pre-classical liberal internationalism' may be found in the 1770s in the first stirrings of the American Revolution – perhaps most vividly in the anti-monarchist tracts of Thomas Paine with their faith in universal self-government inspired by the American example. Virtually all the Founders repeatedly expressed sentiments that with government resting on the consent of the governed, the United States would be a model for other peoples, a beacon to the ages.[13]

As George Washington stated in his First Inaugural Address, 'the preservation of the sacred fire of liberty and the destiny of the republic mode of government, are justly considered as deeply, and perhaps as finally, staked on the experiment entrusted to the hands of the American people'. Moreover, in a part of the draft that he chose not to include, he speculated on the example of the United States:

> I rejoice in a belief that intellectual light will spring up in the dark corners of the earth, that freedom of inquiry will produce a liberality of conduct; that mankind will reverse the absurd position that the many were made for the few, and that they will not continue slaves in one part of the globe when they can become freemen in another.[14]

Accordingly, the United States would cheer on the independence of Latin America and issue the Monroe Doctrine in 1823, not only for commercial and security interests but also because it appeared to signal another retreat of monarchical rule and the advent of governments that might give rise to democratic republics. Or in 1848, the United States would salute the 'springtime of nations' and its promise to undermine imperial rule in central Europe, just as it would support in the following decades constitutional reform movements in countries as different as Japan, Turkey, China and Russia. Nevertheless, in its pre-classical mode, liberal doctrine was provincial – what the United States itself would gain should democracy take root abroad was never clearly articulated – and it was insular – Americans would work by force of example rather than by force of arms to further the liberal cause worldwide.

The Spanish–American War in 1898 marks the transition of pre-classical liberal internationalism towards its 'classic' phase. Now Washington would claim to liberate the peoples of Cuba and the Philippines from autocratic rule and serve its commercial and security interests in the process. However, the stakes were low, and the effort did not compare well to the imperialist passions pushing the European powers to partition Africa, undermine the integrity of the Ottoman Empire and 'slice the Chinese melon'.

The flowering of 'classical liberal internationalism' had to await Wilson's presidency (1913–21). The genius of Wilson was his ability to combine what had been implicit features of American foreign policy into a relatively clear blueprint for world affairs, its centrepiece being the call for the United States to support the expansion of democratic governments abroad as a way of fostering freedom embedded in constitutional institutions that would inevitably strengthen the cause both of American national security and world peace. Scarcely a week into his presidency, Wilson announced his extraordinary 'non-recognition doctrine' with respect to Latin America (and more particularly with regard to Mexico, then in the throes of a momentous revolution):

> We hold […] that just government rests always upon the consent of the governed and that there can be no freedom without order based upon law and upon the public conscience and approval. We shall look to make these principles the basis of mutual intercourse, respect, and helpfulness between our sister republics and ourselves. We shall lend our influence of every kind to the realization of these principles in fact and practice, knowing that disorder, personal intrigue and defiance of constitutional rights weaken and discredit government […] We can have no sympathy with those who seek to seize the power of government to advance their own personal interest or ambition. We are friends of peace but we know that there can be no lasting peace in such circumstance.[15]

In this spirit of democratic anti-authoritarianism, Wilson endorsed the Mexican Revolution but intervened against military leaders who would usurp power in order to see that it was kept on a constitutional, and consequently a democratic, track. 'My passion is for the submerged 85 per cent of the people of the Republic who are now struggling toward liberty,' declared the president in 1914. 'I challenge you to cite me an instance in all the history of the world where liberty was handed down from above. Liberty always is attained by the forces working below, underneath, by the great movement of the people.'[16] But revolt was not enough; only constitutionally based institutions could provide freedom and stability. Otherwise anarchy could be the bitter fruit of a hard-fought uprising. In subsequent interventions in Haiti, Nicaragua and the Dominican Republic, Wilson was more concerned to stop civil strife among rival *caudillos* for the sake of a stable government; supporting the oppressed was not at the top of his agenda. Yet in all cases, as well as in his efforts to create a Pan American Treaty, the president's overriding ambition was to create government institutions based on democratic procedures; this for the benefit not only of the peoples of the countries the United States took over but for regional peace and for American security as well.[17]

Wilson's greatest bid to spread democratic government came with his call for national self-determination for the peoples liberated from imperial rule by the Great War. With the collapse of the Austro–Hungarian, Russian and Ottoman Empires in 1917–18, the moment finally seemed at hand to make a reality of the promise of 1848 and promote the expansion of the nation state at the expense of imperial orders. The president's hope was that these power vacuums would be filled with democratic states. So Wilson worked on the practical questions of national borders, the rights of minority populations, the character of new govern-ments themselves, and problems of regional stability in an area turned over to nationalist forces now that these great empires lay in ruins. He worried that the Russian Revolution would be anti-democratic. He believed that the Kaiser's abdication could lead to the consolidation of democratic government in Germany and on this basis to Franco–German reconciliation, which he saw as the key to peace in Europe. The peace treaty signed at Versailles in the spring of 1919 was to be the basis of a system of collective security lodged in the League of Nations, itself under the sway of democratic countries and especially of the United States.

Nowhere was Wilson's faith in democracy as the cornerstone of peace more evident than in his War Message to the Congress on 2 April 1917:

> A steadfast concert for peace can never be maintained except by a partnership of democratic nations. No autocratic government could be trusted to keep faith within it or observe its covenants. It must be a league of honor, a partnership of opinion. Intrigue would eat its vitals away; the plotting of inner circles who could plan what they would and render account to no one would be a corruption seated at its very heart. Only free peoples can hold their purpose and their honor steady to a common end and prefer the interests of mankind to any narrow interest of their own.

As we have seen, to construct an architecture favouring peace, Wilson proposed the League of Nations. His initial drafts for its founding Covenant (the word itself reflected Wilson's Presbyterian background and democratic insistence on personal responsibility through a group pledge) presupposed that the organization would be restricted to democratic countries (except for those that might enter by virtue of having been formally at war with Germany and Austria–Hungary). Only reluctantly, but then with some hope for later developments based especially on American leadership of the League, did Wilson surrender his insistence on making the League a club of democracies.

In short order, Wilson's efforts were thoroughly discredited. Except in Czechoslovakia, Wilson's hopes came to naught. The failure of the Senate to ratify American entry into the League, the Depression, the expanding appeal of communism in Europe and the rise of fascism, all combined to weaken liberal democracy's appeal in Europe. Yet time was to resurrect the Wilsonian promise. For thanks to Wilson, liberal internationalism had become enough of an ideology that it could survive to offer an alternative to the totalitarian movements of the 1930s.

Given the victory over fascism by 1945, 'classic liberal internationalism' was now set to enter its 'hegemonic' phase. Franklin D. Roosevelt's notion of the United Nations (UN) refined Wilson's version of the League by making it clear that the institution was no embryo of world government. Roosevelt's Bretton Woods system gave far more form to an open international economy than Wilson had ever dreamed. Roosevelt's notion that the occupation of Germany and Japan should be dedicated to the democratization of these two militaristic, autocratic countries embodied the age-old liberal belief that democratic government could profoundly influence the domestic and external behaviour of those who enjoyed it. And the president's call to the European powers to liberate the colonial empires, and to Moscow to permit the peoples of central Europe to organize freely their own governments, revealed his conviction that democracy might take root in lands where it had never been practised. As importantly, Roosevelt understood how indispensable American leadership was to the success of this bold vision. Nor was FDR's (or subsequently Harry Truman's) liberal faith misplaced. With the Marshall Plan announced in 1947 and NATO formalized in 1949, a liberal order was set into place that eventually won the Cold War.[18]

But let us not exaggerate. During the Cold War, liberalism remained a 'track' in Washington's foreign policy, a line of approach that worked to support the 'containment' of communism, a hope for a better tomorrow in a world that otherwise would continue to obey the law of the jungle. In these circumstances, democracy promotion remained a central concern in American foreign policy, but most certainly not the primary concern it was to become at a later stage. Whatever it took to defeat communism, the United States would not be found wanting. Containment based on realist thinking thus predominated over liberal ambitions, much as the two streams of argument might cooperate towards victory in the struggle with communism.[19]

Accordingly, where the prospects for democratic consolidation were evident, the Marshall Plan promised support. Where such prospects were less bright – as in the eastern Mediterranean – the Truman Doctrine nonetheless promised support to governments that were anti-communist. As a consequence, in countries critical to American security such as Greece, China, Turkey and Iran, authoritarian governments were accepted for what they were – necessary expedients in an imperfect world, where American power was not up to any mission of liberalizing regime change. 'Realistic' or 'selective' liberal internationalism was the only sensible way to proceed.

Nor did all presidents express liberal convictions in the same fashion. Dwight Eisenhower (1953–61) focused on the 'captive nations' of eastern Europe that needed to be restored to democratic life by having the boot of Soviet control lifted from their backs. Elsewhere, Eisenhower's stance was more muted, as in Iran and Guatemala, where he gave the green light to the Central Intelligence Agency (CIA) undertakings to topple constitutional governments that could fairly claim to be democratizing their countries. By contrast, the centrepiece of liberal internationalism for John F. Kennedy (1961–63) was the Alliance for Progress, an effort to promote democratic government throughout the Western hemisphere as a way of warding off the possibility that the Cuban Revolution might be repeated. By joining a call for land reform to state restructuring, Washington was engaged in an unprecedented initiative towards Latin America. From the time of Lyndon B. Johnson through to the administrations of Richard Nixon and Gerald Ford (1963–77), however, democracy promotion was at a Cold War low. As for Jimmy Carter (1977–81), the way to democracy ran through his 'human rights crusade', which he conducted against regimes favourable to the United States as well as against those that were hostile, and which he naively believed to be far less political than was actually the case. As this account suggests, the distinctiveness of these various administrations indicates why some question the meaning of democracy promotion in the making of United States' foreign policy.[20]

During the era of 'hegemonic liberal internationalism', two moments stand out as especially important – its opening in the 1940s with a blueprint for world order authored in Washington by Democrats, and its conclusion in the 1980s on terms authored by the Republicans that contributed to victory in the Cold War for the United States. Here are the liberal bookends of the contest with communism, its opening heralded by an extraordinary range of measures to arrange for cooperation among the market democracies, its conclusion marked by the presidency of Ronald Reagan (1981–89), who made liberal internationalism not only respectable in Republican circles but imaginable as part of the 'New Thinking' of Mikhail Gorbachev as well. Prior to George W. Bush (2001–9), no presidency since Wilson's time had been more liberal in world affairs than Reagan's. For some, there is a problem in awarding him this title given his suspicion of multilateral institutions like the UN. However, a distrust of international organizations not dominated by democratic states was something that might legitimately be called Wilsonian, given Wilson's distrust of autocracies and confidence in democratic practices alone. NATO might be cited as an organization far more to a liberal's liking, or the Community of Democracies set in motion at the end of the Clinton administration.

As one would expect from a Wilsonian, Reagan propounded the conviction that Washington had a leadership role in world affairs in good measure because of its moral example, and he asserted repeatedly (as in his most famous foreign policy speech at Westminster on 8 June 1982) that only democratic governments could be considered legitimate and be trusted friends of the United States. He argued that a world order run by democratic states would be more prosperous and peaceful than any other. At home and abroad, Reagan pushed anti-statist economic policies to reduce the strength of government relative to civil society while unreservedly endorsing open markets. And he indicated a willingness to use force for the defence of freedom worldwide.

A critical aspect of Reagan's approach to communism is that while he had a well-nigh religious conviction that democracy was the answer to humanity's problems, in practice he was cautious and restrained, waiting for history to take its course as he and Secretary of State George Shultz often put it, convinced as both men were that communism was fated to collapse from its own internal contradictions.[21] The relative restraint during the hegemonic period of liberal internationalism under Reagan continued during the presidency of George H. W. Bush (1989–93). Bush was well known for saying he did not have 'the vision thing' and announced that he would not 'dance on the Berlin Wall'. He also reassured Chinese leaders in the summer of 1989 that the Tiananmen Square appeals for democracy – even when invoked with the statue of the 'Goddess of Liberty' deliberately modelled on the Statue of Liberty – had no support from his administration. Similarly, Bush and his National Security Adviser Brent Scowcroft refused to engage in regime change in Baghdad after the United States' resounding victory against Iraq in 1991.

Bush nevertheless emerges as a 'selective' supporter of democracy abroad, whose primary emissary to this end was Secretary of State James Baker. After the extra-ordinary accomplishment of securing a reunified Germany as a democratic member of NATO, the great question became 'Whither Russia?' In his efforts to guide political events after the fall of the Iron Curtain and the end of the Soviet Union itself, Baker reiterated five principles governing American policy towards this vast region: that minority rights be considered sacrosanct; that human rights be respected; that borders were inviolable unless changed by peaceful means; and that the Helsinki Final Act and the Charter of Paris confirming these norms and practices were to guide conduct. In Baker's words:

> The opportunities are historic. We have the chance to anchor Russia, Ukraine, and other republics firmly into the Euro-Atlantic community and the democratic commonwealth of nations. We have the chance to bring democracy to lands that have little knowledge of it, an achievement that can transcend centuries of history … This historic watershed, the collapse of communist power in Bolshevism's birthplace, marks the challenge that history has dealt us: to see the end of the Soviet empire turn into a beginning for democracy and economic freedom across the Soviet empire.[22]

Although Bill Clinton campaigned for the presidency in 1992 on the basis of pushing a human rights agenda with respect to China and Haiti more strongly than his predecessor, once in the White House (1993–2001) he became more prudent. Although in 1995 Clinton published the first of his National Security Strategies, entitled 'Engagement and Enlargement', in which the notion of promoting democracy and open markets as the basis of national security and world peace received its first high-level statement, in action this Democratic president turned out to be of much the same mind as his Republican predecessor. He endorsed the expansion of NATO and the incorporation into the European Union of many of the once-communist states of central Europe. Yet Clinton was reluctant to use force to further a liberal agenda despite his eventual involvements in Haiti and Serbia, just as his strikes against Saddam Hussein in Baghdad were more measured than many neoconservatives especially wanted. Like Bush, Clinton backed efforts at expanding the power of the WTO and rescuing countries, from Mexico and Russia to Southeast Asia, that found themselves mired in economic difficulties over aggressive military action.

All this was to change with the presidency of George W. Bush (2001–9). With the rise to power of the neoconservative movement within this administration a new form of liberal internationalism came to the fore, a fourth 'stage' that may best be labelled as 'progressive imperialism'. While the origins of this movement were multiform, the shape that it took by 2001 focused on three central themes, all of which were compatible with traditional liberal internationalism, original though they might be in their own ways. First, neoconservatism embraced 'democratic peace theory', which maintained that should democratic governments expand worldwide, then Kant's and Wilson's vision of an international order of perpetual peace might fall into place. Second, what might be called 'democratic transition theory' reassured American policy-makers that the world was waiting for liberation from bondage. And third, liberal international jurists declared a 'duty to intervene' based on a 'responsibility to protect' (R2P) that amounted to a new 'just war' doctrine allowing democracies to depose authoritarian governments that engaged in gross and systematic human rights abuses and/or that amassed 'weapons of mass destruction'.[23]

It should be emphasized that none of these liberal internationalist arguments was original to neoconservatism. All had been developed by neoliberal academics in the United States' best universities; the only neoconservative who had any role in their generation was Francis Fukuyama, and his contribution was modest. The genius of the neoconservatives was rather the way they joined these neoliberal arguments into a seamless case for progressive imperialist war-making, then organized the political coalition and popular outreach that with Bush in office and the country at arms over the attack of 11 September 2001 eventually led to the invasion of Iraq in 2003.

Obviously, more than theory drove practice. An American president eager to show his father he could move events and a Republican Party that held out as its slogan 'ABC' ('Anything But Clinton') combined with a militaristic vice-president and secretary of defence to give Operation Iraqi Freedom its appeal. A will to power — Iraq was an attractive piece of real estate from a realist perspective, with its oil, its proximity to friends and foes of the United States and its largely desert topography — more than abstract liberal theory, drove the conviction of the neoconservatives lodged in the Pentagon, the National Security Council and the office of the vice-president that crisis meant opportunity.

Nevertheless, the promise of the new liberal internationalism composed by the neo-Wilsonian arguments of democratic peace theory, democratic transition theory and R2P played an indispensable role in persuading a large segment of 'progressive' Democrats that the Bush Doctrine's determination not only to transform Iraq but also thereby what was called 'the Broader Middle East' was a grand strategy appropriate to a period when the United States was the world's sole superpower.[24] The age-old liberal dream gained a new life. Possessed of a blueprint for action, Washington would liberate the Middle East from despotism, increase American national security, and contribute directly and mightily to a new world order of peace, based on the concepts that Wilson had first enunciated: democratic government, open markets, multilateralism and American supremacy.

The first months of the administration of Barack Obama seemed to herald a break with neoliberalism. In his Inaugural Address, the new president did not invoke 'democracy' worldwide as the standard of his vision for international order (in contrast, Bush had used the term or the word 'freedom' some 30 times in his 2005 Inaugural Address). Hillary Clinton reinforced the president's silence in prepared remarks in Senate hearings to confirm her as secretary of state when she spoke of the three pillars of policy being the 'three Ds' of 'defence, diplomacy and development', leaving out 'democracy' as a 'D' to be fostered.[25]

Yet considered from the perspective not of his immediate predecessor, whose liberalism had reached historically unparalleled extremes, but in comparison with administrations where liberalism had been mixed with a prudent realism, Obama's Wilsonian credentials remained quite in order. Well before he became president, Obama defined the United States' role in the world in Wilsonian fashion to be one of undisputed leadership; there was never any hint that he could be labelled an 'isolationist' or 'protectionist' in a 'post-American world'. Obama was not by any measure a 'declinist' either. Addressing the Chicago Council on Global Affairs with the up-beat title 'The American Moment' on 23 April 2007, he declared that his administration would open 'a new chapter in American leadership':

> I reject the notion that the American moment has passed. I dismiss the cynics who say that this new century cannot be another when [...] we lead the world in battling immediate evils and promoting the ultimate good. I still believe that America is the last, best hope of Earth.

In talks he gave and articles he published prior to his election, Obama stayed true to this theme.

Obama's lengthiest discourse on the subject of what may be called an American 'responsibility to protect' by promoting democratic government abroad came in his Nobel Prize acceptance speech of 10 December 2009. Here the president explicitly laid out the concept of 'just war' that had contributed years earlier to the invasion of Iraq:

> Make no mistake: evil does exist in the world. I believe that force can be justified on humanitarian grounds [...] inaction tears at our conscience and

can lead to more costly intervention later. That is why all responsible nations must embrace the role that militaries with a clear mandate can play to keep the peace.

Evoking democratic peace theory, Obama declared, 'Only a just peace based upon the inherent rights and dignity of every individual can truly be lasting'. Again, evoking the Universal Declaration of Human Rights adopted by the UN in 1948, he insisted: 'if human rights are not protected, peace is a hollow promise'. In lines that won the applause of neoconservatives who had supported the preceding Bush administration, the president continued in lines that could have been lifted from Reagan's Westminster address on 8 June 1982:

> In some countries the failure to uphold human rights is excused by the false suggestion that these are Western principles, foreign to local cultures or stages of a nation's development [...] I believe that peace is unstable where citizens are denied the right to speak freely or worship as they please; choose their own leaders or assemble without fear. Pent up grievances fester and the suppression of tribal and religious identity can lead to violence [...] Only when Europe became free did it finally find peace. America has never fought a war against a democracy, and our closest friends are governments that protect the rights of their citizens. No matter how callously defined, neither America's interests, nor the world's, are served by the denial of human aspirations. So even as we respect the unique culture and traditions of different countries, America will always be a voice for those aspirations that are universal.

In visits abroad from 2009 to 2011, Obama reiterated the powerful links that held together free market democracies and made them fundamentally different from authoritarian, protectionist regimes. This was a major theme of his visits to Ghana, India, Indonesia, Brazil and Chile, one repeated before the UN General Assembly in 2009 and 2010. Referring to the 'Arab Spring' during his address to the British parliament on 25 May 2011, Obama extolled respect for human rights and individual freedom.

> That is the beacon that guided us through our fight against fascism and our twilight struggle against communism. And today, that idea is being put to the test in the Middle East and North Africa. In country after country, people are mobilizing to free themselves from the grip of an iron fist. And while these movements for change are just six months old, we have seen them play out before – from Eastern Europe to the Americas, from South Africa to Southeast Asia [...] Let there be no doubt. The United States and the United Kingdom stand squarely on the side of those who long to be free. And now, we must show that we will back up those words with deeds. [...] we must also insist that we reject as false the choice between our interests and our ideals; between stability and democracy. For our idealism is rooted

in the realities of history – that repression offers only the false promise of stability, that societies are more successful when their citizens are free, and that democracies are the closest allies we have.

On 19 May 2011, shortly before leaving for London, Barack Obama had defended his actions once again, referring to North Africa and the Middle East in terms that resonated with his Nobel acceptance speech:

> The status quo is not sustainable. Societies held together by fear and repression may offer the illusion of stability for a time, but they are built upon fault lines that will eventually tear asunder. [. ...] The United States supports a set of universal rights. And these rights include free speech, the freedom of peaceful assembly, the freedom of religion, equality for men and women under the rule of law, and the right to choose your own leaders – whether you live in Baghdad or Damascus, Sanaa or Tehran [...] our support must also extend to nations [other than Tunisia and Egypt] where transitions have yet to take place.

On 22 June 2011, Obama announced the beginning of a troop withdrawal from Afghanistan in an address that implicitly gave up on nation- or state-building there and made no mention of democracy in the region. Acknowledging the serious economic problems at home, the president declared, 'America, it is time to focus on nation building here at home'. Yet in this very speech, where he displayed a realistic sense of how Afghanistan had dragged his administration into a situation that to many observers was highly reminiscent of Vietnam, Obama nonetheless found another liberal objective to serve:

> We protect our own freedom and prosperity by extending it to others. That is why we have a stake in the democratic aspirations that are now washing across the Arab world. We will support those revolutions with fidelity to our ideals, with the power of our example, and with the unwavering belief that all human beings deserve to live with freedom and dignity.

Given what was at times Obama's Wilsonian rhetoric but at other times his more measured realism, one might say of his record that it had more in common with positions taken by George H. W. Bush and Bill Clinton than with his immediate predecessor. Again and again, Obama stressed that democracy should not, indeed could not, be imposed from without. The president also recognized that the road to democratic government was neither sure nor rapid. 'History tells us that democracy is not easy', he remarked before the British parliament on 25 May 2011.

> It will be years before these revolutions [in the Arab world] reach their conclusion and there will be difficult days long the way. Power rarely gives up without a fight [...] We also know that populism can take dangerous turns – from the extremism of those who would use democracy to deny minority

rights, to the nationalism that left so many scars on this continent in the 20th century.

Like Clinton and Bush Sr., Obama was emerging as a 'selective liberal', recognizing that what was desirable might often not be feasible, and that the attempt to force events imprudently could worsen an already bad situation.

The contradictions of liberal internationalism today

By 2012 the liberal internationalist framework for policy that had done so much to establish the United States' pre-eminence in world affairs between 1945 and 2001 had contributed directly to its decline thereafter. Following 1945, American control over West Germany and Japan had allowed it to transform these two lands politically and economically, integrating them into Washington's orbit in a manner that gave the free world a decisive advantage over its Soviet and communist rivals. If containment had been the primary track for American foreign policy during the Cold War, a secondary track, consolidating the political and economic unity of the liberal democratic countries through multilateral organizations under American leadership, had had a decisive influence over the course of the global contest. Certainly, the power advantage the United States enjoyed was fundamental, as were the personalities of Reagan and Gorbachev, who brought the contest to a successful conclusion that very few anticipated. But Wilson's hope to make the United States secure by making the world peaceful through the expansion of what by Clinton's time was called 'free market democracies' meant that the contribution of liberal internationalism to the outcome had shown itself to be fundamental. Yet during the first decade of the twenty-first century, the very forces that had allowed the United States to win the Cold War had created the illusion that with relative ease history now could be controlled and international affairs fundamentally restructured by the expansion of the free market democratic world into an international order of peace. Under neoconservative and neoliberal auspices, democracy was believed to have a 'universal appeal' with peace-giving qualities of benefit to all peoples. A market economy both domestically and globally would compound the process of political stabilization. Under the terms of 'the responsibility to protect', progressive imperialism became a form of 'just war' and the American military that George W. Bush announced was 'beyond challenge' was tasked with ushering in a new dawn of freedom worldwide. For a 'unipolar world' a global mission was conceived, as in neoliberal and neoconservative hands neo-Wilsonianism evolved into a hard ideology, the equivalent in conceptual terms to Marxism–Leninism, with a capacity to give leaders and people a sense of identity and worldwide purpose that liberalism had never before possessed to such a degree.

In this march of folly, fuelled not only by ideology but also by a will to power after triumph in the Cold War, all the earlier reservations about the difficulties of nation- and state-building that were discussed during the Cold War were disregarded so that even after policy-makers understood that democracy did not grow spontaneously in many places, they were reassured by authoritative studies put out by places like the RAND Corporation and the Army/Marine Corps that such missions could be accomplished.[26] As a consequence, although it was widely recognized that the failure to plan properly for Iraq after Baghdad had been captured was a fundamental error, very few voices in positions of power were heard saying that the democratization of Iraq and Afghanistan (or the thought of working with 'democratic' Pakistan) was likely a fool's errand from the start. Instead, efforts to rectify the failures at conceptualizing state- and nation-building turned out to be 'how to' or 'can do' publications. These tracts only prolonged and deepened a misplaced American self-confidence that it was possible to use the window of opportunity at the country's disposition as the world's sole superpower to change the logic of international relations forever.

Much the same mixture of arrogance, self-interest and self-delusion characterized the arguments underlying the 'Washington Consensus', which boldly saw the key to world prosperity and peace in the interdependence generated by economic globalization with its trinity of concepts – privatization, deregulation and openness. Certainly, economic interdependence was indeed capable of delivering on its promise, as the integration of the European Union and the growth in world trade and investment centred on the free market democracies so powerfully demonstrated for half a century after the Second World War. However, a serious problem lay in the inability of political forces, either nationally or internationally, to control the capitalist genie once let out of its bottle. For in due course, deregulation turned against the very system that had given birth to it, unleashing a flight of technology, capital and jobs (to countries in Asia especially) and permitting the irresponsible banking practices that engendered in the United States and the European Union (after having earlier affected Mexico, Russia, Southeast Asia and Argentina more than a decade earlier) an economic crisis second in its devastation only to the Great Depression of the 1930s.

The result in the United States was not only the decimation first of the working and then of the middle classes as the top 10 per cent of the nation (and especially the top 1 per cent) monopolized virtually all the gains of economic openness for a period of more than two decades, but also a decline in national power as technology, capital and jobs moved abroad and as China grew apace.[27] For all the talk by Obama about the example the United States should set for the sake of democracy promotion abroad, the first three years of his administration did not meaningfully address the deep-seated, underlying problems of economic growth and inequality in the country, nor the control by corporations of its political life, nor concerns about national power based on an economy in decline. As a result, liberal economic doctrine and practice were undermining democratic government as well as national power. Aspects of the liberal agenda, once too easily assumed to be automatically mutually reinforcing, were coming to be increasingly at odds with one another.

The Wilsonian tradition thus found itself in crisis. Within only two decades after the Cold War, liberal internationalist overconfidence in the universal appeal of democratic government and in the blessing of unregulated free market capitalism had combined to reduce the effectiveness of multilateral institutions and the capacity of the United States to provide leadership in settling the problems of world order. A liberal order capable of withstanding the challenges of both fascism and communism had come in a short time to be its own worst enemy. Communism was dead, but 'free market democracy' was proving to be a much weaker blueprint for world order than had only recently been anticipated. As Machiavelli had counselled in his *Discourses*, 'Men always commit the error of not knowing where to limit their hopes, and by trusting to these rather than to a just measure of their resources, they are generally ruined.'

One scenario for the future was bleak. It foresaw economic chaos as feeding on itself; more self-defeating military interventions being undertaken; and all the while the banner of freedom and democracy being lifted at the very moment that self-government was being undermined at home by vested interests and delusional thinking undergirding an imperial presidency. Yet if liberalism for the moment was its own worst enemy, other forces challenged its future role as well. As the fate of the Rose Revolution of 2003 in Georgia, the Orange Revolution in Ukraine in 2004–5 and the Cedar Revolution in Lebanon in 2005 all illustrated, transitions from authoritarian government were often quite difficult to accomplish. More critically, the model of state capitalism in conjunction with authoritarian states was giving increasing evidence that it might prove more successful in creating national power than the free market democratic blueprint prevalent in the West. Not only China, but also Russia, had deep-set cultural and political forces resisting the liberal appeal. More ominously, there was increasing reason to think that in time authoritarian state capitalism might consolidate itself in a way that could markedly increase the national power of China and Russia relative to the West and Japan, and this in a fashion that diminished the international standing of the United States while breaking the back of the unity that had held together the world of free market democracies.[28]

Perhaps this pessimism characteristic of 2012 was exaggerated. The June Democracy Movement of 1987 had led to the establishment of what subsequently appeared to be a solid democracy in South Korea, as did a plebiscite in Chile in 1988 and one in Slovenia in 1990. Poland and the Czech Republic were among the countries that moved with relative ease to democracy once the Soviet empire collapsed. Brazil, the most important of Latin American countries, demonstrated the ability of a country outside the perimeter of American hegemony to combine responsible government with strong economic growth and successful projects of social justice. The Brazilian model had obvious relevance for all of Latin America, with the potential to displace the appeal of the 'illiberal' variant of democracy, such as was evident with Hugo Chavez in Venezuela and his imitators.[29]

So, too, the Arab world was finally in movement in the aftermath of the Tunisian uprising that began late in 2010, giving birth to the 'Arab Spring'. Stirred by the success of popular democracy movements in Tunisia and Egypt that resulted in the fall of long-term dictators in January and February 2011, a popular revolt began in Libya, one that Muamarr Qaddafi moved savagely and unsuccessfully to repress. In March, the Arab League and the UN Security Council voted to sanction intervention to stop the threat of mass murders by government forces in eastern Libya. On 19 March 2011 (the eighth anniversary of the invasion of Iraq), American and British missiles fell on Libyan government forces that French and British war planes were attacking simultaneously. Non-violent mass protests based on politicized youths explicitly demanding democratic government (and to all appearances uninterested in the rhetoric of Islamic fundamentalism) demonstrated the weakness of brutal and ineffective authoritarian government and the appeal of constitutional order, with its emphasis on transparent and accountable government capable of providing a tangible margin of freedom, prosperity and national dignity. The Wilsonian promise appeared to be bearing fruit where few had thought to see it appear so robustly.

But would the Arab world be capable of embracing democracy? If Tunisia had the good fortune to possess most of the ingredients for success – no serious ethno-religious cleavages; a well-organized, moderate trade union movement; a large, educated middle class; a small military; a moderate mainstream Islamist movement; and no oil or gas resources to fund a state independent of popular will – nowhere else in the Arab world (allowance perhaps made for the monarchies in Jordan and Morocco) was there the same likelihood of making a transition to democracy.[30] That said, the Turkish model – where responsible government, economic growth, Islamic secularism and social justice were emerging with a character that was indigenous – might have influence in many countries where historically the Ottoman Empire has left its mark.

Just as it was possible that liberal internationalism's dedication to democracy promotion might still have life whatever the reversals in Iraq and Afghanistan, so too economic reform was possible whatever the damage inflicted by the crisis that began in 2008 and that had not abated three years later. For it is in the interest of capitalism to be regulated; effective markets cannot exist without the same kind of accountability and transparency we expect from democratic governments. Moreover, supranational institutions may experience growth as they take on the task of supervising at regional or international levels reforms that will also involve increased political harmonization if not integration. While the hold of corporate influence on political elites in the United States and national differences in the European Union could block the very changes that it would be to their long-term benefit to have, it might also turn out that dramatic innovations could be adopted, should the Democrats insist on thoroughgoing reforms in the spirit of the Progressive Era or the New Deal when their party gave critical leadership, or should the European Union manage not only to survive the challenges to the unity of the euro zone but actually to grow supranationally in the process.

The fate of liberal internationalism thus depended for the most part by 2012 on the behaviour of those who guide the policies of the democratic world. If leaders of a Wilsonian persuasion could rein in the inflated self-confidence that too many of them had in the two decades after the end of the Cold War with respect to the merits of an indiscriminate promotion of democratic nation- and state-building and with regard to their unquestioning support for a deregulated capitalism – if they could regain the modesty and realism that Reinhold Niebuhr called for 60 years ago and that in many respects Woodrow Wilson displayed a century ago – then liberal internationalism might continue to play a beneficent role in world politics. The choice was for the United States to make, as Niebuhr had insisted in the final lines of *The Irony of American History*:

> If we should perish, the ruthlessness of the foe would be only the secondary cause of the disaster. The primary cause would be that the strength of a great nation was directed by eyes too blind to see all the hazards of the struggle; and the blindness would be induced not by some accident of nature or history but by hatred and vainglory.[31]

Notes

1 On what he calls 'the protean nature of Wilsonianism and the diverse adjectives that the term continues to host', see Thomas Knock, 'Playing for a Hundred Years Hence', in G. John Ikenberry *et al.*, *The Crisis of American Foreign Policy: Wilsonianism in the Twenty-First Century*, Princeton University Press, 2009, 26ff. See also Brian C. Rathbun, 'Is Anybody not an International Relations Liberal?', *Security Studies,* 19, 2010, and Frank Ninkovich, 'Wilsonianism after the Cold War: Words, Words, Mere Words', in John Milton Cooper Jr. ed., *Reconsidering Woodrow Wilson: Progressivism, Internationalism and Peace*, Woodrow Wilson Center Press and Johns Hopkins University Press, 2008.

2 For an extended discussion of types of international relations thinking, see also Michael W. Doyle, *Ways of War and Peace: Realism, Liberalism and Socialism*, Norton, 1997.

3 Bruce Russett and John Oneal, *Triangulating Peace: Democracy, Interdependence, and International Organizations*, Yale University Press, 2001. For a critique, see Tony Smith, *A Pact with the Devil: Washington's Bid for International Supremacy and the Betrayal of the American Promise*, Routledge, Taylor & Francis, 2007, pp. 101ff, 116ff.

4 Whereas Russett and Oneal use a three-sided *triangle* throughout their book to illustrate the interaction of democracy, economic openness and multilateralism on one another, we suggest instead a four-sided *diamond*, adding as an indispensable additional concept the character of a hegemonic power; in this case the United States.

5 Neo-Marxist arguments of this sort appeared as 'dependency' theories in the 1970s and remain current in some leftist circles today, in the United States perhaps most prominently in the work of Noam Chomsky. The roots of such thinking are to be found in early twentieth-century debates among Rosa Luxemburg, Karl Kautsky, Vladimir Lenin and John Hobson. On Wilson, see Arno Mayer, *Politics and Diplomacy of the Peacemaking: Containment and Counter-revolution at Versailles, 1918–1919*, Knopf, 1967.

6 For a historical perspective that starts in 1815, see G. John Ikenberry, *After Victory: Institutions, Strategic Restraint, and the Rebuilding of Order after Major Wars*, Princeton University Press, 2001; see also Ikenberry, *Liberal Leviathan: The Origins, Crisis and Transformation of the American World Order*, Princeton University Press, 2011.

7 On the importance of multilateralism to Wilsonianism, see Thomas Knock, 'Playing for a Hundred Years Hence', and Anne-Marie Slaughter, 'Wilsonianism in the Twenty-first Century', in G. John Ikenberry *et al.*, *The Crisis of American Foreign Policy*, op. cit.

8 Such a conviction is apparent in Wilson's thought from his earliest ruminations on democratic character and government to his latest writings. For an early statement, see Wilson, 'The Modern Democratic State', in Arthur S. Link, *The Papers of Woodrow Wilson*, Princeton University Press, December 1885, 5:54ff; see also his last academic publication, *Constitutional Government in the United States*, 1908.

9 See Woodrow Wilson, *The New Freedom: A Call for the Emancipation of the Generous Energies of a People*, Doubleday, Page and Company, 1918. See also Emily S. Rosenberg, 'Progressive Internationalism and Reformed Capitalism: New Freedom to New Deal', and J. Elliot Brownlee, 'Wilson's Reform of Economic Structure: Progressive Liberalism and the Corporation', in John Milton Cooper Jr., ed., *Reconsidering Woodrow Wilson: Progressivism, Internationalism, War, and Peace*, Woodrow Wilson Center Press and the Johns Hopkins University Press, 2008.

10 See Wilson's discussion of demagogic democracy in 'The Modern Democratic State', in Link, *The Papers*, op. cit., 5:87ff.

11 To review the evolution of Wilson's thinking during the Peace Conference, see the various drafts of the Covenant and meetings of the Commission in what remains an indispensable source, David Hunter Miller, *The Drafting of the Covenant*, G.P. Putnam's Sons, 1928, two volumes.

12 Hence the importance of the rule of law in Wilson's thinking throughout his life, most fully expressed in his final academic publication, *Constitutional Government in the United States* (1908).

13 See Smith, *A Pact*, op. cit., ch. 3, for a more extended discussion.

14 Matthew Spalding and Patrick J. Garrity, *A Sacred Union of Citizens: George Washington's Farewell Address and the American Character*, Rowman & Littlefield, 1996, 113f.

15 In Link, *The Papers*, op. cit., 27:172. See also 30:231ff and 37:36f. On the Caribbean, see Arthur S. Link, *The Struggle for Neutrality, 1914–1915*, Princeton University Press, 1960, ch. 15, and for Mexico, chs 8, 14, 18.

16 Wilson cited in Ray Stannard Baker and William E. Dodd, *The New Democracy: Presidential Messages, Addresses and Other Papers, 1913–1917*, Harper and Brothers, 1926, 1:111f.

17 On Wilson's efforts to bring into existence a Pan American Union based on a treaty pledging all countries to be democracies, see Link, *The Papers*, op. cit., 35:111f, 188f, 241f.

18 Fuller discussion in Tony Smith, *America's Mission: The United States and the Worldwide Struggle for Democracy*, Princeton University Press, second ed., 2012, chs 5–6.

19 G. John Ikenberry, *After Victory*, op. cit., chs 6–7.

20 Smith, *America's Mission*, op. cit., chs 7–11.

21 For a fuller discussion of the Reagan years, see Smith, *America's Mission*, op. cit., ch. 10.

22 On James Baker and the Bush administration, see *America's Mission*, op. cit., 310ff. In the name of democracy promotion, the administration also intervened in the Philippines to protect the government of President Corazon Aquino, and assured the Sandinista government in Nicaragua that, if it would abide by free elections, Washington would recognize whatever faction won the popular vote there.

23 For an extended discussion of these three concepts, see Smith, *A Pact*, op. cit., chs 4–6.

24 On the Progressive Policy Institute as a think tank founded by the Democratic Leadership Council in 1989, which roundly endorsed these neoliberal views for policy reasons, see Smith, ibid., 179–90.

25 Nicolas Bouchet, 'Barack Obama's Democracy Promotion at Midterm', *The International Journal of Human Rights*, 15, 4, May 2011, 572.

26 James Dobbins *et al.*, *America's Role in Nation Building: From Germany to Iraq*, RAND, 2003; *The U.S. Army/Marine Corps Counterinsurgency Field Manual*, University of Chicago Press, 2007. For a fuller discussion, see Smith, *America's Mission*, op. cit., ch. 13.

27 Jacob S. Hacker and Paul Pierson, *Winner-Take-All Politics: How Washington Made the Rich Richer and Turned its Back on the Middle Class*, Simon and Schuster, 2010; Robert B. Reich, *Aftershock: The Next Economy and America's Future*, Knopf, 2010; Robert G. Kaiser, *So Damn Much Money: The Triumph o f Lobbying and the Corrosion of American Government*, Knopf, 2009. See also the articles by Paul Krugman in *The New York Times* in spring and summer 2011.

28 For a cogent argument, see Azar Gat, 'The Return of Authoritarian Great Powers', *Foreign Affairs*, July/August 2007. On the rise of the Chinese model, see Bruce J. Dickson, *Wealth into Power: The Communist Party's Embrace of the China's Private Sector*, Cambridge

University Press, 2008, and Stefan Halper, *The Beijing Consensus: How China's Authoritarian Model Will Dominate the Twenty-First Century*, Basic, 2010, especially chs 3–4.

29 Fareed Zakaria, *The Future of Freedom: Illiberal Democracy at Home and Abroad*, W.W.Norton, 2004.

30 Lisa Anderson, 'Demystifying the Arab Spring', and Jack A. Goldstone, 'Understanding the Revolutions of 2011', *Foreign Affairs*, 90, 3, July–August 2011.

31 Reinhold Niebuhr, *The Irony of American History*, University of Chicago Press, 1952.

2

THEODORE ROOSEVELT

Adam Quinn[1]

Sometimes when we read the words of statesmen long dead it is the sense of uncanny familiarity that seems most striking. We find it easy to imagine their phrases and sentiments transplanted down the generations to emerge little altered from the mouths of present-day successors. At other times, it is the jarring sense of difference that strikes us more forcefully. Even those historical figures whose thinking we consider richest in contemporary resonance often also harboured thoughts and dealt in turns of phrase that seem alien, even offensive, to the sensibilities of today.

As L. P. Hartley commented, 'the past is a foreign country: they do things differently there'. There are two sides to this proverbial coin: first, we have to guard against the mistake of assuming we have an uncomplicated bond of common understanding with a speaker from distant history simply because they used words with which we think ourselves still familiar. Inhabiting a formative context and intellectual milieu quite different from our own, a voice from decades past may speak words that sound superficially familiar to our ear, but have intended a meaning quite different from what we would in invoking the same words today. This is most obvious when it comes to terms like 'empire', which have acquired a caravan of pejorative baggage over the years that did not previously exist, but less immediately suspicious words can be nearly as slippery; 'liberty' and 'democracy' being examples that spring to mind. Likewise we must be careful to avoid the converse misunderstanding: allowing differences in phraseology to blind us to close similarities of concept and attitude. Sometimes thoughts may have been expressed whose substance speaks readily to today's debates, but been couched in language familiar more to a bygone era than to our own.

All of this is by way of a prologue to the simple observation that the rhetoric of some statesmen has travelled better down the years than that of others, falling more gently upon the twenty-first-century ear. One example particularly close to the heart of the topic under focus in this book is the comparison between Theodore Roosevelt and his contemporary Woodrow Wilson.[2] To those in search of chiming resonances between today's rhetoric and the traditions of America's past, Wilson provides the readiest of material. Over a period of years, especially after the United States' entry into the First World War, Wilson delivered an array of pronouncements that seem to map directly onto the ideological preoccupations of American leaders during the century that followed. He spoke often, in terms that with only minor amendment could sit within a presidential address today, about the empowerment of peoples over governments, the creation of a world order based upon cooperation rather than rivalrous balances of power, and of the spread of liberty as a transformational force for good. In doing so he seems to signify himself down the decades to us as a forerunner, perhaps the founding father, of America's modern leaning towards liberal universalism. Indeed, in the term 'Wilsonianism', his name has itself become a byword for that tradition. All this being the case, the justification for Wilson's prime location in any survey of the tradition of American democracy promotion is intuitively clear, requiring little in the way of audience persuasion.

Theodore Roosevelt was an animal of a rather different stripe. Where Wilson's rhetoric and statecraft centred on modern-sounding concepts like freedom, national self-determination and the 'new world order', Roosevelt focused on national greatness, martial virtue and unashamedly hierarchical, sometimes race-oriented, thinking about civilization and progress. Though Roosevelt's presidency, from 1901 to 1909, preceded Wilson's by only four years, and though Wilson was actually by a slight margin the older man, Wilson's soaring liberal rhetoric seems to connect in a straight line with the idealistic pronouncements of American leaders in subsequent generations. Roosevelt's unabashedly imperialist and militarist ideals, on the other hand, often seem to speak to us as epistles from a lost world, predating the onset of the world wars and ideological struggles of the twentieth century.

This is not just a matter of appearances deceiving. It is indeed true that in various respects Roosevelt was more in tune with the diplomatic mores of the nineteenth and early twentieth century, while Wilson's mindset, for better and for worse, was built around the core liberal notions at the heart of much of the United States' later twentieth-century international strategy, especially after the Second World War.[3] As is discussed below, there is a basis for applying a variety of labels to Roosevelt's approach to foreign policy – imperialist, moralist, nationalist, realist – but 'promoter of democracy' would be a quirky choice, and not one he would likely have embraced himself. Nevertheless, in spite of his often period-stamped preoccupations, Roosevelt remains a significant figure if we seek to understand the emergence of the United States as an assertive global power actively embracing value-laden intervention in the internal affairs of other nations, and that in turn is important in understanding the evolution of the democracy promotion tradition. His convictions – minority positions in his own time, entirely mainstream later – regarding the importance of a militarily strong, internationally active United States, and his efforts to translate them into policy as best he could within an often constrained political context, represent a crucial staging post in the nation's journey from being a deliberately inward-looking and militarily insignificant country to a globally entangled great power with both the capacity and the disposition to seek to engineer the political destiny of foreign societies.

This chapter proceeds as follows. First, it sets out the context in which Roosevelt's presidency occurred and sketches the mindset he brought to foreign policy, especially his preoccupation with national greatness and a bigger role for the United States in global diplomacy. Second, it sets out the aspects of his policy that had particular bearing on the question of interference with the internal affairs of other nations: his reinvigoration of the Monroe Doctrine as a charter for deeper regional hegemony in Latin America, as well as his policy in Asia. Third, it concludes by evaluating the connection between the Roosevelt era and democracy promotion. It argues that Roosevelt was significant not only for seeking, with some success, to expand the United States' strategic horizons, but also for attaching that goal to the missionary objective of placing national power in the service of furthering 'civilization'. It is clear that Roosevelt did not draw an uncomplicated equivalence between 'civilization', the thing of highest value to him, and 'democracy', but he did regard 'orderly liberty' as 'both the foundation and the capstone of our civilization', and was convinced it could be 'gained and kept only by men who are willing to fight for an ideal'.[4]

Roosevelt's context: accidental president in a changing word

Roosevelt came to power not long after the watershed moment symbolizing the emergence of the United States as a global power, namely the Spanish–American war of 1898. In spite of entering that conflict with armed forces that were relatively small in number and little prepared for war with a major power, however declining, the United States had emerged with a surprisingly speedy and comprehensive victory. In the space of only a few months, American forces in the Caribbean successfully occupied Cuba and Puerto Rico, while in the Pacific American ships pulverized the Spanish fleet at Manila, adding the Philippines to the haul. It was, in the phrase of the soon-to-be secretary of state John Hay, 'a splendid little war', at least from the perspective of the American government and press.[5]

Roosevelt himself played two significant parts in the unfolding of these events. First, as assistant secretary of the navy, he helped put in place the plans that would ultimately result in the naval triumph at Manila and seizure of the Philippines. With that scheme in place, he then resigned his desk in Washington and took personally to the battlefield in Cuba, where his heavily publicized service with a volunteer cavalry regiment, the so-called 'Rough Riders', earned him status as an overnight popular hero. This was the springboard from which Roosevelt propelled himself into elected politics as governor of New York, and from there, thanks first to internal rows within the Republican Party and then to the dark chance of President William McKinley's assassination by an anarchist in September 1901, almost immediately upward to the vice-presidency and presidency. Within three years he had gone from a second-tier bureaucratic post in the executive branch to being president of the United States. At 42, he was the youngest ever to hold the office.

Roosevelt took office at a time of increasing strength and confidence for the nation, though in a world undergoing shifts in the distribution of power whose outcome could not yet be foreseen. The United States' wealth, territory and population had all grown hugely over the preceding decades, granting it a new significance, in potential at least, in the global scales. Dealing the deathblow to the sickly Spanish empire served to underline the impression of an emergent great power. The world of Roosevelt's era was still dominated, as it had been for centuries previously, by powerful European states, including Britain, France and Russia, but the prevailing balance of power was increasingly being challenged, at Europe's centre by the rise of the recently unified Germany, and in the East by Japan, the first nation populated neither by Europeans nor their colonial descendents to 'modernize' in pursuit of great power status. This opportune combination of internal and external circumstances meant that a larger world role was the United States' for the asking. The question was whether the country had the stomach for the undertaking.

The expansion of American horizons: national greatness as national mission

Though conspiracy of events placed him in office young and unexpectedly, Roosevelt did not enter the White House without firm ideas about the United States' role in the world. Perhaps most central to his worldview was an almost obsessive-compulsive devotion to the importance of energy and activity.[6] Roosevelt the man was notable – indeed notorious – for being convinced of the virtue of constant physical and mental exertion. Several contemporary observers, as well as subsequent biographers, remarked on how those in his company, regardless of age or station, were conscripted into to an unceasing sequence of physically demanding pastimes and subjected in conversation, willingly or otherwise, to a cascading torrent of words and thoughts.[7] This compulsive dynamism was buttressed with an explicitly articulated philosophy of self-improvement through active participation. Moral virtue, he believed, and would later tell the world from a podium, could be attained only by being 'the man who is actually in the arena, whose face is marred by dust and sweat and blood'. Win or lose, such a man was superior to the 'cold and timid souls who know neither victory nor defeat'.[8] Leon Bazalgette, author of the first Roosevelt biography, noted that:

> To live, for him, has no meaning other than to drive oneself, to act with all one's strength. An existence without stress, without struggle, without growth has always struck him as mindless. Those who remain on the sidelines he sees as cowards.[9]

It is not difficult to see how such an outlook on life might sit ill with the traditions of hemispheric detachment and non-entanglement that had prevailed in American foreign policy since the era of the founding fathers, and one way of understanding Roosevelt's approach to foreign policy is as an extension of these beliefs about individual virtue to the level of nations. By the time he rose to national prominence, it was clear that the United States possessed the size and resources necessary to claim a place at the table of the great powers. What remained uncertain was whether it had the political will to stake such a claim, and in so doing to take on the burdens – financial, military, political and moral – of global power-broking inherent in doing so. Knowing that the American populace and its representatives had grave and long-standing reservations about setting aside the nation's traditions of non-entanglement and hemispheric separatism, Roosevelt made it his mission to use all means at his disposal to overcome this national reluctance.

As Roosevelt saw it, the nation, as the individuals within it, had a moral calling to test itself in the 'arena' – to live what he termed 'the strenuous life' – rather than seek a life of quiet prosperity through withdrawal from the world.

> Far better it is to dare mighty things, to win glorious triumphs, even though checkered by failure, than to take rank with those poor spirits who neither enjoy much nor suffer much, because they live in the grey twilight that knows not victory nor defeat.[10]

The country most to be admired was that prepared to 'boldly face the life of strife ... provided we are certain that the strife is justified, for it is only through strife, through hard and dangerous endeavour, that we shall ultimately win the goal of true national greatness'.[11]

This was not so much a choice, really, as it was a duty, to be either undertaken honourably or shirked. 'There is scant room in the world at large for the nation with mighty thews that dares not to be great', he told Americans in 1901.[12] Having comfortably won a presidential term in his own right in 1904, he used his Inaugural Address to tell the nation that

> Much has been given us, and much will rightfully be expected from us ... We have become a great nation, forced by the fact of its greatness into relations with the other nations of the earth, and we must behave as beseems a people with such responsibilities.[13]

It would be an impermissible display of weak character, Roosevelt thought, for America to seek to 'opt out' of its responsibility to act as a global power. Drawing a parallel with the simultaneous responsibilities of individuals to both family and society, he argued that

> a nation's first duty is within its own borders, [but] it is not thereby absolved from facing its duties in the world as a whole; and if it refuses to do so, it merely forfeits its right to struggle for a place among the peoples that shape the destiny of mankind.[14]

Nations might ultimately be transient, like men, but 'the nation that has dared to be great, that has had the will and the power to change the destiny of the ages … really continues, though in a changed form, to live forevermore'.[15] In painting this romantic narrative of achieving national immortality through shaping the course of history, Roosevelt was more than happy to draw explicit parallels with the historical legacies of the Roman and British empires.[16] As Britain had done in Egypt and India, he mused in his 'strenuous life' address, 'we will play our part in the great work of uplifting mankind'.[17]

Doing this 'great work of uplifting' would require investment in the United States' capacity to wield power, to allow it to harness its size and wealth for strategic purposes. This meant enlarging and modernizing its armed forces, particularly its navy, and the effort to do so was perhaps the single most prominent and recurrent concrete policy objective sought by all his political pronouncements. One of the first addresses of importance he made in national office to the Naval War College in 1897 was on the theme of 'Washington's Forgotten Maxim', by which he meant the old epigram that 'to be prepared for war is the most effectual way to promote peace'.[18] Attacking the prevailing Jeffersonian tradition in the United States' political culture, which was suspicious of standing armies, he explained that in his view there was 'not the slightest danger of an over-development of warlike spirit' in the United States.[19] On the contrary, the true danger lay in its underdevelopment. A popular movement of the time sought to push governments to enter arbitration treaties to avert war in cases of dispute, but Roosevelt was convinced these were quite insufficient to serve as guarantors of the peace:

> Arbitration is an excellent thing, but ultimately those who wish to see this country at peace with foreign nations will be wise if they place reliance upon a first-class fleet of battleships rather than on any arbitration treaty which the wit of man can devise.[20]

Regarding the United States' relations with the European great powers, he was of the unsentimental view that

> we shall keep the respect of each of them just so long as we are thoroughly able to hold our own, and no longer. If we got into trouble, there is not one of them whose friendship we could count on to get us out; what we shall need to count upon is the efficiency of our own fighting men and particularly of our navy.[21]

As well as shipbuilding, national preparedness meant something less tangible: the inculcation of fighting spirit in the people, ensuring that they developed 'those most valuable of all qualities, the soldierly virtues'.[22] To one regular correspondent he wrote in 1907: 'I abhor and despise that pseudo-humanitarianism which treats advance in civilization as necessarily and rightfully implying a weakening of the fighting spirit and which therefore invites destruction of the advanced civilization by some less-advanced type.'[23]

Weaker nations, intervention and the spreading of 'civilization'

During Wilson's presidency a decade later, the United States would emerge explosively from its tradition of 'isolation', waging war in Europe, preaching the gospel of universal liberty and proposing a grand new scheme for the reform of the global order. During Roosevelt's tenure, in the absence of the extraordinary turbulence confronting Wilson's America on the international scene, such a bold break with the past was politically inconceivable, however keen on a new activism abroad the president personally might have been. Roosevelt did find some smaller opportunities to realize his desire to develop the muscles of American intervention, however, in Latin America and Asia. In the Americas, he oversaw the expansion of the Monroe Doctrine from a largely symbolic expression of American hostility to outside interference into a regime of hegemonic American dominance. In Asia, he joined the great-power consortium in facing down native resistance to the exploitation of China, and also learned the downside costs of imperialism as the United States struggled to decide what to do with the Philippine prize it had won in 1898.

The initial spur to a new interventionism in the Americas was not any great interest in the affairs of the Latin American states and Caribbean states *per se*, but rather a desire to forestall land-grabbing on the part of European powers. It had been an increasing source of concern over the preceding years that Latin American nations had been running up debts to European powers, with their ability to pay in doubt. This came to a head during Roosevelt's presidency in 1902, when it seemed that Venezuela's inability or unwillingness to pay its debts to Germany and Britain might result in the use of force on the part of those powers to coerce the Venezuelan government and perhaps seize territory in lieu of cash. Roosevelt managed to see off the short-term danger, apparently using back-channel threats in combination with American naval deployments to deter Germany from seeking to establish a new colonial foothold.[24] But he was acutely aware that this action on his part had created a moral hazard. If the United States was determined to uphold the Monroe Doctrine, which prohibited European intervention against states in the Americas, did this not provide those nations with every incentive to run up bad debts under cover of a blanket American guarantee of protection against the consequences? In the Venezuelan case, the heat of crisis had allowed the United States to corral the government into arbitration to resolve the original dispute. But what of future such cases?

It was the need to resolve this dilemma that gave rise to Roosevelt's well-known 'corollary' to the Monroe Doctrine, which expanded the doctrine into the interventionist's charter that the term conjures today. The Roosevelt Corollary stated that since the United States was to be expected to defend Latin American states against European intervention in a crisis, it must be entitled to act preventively against any actions on their part that might provoke such a turn of events. This ideological quid pro quo served – from the American perspective, at least – to legitimize interventions on the part of the United States, including if necessary the use of force and the seizure of parts of a state's financial apparatus, to ensure 'sound' management. This was the principle that underwrote what would become a pattern of recurring regional interventionism unfolding under Roosevelt and his successors, including interventions in Cuba, Nicaragua, Haiti and the Dominican Republic.

Roosevelt's conception of 'civilization', and his understanding of it as a progressive phenomenon in which some peoples were more advanced than others, played an important part in legitimizing this framework for hemispheric relations. The corollary was based on the idea that more advanced nations had a duty to monitor and educate those less developed. Under conditions where 'chronic wrongdoing, or ... impotence ... results in a general loosening of the ties of civilized society', Roosevelt argued, 'intervention by some civilized nation' would be entirely justified, and perhaps morally required. Within the area covered by the Monroe Doctrine this meant the 'exercise of an international police power' by the United States, 'however reluctantly'. He was naturally eager to disavow any 'land hunger' on the part of the United States, insisting that any American intervention should be understood as serving the long-term interests of the nations affected. 'All that this country desires is to see the neighbouring countries stable, orderly, and prosperous', he professed.[25] So long as 'the reign of law and justice' held sway within their borders and they obeyed 'the primary laws of civilized society', no Latin American state need fear interference.[26]

On one level, Roosevelt's approach could be read as straightforwardly self-interested realist policy on the part of the United States, excluding rival powers from its sphere of influence and exercising dominion over the weaker states in its immediate environs. Within the American sphere, however, Roosevelt's ideological vision could more accurately be characterized as a sort of liberal quasi-imperialism rather than the realist image of morally equivalent states competing for advantage in a fundamentally neutral system.[27] Roosevelt did not envision the 'American system' in the Western hemisphere as operating based upon raw coercion on the part of the United States in the service of exploiting its neighbours. Rather, the purpose was to serve a sort of imagined 'common interest', albeit one that the United States presumed the right to define and act upon unilaterally. This principle of American leadership, unaccountable yet somehow still thought to be legitimate by reference to its benign quality, would prove central to understanding the ideology of American interventionism that would follow, including Wilsonianism and its successor creeds.

Without an understanding of the self-justificatory role played by this ideological perspective, subsequent American policy appears entirely cynical and disingenuous. Giving some credence to the reality of its place in Roosevelt's mind, and those of many of his supporters and contemporaries, however, American policy takes on the aspect of an often well-intentioned, if profoundly chauvinistic, enterprise, and this is on balance probably a more accurate characterization of the bulk of American thinking. Roosevelt's ideological position did contain elements of the liberal, in that it treated self-government as the ideal for all peoples and aiding it as a primary purpose of outside intervention. But it also contained an unmistakable strain of imperialism in presuming to impose American parameters on the values and practices 'free' societies should adopt. '[E]very nation ... which desires to maintain its freedom, its independence,' he argued, 'must ultimately realize that the right of such independence cannot be separated from the responsibility of making good use of it.'[28]

Beyond the Americas, elements of the same framework could be discerned, albeit tailored for the different circumstances confronted. In the Philippines, the United States inherited from Spain a restive native population convinced of its right to independence and disposed to resist further subordination. Between 1899 and 1902 this took the form of active and violent resistance against American presence on the islands. Thereafter, with rebellion quieted and American administration imposed, it took the form of dominance on the part of independence-supporting groups within what institutions existed to represent the local population.[29]

Roosevelt is rightly associated, because of his writings and lobbying at the time, with the wave of unabashed imperialism that swept the United States immediately before and after the territorial acquisitions of 1898.[30] By the time of his presidency only a couple of years later, however, the realities of dealing with newly acquired territory populated with unwilling subjects had battered the nation's brief enthusiasm for openly embracing empire. The Philippines and Cuba both presented difficulties for the American government, since under prevailing political sensibilities their large non-white populations could nether be displaced and replaced as the American Indians had been in the continental United States, nor assimilated as citizens into the existing structures of the American government. Yet any declaration that the new territories were to be administered under perpetual colonial rule in the European style would generate discomfiting friction with the dominant American political creed, which defined itself by opposition to colonialism and unrepresentative government. But Roosevelt (and others) also had grave doubts, especially in the case of the Philippines, about capacity of the locals to govern themselves 'properly' if granted immediate independence. The only option remaining, therefore, was a sort of liberal-imperialist 'middle way': to embrace ultimate liberation for the subject peoples as an objective, while justifying continued American administration as necessary to ensure their 'education' in how to make 'good use' of their freedom.

Thus the legacy of 1898, in combination with Roosevelt's imperial instincts and desire for a larger American foreign policy, was a commitment to civilizational 'uplift' in those places where American action could, to varying degrees, carry the necessary authority. 'Barbarism', Roosevelt explained to Americans in an address in 1902, could have 'no place in a civilized world'. 'It is our duty toward the people living in barbarism to see that they are freed from their chains, and we can free them only by destroying barbarism itself ... We must raise others while we are benefiting ourselves.'[31] In the Philippines, it was his view that: 'We are not trying to subjugate a people; we are trying to develop them.'[32] This meant attempting to instil North American political mores in the hope they would ultimately become self-sustaining, allowing for true independence. As Morris has observed, 'Expansion to [Roosevelt] meant a hemispheric programme of acquisition, democratisation and liberation.'[33] This would by necessity be a gradual process at best. Those who insisted that the

United States should steer clear of an educative imperialism and grant total self-government immediately, Roosevelt told one sympathetic correspondent, were 'jack fools who seriously think that any group of pirates and head-hunters needs nothing but independence in order that it may be turned forthwith into a dark-hued New England town meeting'. Nevertheless, he was confident – up to a point – that it was possible to 'rapidly teach the people of the Philippine Islands ... how to make good use of their freedom'.[34]

Similar tensions between the notional ideal of self-government and an insistence on the need for less advanced peoples to be subordinate to more civilized nations were apparent in continental Asia, in Roosevelt's attitude towards China. Though in theory united and sovereign, in practice China was being carved up with increasing explicitness into spheres of influence controlled by the European great powers and Japan. Though the United States had objections to spheres of influence, preferring a commercial 'open door' for all powers to the whole country, Roosevelt broadly supported the other powers in opposing Chinese demands for greater autonomy, and was vehemently hostile to the Boxer Rebellion, which was ongoing at the time of his rise to power. As in the Philippines and Latin America, Roosevelt's logic was an imperialist one: the Chinese were not equipped to cope with full sovereignty, and needed continued tutelage to protect them from doing themselves harm. There was an ironic but unyielding circularity in Roosevelt's thought on this point, albeit apparently unconscious: in his eyes a people could only earn respect by demonstrating strength and independence, something for which he praised the 'civilized' Japanese; yet he simultaneously accused those who pushed for more independence by forceful means, as the Chinese did, of child-like irresponsibility in doing so.[35]

Roosevelt, not alone among imperialist thinkers, was prone to imagine himself and his country as the reactive party in the relationship, forced by the actions of others to intervene when in truth he would have preferred otherwise. Further, he considered his interventionist policies to be so self-evidently for the benefit of all involved that they ought to merit both compliance and gratitude. Faced with the manifest absence of either on the part of those on the receiving end, he was therefore given to disillusionment and anger. Forced, as he saw it, into renewed intervention to suppress disorder in 'independent' Cuba in 1906, he took on the rhetorical character of an enraged Caesar:

> Just at the moment I am so angry with that infernal little Cuban republic that I would like to wipe its people off the face of the earth. All that we wanted for them was that they would behave themselves and be prosperous and happy so we that we should not have to interfere.[36]

When pressure mounted for the United States to take the Dominican Republic's finances into receivership, he lamented: 'I have about the same desire to annex it as a gorged boa constrictor might have to swallow a porcupine wrong end to.'[37] Even before he proclaimed the Roosevelt Corollary, he had arrived at the view that sooner or later it seems to me inevitable that the United States should assume an attitude of protection and regulation to all these little states in the neighbourhood of the Caribbean. I hope it will be deferred as long as possible, but I fear it is inevitable.[38]

In the process of constructing his self-image in this way – as the reluctant, put-upon agent of civilization's spread, he often seemed to assume, in line with other American progressives, that a free nation was in a sense defined as truly free not by the absence of external compulsion but by its choosing to become the 'right' kind of society. Variation between free societies might be acceptable in theory, but in practice such difference could only be superficial: on central political and economic principles they were expected to share values and practices roughly approximating the civilized path exemplified by the United States. In this way, 'liberty' was not viewed as a condition allowing for a multiplicity of alternative paths of development. Rather, 'true' liberty was taken to contain fixed social outcomes within it, or at least narrow parameters limiting acceptable outcomes, within which 'free nations' should develop. To put it more concisely, it was assumed by a great many American thinkers that liberty for a state ought to produce something resembling American liberalism within that state, for such was the meaning of 'progress' as they understood it. If this proved not to be the case, it was axiomatic that the nation in question had not truly become free, thus rendering legitimate any further intervention required to rectify the flaw.

This was the ideological basis of Roosevelt's liberal quasi-imperialism. In the Philippines, it meant a relatively long-term project to restructure the social order while maintaining occupation. In Cuba, it meant doing away with direct American administration sooner, but continuing to underwrite a brittle liberal order with intervention as a last resort should backsliding occur. In other Latin American states less entirely under American sway it meant stepping in to ensure 'proper' governance and appropriate economic management if crisis should present need and opportunity. And in East Asia it meant paying lip service to the unity independence of China while in practice being complicit in the suppression of indigenous resistance movements and the maintenance of the great power consortium's quasi-colonial control.

Roosevelt's place in the American tradition of democracy promotion

As the above sketch of Roosevelt's approach to relations with less powerful nations illustrates, it would be dubious to classify him in any unqualified sense as an evangelist for the promotion of democracy. If we define democracy as a system of government in which ultimate power over the actions of government lies in the hands of the governed, then neither his beliefs nor his policies supported its immediate realization in non-white nations, and in some places he was active in denying it, at least in the short term.

In Latin America he was instrumental in creating a hegemonic order in which the governments of weaker states, whether elected or not, could be overridden by the United States when it came to key aspects of their economic order. This did not mean American troops on every street corner south of the Rio Grande, but it did establish the principle that unless other nations did what the United States considered to be in their own best interests, intervention to restore them to the proper path of order and liberty was entirely justified. Roosevelt's corollary to the Monroe Doctrine subscribed to an ideal of self-sustaining liberal order within the nations of the Americas, but in its ascription of a 'police power' to the United States to enforce good governance it could be argued to have undermined liberal democratic ideals as much as it advanced them. Certainly it laid the ideological basis for a generation of interventions in the region under Roosevelt's successors, which were greatly resented by the nations affected, whatever one may think of the motives underlying them.

In the Philippines, the closest thing the United States ever came to governing a colony in the classic nineteenth-century European sense, Roosevelt was initially enthusiastic about the prospect of a full-blown American imperialism, involving the indefinite subordination of native political institutions to American administration. This was connected to a narrative that portrayed American rule as a form of educative oversight necessary to endow the native peoples with the level of cultural, political and intellectual maturity required to safely run their own affairs. In effect, it was believed that democratic self-government was indeed a desirable end goal, but the higher priority was that the natives should be 'civilized' first, in order that this should be possible. In contributing to this process, the United States could add to its own national greatness as an agent of the advance of civilization, defined as imitation of the rich, modernized states of the period and particularly itself, as a global phenomenon. Roosevelt never really gave ground on the substance of this view, though he did ultimately shift towards advocacy of a faster timetable for the granting of independence to the Philippines. This was for two reasons little to do with the substantive principle of swift democratization versus civilizationally educative empire: first, he was concerned that the ill-defended Philippines could serve as a strategic Achilles' heel in any future conflict with Japan; and second, he increasingly recognized that the political culture in the United States remained resolutely hostile to imperialist projects, and that he was unable to change that fact.[39]

In China, Roosevelt was not in any sense an agent for democracy's promotion. He did maintain an American position that China should be treated as a unified entity with equal rights for all outside powers throughout, but that was a question with only tangential bearing on the question of Chinese democracy and sovereignty. On the whole Roosevelt was as dismissive as European heads of government were of the right of the native Chinese or their government to exercise genuine control over their own territory, especially if that should come at the price of inconvenience to foreign economic interests.[40] More obviously even than in other cases, Roosevelt's policy in this part of the world revealed the limits on his commitment to self-government for peoples, circularity noted earlier in his thinking about how they might demonstrate their fitness for self-rule.

But for all this, Roosevelt is neither to be dismissed as irrelevant to the American tradition of democracy promotion, nor written off entirely as an illiberal anti-democrat. While, as has been set out, he was not himself a particularly eager or effective promoter of democracy, he did contribute significantly to the tradition in three respects.

First, Roosevelt was a key figure in expanding the horizons of American foreign policy, and in doing so attaching it to a sense of mission and purpose requiring entanglement in the affairs of foreign nations. If American foreign policy is divided, as some have suggested, between those who believe the nation should provide an example to others and those who believe it should find greatness by its efforts to change the behaviour of others, then Roosevelt was a major figure in pushing forward an ideological shift from the former to the latter.[41] In the terminology of another analyst, Roosevelt, in his drive for activity abroad, was instrumental in moving the United States part of the way along the spectrum from seeing itself as a detached 'promised land' towards adopting the demeanour of a 'crusader state'.[42] This led him to advocate, with significant success, increased activity on the part of the United States abroad, and increased development of the military and naval resources that would prove essential for the era of interventionism ahead.

Second, Roosevelt had a fervent ideological attachment to the concept of 'civilization' and the importance of its defence and spread. He viewed it as the purpose of all nations, or at least all respectably vigorous ones, to pursue greatness through their contribution to this broader phenomenon. This served three major purposes in Roosevelt's worldview: (a) To allow him to view peoples and nations hierarchically, based upon their attainment of advanced civilized attributes or failure to do so; (b) to add a sense of mission to American activity in the world, transcending cold-blooded pursuit of narrow advantage or financial gain; and (c) to provide a clear basis of justification for interference on the part of the United States in the internal affairs of others, even at the cost of denying them full self-government at the point of a gun. If other nations were objectively less civilized than the United States, and if the furtherance of civilization was the standard against which a nation's historical greatness was to be judged, then it is not difficult to see how the niceties of sovereignty might fall by the wayside as Roosevelt constructed a broader mandate for American action abroad.

Thus Roosevelt's thought and policy had much to link them to the mindset that would subsequently undergird Wilsonianism and the tradition of democracy promotion, even if they were by no means Wilsonian in themselves. The gap between the two hinges upon the degree to which 'democracy' and 'civilization' can be read as equivalent. Since Roosevelt was unequivocally devoted to the promotion of the latter, but his record in embracing the former is, as has been discussed, patchy at best, one can infer the existence of at least some clear intellectual water between the two. Roosevelt unapologetically believed in the universal validity and superiority of the features of the most successful states of his era, including his own – speaking in broad terms, the features of 'modernity': relatively stable, formally constituted political institutions of a liberal sort; a relatively liberal economy (in the broad sense of 'liberal', in a domestic context Roosevelt became increasingly 'progressive' during his time in power, favouring government-imposed limits on the autonomy of private enterprise); a culture promoting Victorian ideals of self-control and self-command; organized armed forces with some basic capacity.

And thus Roosevelt's thinking was, as was usual for 'progressives' of the era, teleological, i.e. convinced of the existence of an objective destination for social development, with alternatives classified as aberrant. A major part of his mindset was a serene confidence that in doing anything that served the advance of this social model, the United States would be performing the 'world work' of civilization's advance. Where he differed with some American liberals in his own era, and a great many in subsequent eras, was in his scepticism that delivering 'democracy', meaning sovereign self-government and majority rule, to those peoples who did not already possess it, would naturally lead to the advance of the 'civilized' values he prized. Unconstrained freedom delivered to a civilizationally immature people (such as that in the Philippines), Roosevelt worried, could as easily lead to political instability and violence and economic recklessness as to progress in civilization. Those, whether Filipino, Chinese or American, who demanded total independence for subject peoples immediately, were guilty in his eyes of either childishly naive optimism or cavalier recklessness in assuming that all it would take for civilized societies to flower the world over was for colonial powers to pack up and go home. In this regard Roosevelt perhaps had as much or more in common with the liberal imperialist tradition of educating other peoples to be 'ready' for their freedom, to be granted at some point over an often retreating horizon, than with those in the tradition of democracy promotion past and present believing that democratic self-government is an intrinsic good to be put in place with urgency wherever it should be absent.[43]

Finally, it might be noted that while the divergence is more extreme in the case of Roosevelt, neither Wilson nor his imitative successors were unequivocal either in defining the promotion of democracy as granting freedom to other peoples to do whatever a majority saw fit to vote for within their own borders. Wilson may genuinely have had faith in the likelihood of free peoples deciding to 'do the right thing' from the American perspective and pursue values and practices more or less in line with American preferences, but his use of the language of liberty and self-determination also sometimes served to obscure his assumption that being 'free' meant spontaneously embracing American ideals. Meanwhile, Roosevelt's comfort with the conceptual framework of civilizational hierarchy and benign imperialism encouraged more explicit discussion of what should be done when faced with a choice between allowing a weaker nation to go its own way and using American power to coerce other peoples 'for their own good'.[44] In short, while Wilson's familiar language of universal liberty may serve to obscure the elements of international hierarchy and progressive determinism at work in his mindset, the old-fashioned openness with which Roosevelt cast his views in terms of more civilized peoples knowing best and needing armed strength to enforce their views may serve to blind us to how durable the substance of such thinking in fact proved over the years to come. It is only mild hyperbole to suggest that in substance if not in language, much of Roosevelt's mindset remains at play in the debates of today surrounding American democracy promotion.

Notes

1 The content of this contribution is based primarily on material derived from Adam Quinn, 'Theodore Roosevelt: the nation that has dared to be great', in Adam Quinn, *US Foreign Policy in Context: National Ideology from the Founders to the Bush Doctrine*, Abingdon and New York: Routledge, 2010, pp. 61–85.
2 Because of their status as contemporaries, and their open rivalry, it has not been uncommon to compare and contrast the two. This has been done most effectively in J. M. Cooper, *The Warrior and the Priest: Woodrow Wilson and Theodore Roosevelt*, Boston: Harvard University Press, 1985.
3 It is worth noting in passing here that Wilson's credentials as a modern liberal are not entirely unimpeachable. Although Roosevelt wrote much more over his life on the issue of race as a component in his thinking about global affairs, Wilson was by no means a pioneer of racial equality. In regard to the domestic politics of the United States he was actually more retrograde on racial questions than his immediate predecessors. Meanwhile, Wilson's commitment to universal liberty and national self-determination were sufficiently bound up with notions of the United States' special leadership status that they cannot be neatly divorced from nationalist ideology. On the former point, see Michael Dennis, 'Looking Backward: Woodrow Wilson, the New South, and the Question of Race', *American Nineteenth Century History*, 3:1, 2002, pp. 77–104.
4 Theodore Roosevelt, 'Washington's Forgotten Maxim', in Theodore Roosevelt, *The Man in the Arena: Selected Writings of Theodore Roosevelt*, New York: Forge, 2003, edited by Brian M. Thomsen, p. 318.
5 Quoted in M. A. Jones, *The Limits of Liberty: American History 1607–1980*, Oxford: Oxford University Press, 1983, p. 401.
6 In this chapter biographical information on Roosevelt originates mainly from Edmund Morris, *The Rise of Theodore Roosevelt*, New York: Random House, 2001; Edmund Morris, *Theodore Rex*, New York: Random House, 2002. Direct Roosevelt quotations come chiefly from Theodore Roosevelt, *Letters and Speeches*, New York: Library of America, 2004, edited by Louis Auchincloss and Theodore Roosevelt, *The Man in the Arena: Selected Writings of Theodore Roosevelt*, New York: Forge, 2003, edited by Brian M. Thomsen, hereafter labelled 'L&S' and 'MIA', respectively. More specific references accompany each quotation. Also consulted for background and interpretation were N. Miller, *Theodore Roosevelt: A Life*, London: Harper Perennial, 1994; K. Dalton, *Theodore Roosevelt: A Strenuous Life*, New York: Knopf, 2002. Specifically on his foreign policy, see H. K. Beale, *Theodore Roosevelt and the Rise of America to World Power*, Baltimore: Johns Hopkins Press, 1956; F. W. Marks III, *Velvet on Iron: the Diplomacy of Theodore Roosevelt*, Lincoln: University of Nebraska Press, 1979.
7 For discussion of Roosevelt's extraordinary range of activities and overbearing verbal habits, see Morris, *Rex*, pp. 81, 82, 108, 246, 307, 376, 532.
8 'Citizenship in a Republic', Address at the Sorbonne, Paris, 23 April 1910, in Roosevelt, *L&S*, p. 783.
9 Quoted in Morris, *Rex*, pp. 420–21.
10 'The Strenuous Life', Speech to the Hamilton Club, Chicago, 10 April 1899, in Roosevelt, *L&S*, pp. 755–66, quotation pp. 756–67.
11 ibid., pp. 765–66.
12 'National Duties', Speech at the Minnesota State Fair, St Paul, 2 September 1901, in Roosevelt, *L&S*, p. 768.

13 Inaugural Address, 4 March 1905. <http://www.homeofheroes.com/presidents/inaugural/ 26_teddy.html> (accessed 3 April 2009). His opponent had declared in the campaign that 'I protest against the feeling, now far too prevalent, that by reason of the commanding position we have assumed in the world we must take part in the disputes and broils of foreign countries.' Quoted in Morris, *Rex*, p. 350.

14 'To Munsterberg', in Roosevelt, *L&S*, p. 763.

15 Quoted in Morris, *Rex*, p. 24.

16 See Morris, *Rex*, p. 229; 'To Henry Cabot Lodge', in Roosevelt, *L&S*, p. 186.

17 'The Strenuous Life', in Roosevelt, *L&S*, p. 765.

18 'Washington's Forgotten Maxim', in Roosevelt, *MIA*, pp. 315–31.

19 ibid., p. 315.

20 ibid., p. 316.

21 'To Finley Peter Dunne', 23 November 1904, in Roosevelt *L&S*, p. 366.

22 Washington's Forgotten Maxim', in Roosevelt, *MIA*, p. 316.

23 'To Cecil Spring-Rice', 21 December 1907, in Roosevelt, *L&S*, p. 544.

24 Morris, *Rex*, pp. 177–91.

25 'The Roosevelt Corollary', op. cit.

26 ibid.

27 'Quasi' because it was based on hegemonic domination but not formal territorial conquest.

28 'The Roosevelt Corollary', op. cit.

29 For some detail on the American approach to governance of the Philippines under Roosevelt's presidency, see Stephen Wertheim, 'Reluctant Liberator: Theodore Roosevelt's Philosophy of Self-Government and Preparation for Philippine Independence', *Presidential Studies Quarterly*, 39:3, September 2009.

30 On the imperialist ideology of Roosevelt and his supporters both in the heat of 1898 and later, see Beale, *Theodore Roosevelt*, pp. 14–80.

31 National Duties Speech at the Minnesota State Fair, St Paul, 2 September 1901, in Roosevelt, *L&S*, p. 775.

32 ibid., p. 776.

33 Morris, *Rex*, p. 24.

34 Quoted in Morris, *Rex*, p. 110; 'To Rudyard Kipling', 1 November 1904, in Roosevelt, *L&S*, p. 357.

35 On Roosevelt's China policy, see Beale, *Theodore Roosevelt*, pp. 172–252.

36 Quoted in Morris, *Rex*, p. 456.

37 ibid., p. 319.

38 'To Theodore Roosevelt Jr', 10 February 1904, in Roosevelt, *L&S*, p. 312.

39 For discussion of movement over time in Roosevelt's attitude towards the United States' continued imperial rule over the Philippines and the reasons for it, see Wertheim, 'Reluctant Liberator', especially pp. 505–17.

40 See Beale, *Theodore Roosevelt*, pp. 172–252.

41 For an argument outlining this view, see H. W. Brands, *What America Owes the World*, Cambridge: Cambridge University Press, 1998.

42 W. A. McDougall, *Promised Land, Crusader State: The American encounter with the World since 1776*, Boston: Mariner Books, 1997.

43 In this regard Roosevelt's argument. Understandably, few theorists of either democracy or liberalism would today wish to be associated with either Roosevelt in particular or imperialism in general, so it should be emphasized that this is not a general claim that Zakaria's views resemble Roosevelt's; this is merely to note that it has been a long-running concern among serious American foreign policy thinkers that there might be some tension between the advance of 'civilized'/liberal institutions and values and the spread of the formal procedures of voting and majority rule.

44 For extended discussion of Wilsonianism, see Adam Quinn, 'Woodrow Wilson: conquest of the spirits of men', in Quinn, *US Foreign Policy*, pp. 86–113.

3

WOODROW WILSON

John A. Thompson

Woodrow Wilson is commonly seen as the president who first made the promotion of democracy in other countries a central purpose of American foreign policy, and one which at times justified the use of force. However, a closer look at both Wilson's thinking about the subject and his conduct of American policy complicates this picture considerably. Neither in thought nor in action did Wilson hold to a consistent position on the issue. The various views he expressed have to be understood in the context of his concerns at the time. In his earlier life as an academic, Wilson wrote a good deal about democracy but almost never with any reference to American foreign policy. Rather, he focused on the factors that had shaped the evolution of modern democracy, and the ways in which its workings, particularly in the United States, could be improved. Similarly, the extent to which his commitment to democracy affected his foreign policy can only be assessed by considering its place in relation to his other goals, both his tactical ones in particular situations and the broader strategic conception of the nation's long-term interests that he developed.

Wilson and democracy

Wilson's academic career was launched by the success of his first book, *Congressional Government*, published in 1885 when he was 28. Later that same year, he drafted a substantial typescript on 'The Modern Democratic State' that he envisaged as the basis of a major work on politics, the writing of which remained his ambition for the rest of his life. Wilson's account in this paper of the essential pre-conditions of a successful democracy was hardly reconcilable with the idea that democracy is a universal panacea that could be spread to other countries through the application of external influence or force. As a graduate student at the Johns Hopkins University, Wilson had been schooled in the evolutionary approach to the understanding of social phenomena and, related to this, he had absorbed from Edmund Burke (whom he referred to as 'my master') the idea that society should be seen as a living organism. It followed that democracy was

> wrongly conceived when treated merely as a body of doctrine. It is a stage of development. It is not created by aspirations or by new faith; it is built up by slow habit. [...] immature peoples cannot have it, and the maturity to which it is vouchsafed is the maturity of freedom and self-control.

That Wilson retained this view was shown when in 1901, after the American acquisition of the Philippines and Puerto Rico, he warned against supposing that 'institutions and principles like our own [...] could be put into practice amidst conditions totally unlike those with which, and with which alone, we have been familiar'.[1]

In Wilson's 1885 paper, he observed that 'only the United States and a few other governments begotten of the English race have yet furnished examples of successful democracy of the modern type'. This conservative perspective was, however, somewhat modified by Wilson's confidence that democracy was the product of modernity. Depending as it did on open discussion and broad 'enlightenment', democracy was fostered by the growth of commerce, the rise of a free press and, above all, 'popular education'. So Americans were right to regard their system of government 'as standing at the front of the world's progress'. Also possibly pertinent to Wilson's later policy was his assertion that democracy required a homogeneous society; it could not 'harmoniously unite races of diverse habits and instincts'.[2]

Entry into politics led Wilson to modify somewhat his position on the accessibility of democracy and to place even more emphasis on the value of democracy as a form of society as well as government. After his political opponents exploited some derogatory comments about southern and eastern European immigrants in Wilson's popular *History of the American People*, he made less of the special democratic capability of Anglo-Saxons.[3] More fundamentally, in running for the governorship of New Jersey in 1910 and the White House in 1912, Wilson adopted the language and assumptions of the then surgent progressive movement. Progressive reformers remained a key element in his political support, not least in his re-election campaign of 1916. In the social criticism and political tracts generated by the progressive movement, 'democracy' was *the* central value.[4] The domestic evils that progressives sought to expose and reform, particularly 'boss' politics and the power of 'the trusts', were seen as essentially anti-democratic in both their provenance and their effects, and the political battles to eliminate these evils were often portrayed in the simple terms of 'the people' versus 'the interests'. Translated into international affairs, this led to a deep suspicion of economic imperialism, which was seen both as wrong in itself and also as the source of conflict. This anti-imperialist perspective, which was particularly strong in his own Democratic party, significantly influenced Wilson's approach to foreign policy.

The place of democracy in Wilson's foreign policy

'It would be an irony of fate if my administration had to deal chiefly with foreign affairs', the president-elect reportedly said to a friend shortly before his inauguration in March 1913.[5] The remark reflected the fact that whereas Wilson entered office with a clear and specific domestic agenda, the same was not true of foreign policy, which he made no reference to in his inaugural address. He certainly had no free-standing project to promote democracy in other countries. Wilson's foreign policy took shape in response to developments abroad, when these presented situations on which the United States had to take a position.

Mexico and the Caribbean

The first major issue confronting Wilson arose from the revolution in Mexico. This had begun in 1911 with the overthrow of the long rule of Porfirio Diaz, whose policies had attracted much foreign, including American, investment. A few weeks before Wilson took office, the revolutionary president Francisco Madero had been deposed and murdered in a coup led by General Victoriano Huerta in which the Taft administration's ambassador Henry Lane Wilson was implicated. Appalled by the brutality of the coup and suspecting the role of foreign capitalist interests, Wilson disregarded State Department advice and withheld diplomatic recognition from Huerta's government. His stand gained additional justification when revolutionary leaders, calling themselves the Constitutionalists, launched a military movement against Huerta, bringing into question his government's *de facto* control of the country. Wilson demanded that the Mexican leader schedule elections and stand down. After Huerta's defiant assumption of dictatorial powers in October 1913, Wilson recognized the belligerent status of the Constitutionalists, allowing them to buy arms. By the spring of 1914, he had moved from his initial concern with constitutional process to a desire to align the United States with, rather than against, what he saw as 'the struggle of a people to come into its own'.[6] 'My ideal,' he told a reporter, 'is an orderly and righteous government in Mexico; but my passion is for the submerged eighty-five per cent of the people of that Republic, who are now struggling toward liberty.' That was not all. 'They say the Mexicans are not fitted for self-government,' he observed of conservative demands for intervention to restore order, 'and to this I reply that, when properly directed, there is no people not fitted for self-government.'[7]

Determined to prevail in a public contest of wills with Huerta in which he evidently felt his own prestige as well as his country's was at stake, Wilson took advantage of an incident at Tampico in April 1914 to seize the Mexican city of Veracruz. Intended to aid the Constitutionalists, this action, in which over a hundred Mexicans were killed, was fiercely denounced by them. This reaction, as well as Huerta's departure in July, led Wilson to step back from his attempts to influence how Mexico was governed. As the country descended into civil war, with revolutionary factions fighting each other, Washington's policy followed a somewhat wavering course, but a constant theme was that the Mexicans had a right to determine their own affairs in their own way.[8] The president wrote to his militant Secretary of War Lindley M. Garrison, stating that

> there are in my judgment no conceivable circumstances which would make it right for us to direct by force or by threat of force the internal processes of what is a profound revolution, a revolution as profound as that which occurred in France. All the world has been shocked ever since the time of that revolution in France that Europe should have undertaken to nullify what was done there, no matter what the excesses then committed.

When later assailed domestically about affairs in Mexico, he declared: 'If the Mexicans want to raise hell, let them raise hell. We have got nothing to do with it. It is their government, it is their hell.'[9] In saying this, Wilson incidentally implied that the anti-imperialist principle of self-determination took precedence over any concern with democracy promotion. He later stated this explicitly in connection with the European settlement after the First World War, maintaining that 'there isn't any one kind of government under which all nations ought to live. [...] I am not fighting for democracy except for the peoples that want democracy. [...] If they don't want it, that is none of my business'.[10]

Wilson's experience in Mexico in 1913–14 reinforced the lesson he had already drawn from his reading of the French revolution that outside intervention in such situations was not only illegitimate but likely to be counter-productive. He was to reiterate this point continually in resisting pressure from France and Britain for the use of force against the Bolsheviks in 1918–19.[11] When Wilson authorized military action on Mexican soil for a second time in 1916, it was in response to Pancho Villa's provocative killing of Americans, and raids in New Mexico and Texas. The aim of 'the punitive expedition' was to protect American lives and the nation's borders, not to promote democracy in Mexico. Similarly, Wilson's interventions in the affairs of small states in the Caribbean basically arose from a non-ideological perception of national interest. Since at least the 1890s, all American administrations had assumed a hegemonic responsibility for order in a region seen as vital for American security. In Nicaragua, Haiti and the Dominican Republic, Wilson deployed American power to influence how these countries were governed. But, although he initially proclaimed the desirability of free and fair elections, in practice what he sought were honest leaders who could maintain order and ensure that contractual obligations were met; an authentic democratic mandate was distinctly secondary. The difficulty of achieving this objective by outside pressure led in Haiti and the Dominican Republic to military occupation and more or less direct American rule.

Europe and world order

By far the greatest foreign policy challenge that Wilson encountered was, of course, the European war that broke out in August 1914. It was in response to this that he led his country into a quite unprecedented involvement in great power politics. This was a step-by-step process and it is only by tracing its evolution that we can assess how far and in what ways Wilson's policy-making reflected a concern with democracy.

That Wilson began with no proactive commitment to reforming the international order or promoting democracy in the world is confirmed by his stance in the first phase of the war. His primary objective then seems to have been to insulate the United States as far as possible from the war's effects. He evinced no anxiety about the nation's external security (particularly after the first battle of the Marne apparently removed any danger of an outright German victory), but he did express great concern about the potential effect on domestic harmony of the naturally divided sympathies of a people 'drawn from many nations, and chiefly from the nations now at war'. He sought to counter this not only by calling on his fellow countrymen to be 'impartial in thought as well as in action' but also by appealing to a higher loyalty to the United States; he explained to his Ambassador in London, Walter Hines Page, that this was why he had to do 'everything that is possible to do to define and defend neutral rights'.[12] Asserting the United States' rights as a neutral became the major thrust of the administration's diplomacy, driven not only by their symbolic national significance but also by a desire to minimize the effects of the war on the United States' own life. Nor did Wilson see any need for change in the nation's defence posture. Rejecting the demands for military 'preparedness' that arose from some Republicans close to Theodore Roosevelt, the president told Congress that for the United States to abandon her 'ancient principles of action' by building up a standing, or even a reserve, army 'would mean merely that we had been thrown off our balance by a war with which we have nothing to do, whose causes cannot touch us'.[13]

In rejecting preparedness, as in appealing for impartiality, Wilson spoke of the United States' unique capability, as the one great power not involved, to help Europe back to peace. This was seen from the beginning as a desirable objective for American diplomacy, although there were differences within the administration (notably between the Secretary of State William J. Bryan, and the president's influential friend and adviser Colonel Edward House) over how and when it should be pursued. There were also the questions of what sort of peace should be sought and what contribution the United States might make to achieving it. In an interview with a journalist in December 1914, Wilson said that he hoped for 'a deadlock' because it would show all countries 'the futility of employing force in the attempt to resolve their differences'. Like most Americans, particularly progressives, he attributed the war to the imperialistic ambitions of Europe's ruling elites, and he argued that 'the settlement should be for the advantage of the European nations regarded as Peoples and not for any nation imposing its governmental will upon alien peoples'.[14] But that these were little more than the observations of an interested spectator was indicated by the firm limits placed at this time on the United States' role. When House was in Europe in early 1915 to explore the feasibility of American mediation, the British Foreign Secretary, Sir Edward Grey, indicated that

if the United States was prepared to take an active part in 'the making of a programme of forcible security for the future – in that event England might consent to
end the war in a drawn contest and trust to the subsequent discussion and world-wide
agreement to secure safety for the future'. House emphatically repudiated the
suggestion; it would be contrary to 'not only the unwritten law of our country but
also our fixed policy not to become involved in European affairs'.[15]

What shook Wilson's policy out of these traditional grooves was the German use
of submarines against merchant shipping. Responding to the sense of outrage
caused by the sinking of the *Lusitania* in May 1915, Wilson effectively demanded
the abandonment of this form of warfare, thus raising for the first time the possibility
that the United States might enter the conflict as a belligerent. However, it soon
became apparent to the president that, as he wrote to his future wife, 'the people
of this country rely upon me to keep them out of war'.[16] Aware that German
acquiescence in his demands was both partial and provisional, Wilson now became
much more anxious to bring about an early end to the European war. This was the
only secure way in which he could avoid having to choose at some point between
a humiliating climb-down over the submarine issue and an unwelcome war. It was
as part of a new and more urgent initiative to bring the war to an end that Wilson
indicated to Grey in the autumn of 1915 that he would, after all, be prepared to
lead the United States into a post-war league of nations.[17]

On the face of it, this represented a striking departure from the United States'
time-honoured policy of non-entanglement. When Wilson proclaimed the commitment publicly in May 1916, he argued that events had shown that it was no
longer practicable for the United States to isolate itself from major international
conflicts: 'Our own rights as a nation, the privileges, and the property of our
people have been profoundly affected. We are not mere disconnected lookers-on. [...]
We are participants, whether we would or not, in the life of the world.' If foreign
wars were going to impinge so powerfully on the United States, it had as much
interest as the belligerent nations in the establishment of a lasting peace. Achieving
such a peace became Wilson's strategic goal for the rest of his presidency, and the
basic argument that he made for it – that to protect the security and tranquillity of
the United States' own life it had to take the lead in establishing a system of world
order – forms the core of his legacy.

In fleshing out the shape that the post-war settlement should take in his speech
to the League to Enforce Peace in May 1916 and in his Address to the Senate in
January 1917, Wilson focused exclusively on the nature of relations between states.
At no time during the period of American neutrality did he link this with the way
that states were governed internally or the character of their regimes. In his two
major public statements he specified the following elements of a lasting peace. First
and foremost, the establishment of 'an universal association of the nations [...] to
prevent any war begun either contrary to treaty covenants or without warning and
full submission of the causes to the opinion of the world – a virtual guarantee of
territorial integrity and political independence'. Wilson also called both for a
reduction of armaments and for 'a new and more wholesome diplomacy' that

eschewed 'secret counsels' and expected nations to 'be governed by the same high code of honor that we demand of individuals'. Beyond this, Wilson set out certain guidelines that accorded with the anti-imperialist perspective on international affairs and which could also be seen as deriving from the principles of the Declaration of Independence. Thus, he insisted that small states should 'enjoy the same respect for their sovereignty and territorial integrity that great and powerful nations expect and insist upon'. He stated that 'every great people [...] should be assured a direct outlet to the great highways of the sea', and that these highways should be free for all to use securely. He declared that 'no nation should seek to extend its polity over any other nation or people' and that 'no right anywhere exists to hand peoples about from sovereignty to sovereignty as if they were property'.

It was in this connection that he asserted that 'every people has a right to choose the sovereignty under which they shall live'. He did not give any indication of how 'a people' was to be defined but it was clear that he had in mind possible new annexations rather than the integrity of existing empires. Privately, he indicated that he did not wish to see the destruction of the Habsburg Empire; nor was he intending to challenge the principle of colonialism. He raised the issue, he said, 'not because of any desire to exalt an abstract political principle' but because 'any peace which does not recognize and accept this principle will inevitably be upset'. Wilson's recognition that a lasting settlement required a sensitivity to psychological factors also underlay his call for 'a peace without victory':

> victory would mean peace forced upon a loser, a victor's terms imposed upon the vanquished. It would be accepted in humiliation, under duress, at an intolerable sacrifice, and would leave a sting, a resentment, a bitter memory upon which terms of peace would rest, not permanently, but only as upon quicksand.

But a peace without victory would presumably be one between the pre-existing states and regimes.[18]

It was when the United States moved from neutrality to belligerency in April 1917 that Wilson argued that a peaceful world order would require the extension of democracy. In asking Congress to recognize that, through its inhumane and unrestricted submarine campaign, Germany was in effect making war upon all nations including the United States, Wilson declared that

> neutrality is no longer feasible or desirable where the peace of the world is involved and the freedom of its peoples, and the menace to that peace and freedom lies in the existence of autocratic governments backed by organized force which is controlled wholly by their will, not by the will of their people.

He now advanced a version of what has become known as democratic peace theory when he asserted that 'self-governed nations do not fill their neighbor states with spies or set the course of intrigue to bring about some critical posture of affairs which will give them an opportunity to strike and make conquest'. Whereas before he had spoken of 'an universal association of nations' without reference to forms of government, now he said that 'a steadfast concert of peace can never be maintained except by a partnership of democratic governments. No autocratic government could be trusted to keep faith within it or observe its covenants'. Accordingly, the United States would be fighting 'for the things which we have always carried nearest to our hearts, – for democracy, for the right of those who submit to authority to have a voice in their own governments'.[19]

This appeal to the nation's historic ideals and sense of mission was clearly part of Wilson's attempt to mobilize support for a war that Americans had been very reluctant to enter. Framing the issues in this way also served other, more specific, purposes during the period of American belligerency. Emphasizing that the enemy was 'the Imperial German Government' and that 'we have no quarrel with the German people' was seen as making it easier for German–Americans to justify the president's declared confidence that most of them were 'as true and loyal Americans as if they had never known any other fealty or allegiance'. The distinction between the German people and their government was to be employed by Wilson to evade pleas for peace that, as the leader of a belligerent nation, he now came to view as premature. In August 1917, when Pope Benedict XV appealed to the warring powers to make peace on a basis very similar to that which Wilson had called for in January, the president replied that this was impossible because 'we cannot take the word of the present rulers of Germany as a guarantee of anything that is to endure'. The object of the war, he explained,

> is to deliver the free peoples of the world from the menace and the actual power of a vast military establishment controlled by an irresponsible government which, having secretly planned to dominate the world, proceeded to carry the plan out [...] That power is not the German people. It is the ruthless master of the German people.[20]

The same distinction helped Wilson in the fall of 1918 to reconcile his wish to accept the German request for an armistice on the terms he had set out in the Fourteen Points address of January 1918 and other speeches with the strong public and congressional demand for an unconditional victory. In the exchange of notes that followed the German overture, Wilson insisted that if the American government had to deal with 'the military masters and the monarchical autocrats of Germany, [...] it must demand, not peace negotiations, but surrender'. This contributed greatly to the pressures that shortly led to the abdication of the Kaiser.[21]

Here, then, Wilson may be seen as using American power to effect regime change and establish democracy in a foreign country. However, Germany was a very special case, and not only because ever since the Revolutionary War Americans have tended to demonize the leadership of the countries they have been fighting. Wilson had good reason for thinking that the launching of an unrestricted submarine campaign showed that the civilian authorities in Berlin had been subordinated to the military High Command. That this represented a sort of *coup d'état* seemed confirmed when in July 1917 the Reichstag passed by a large majority a resolution calling for 'a peace of understanding and the permanent reconciliation of the peoples' and abjuring 'forced acquisitions of territory'.[22] In his Fourteen Points address, Wilson stated that he did not 'presume to suggest' to Germany 'any alteration or modification of her institutions', but it was 'necessary [...] that we should know whom her spokesmen speak for when they speak to us, whether for the Reichstag majority or for the military party and the men whose creed is imperial domination'.[23] That it was the latter who were determining German policy was confirmed by the terms of the treaty of Brest–Litovsk in March 1918, and in response (at a time when the Allies were being extremely hard pressed on the western front) Wilson called, rather extravagantly, for 'Force, Force to the utmost, Force without stint or limit, the righteous and triumphant Force which shall make Right the law of the world and cast every selfish dominion down in the dust.'[24]

During the period of American belligerency Wilson also came to give a somewhat more revisionist interpretation to his previously proclaimed principle that 'every people has a right to choose the sovereignty under which they shall live'.[25] This was both a more gradual and a more limited development than one might expect from the image of Wilson as the prophet of national self-determination. The issue was pushed to the fore in 1917 not by Wilson but by the propaganda of the Bolsheviks after the Russian Revolution. The European Allies endorsed the claims of the subject nationalities of the Habsburg Empire long before Wilson did, and they were also earlier in granting recognition to the Czechoslovak National Council.[26] The United States did not declare war on Austria–Hungary until December 1917, and even then Wilson, hoping that Germany's chief ally might be induced to make a separate peace, declared that 'we do not wish in any way to impair or to rearrange the Austro–Hungarian Empire'.[27] In his Fourteen Points address, he said no more than that the peoples of the empire 'should be accorded the freest opportunity of autonomous development'. Although in that speech, he called for the frontiers of Italy, Poland and the Balkan states to be fixed along 'lines of nationality', he did not proclaim this to be a universal principle until the following month, and then in a carefully qualified way:

> all well defined national aspirations shall be accorded the utmost satisfaction that can be afforded them without introducing new or perpetuating old elements of discord and antagonism that would be likely in time to break the peace of Europe and consequently of the world.[28]

However, after it became clear in April 1918 that there was no chance of inducing Vienna to break with Germany, the American government supported the claims of the subject nationalities with increasing strength. This not only led to Wilson's name being much honoured in an independent Czechoslovakia as a liberator but also raised expectations that in the post-war settlement he would champion the principle of national self-determination universally and unequivocally.[29]

As Wilson was well aware, the peace programme he set out, most specifically in the Fourteen Points, did not command unequivocal support in the Allied capitals.[30] But to his supporters, the political alignments in 1918 seemed to confirm that the president was advocating 'a democratic peace'. Walter Weyl of the *New Republic* observed that, 'When we look about the world for the allies of internationalism, we find them in the democratic, liberal and socialistic groups of all nations.' Progressives saw the conflict as one between the desire of ordinary people everywhere for a lasting peace and the vested interest of privileged and powerful groups in militarism and imperialism.[31] As the resistance of the German army was at last crumbling, Wilson himself invoked the 'assemblies and associations of many kinds made up of plain workaday people' who

> still seem to fear that they are getting what they ask for only in statesmen's terms, only in the terms of territorial arrangements and divisions of power, and not in terms of broad-visioned justice and mercy and peace and the satisfaction of those deep-seated longings of oppressed and distracted men and women and enslaved peoples that seem to them the only things worth fighting a war for that engulfs the world.[32]

Anticipating the coming confrontation with his wartime partners, Wilson made little secret of his belief that 'the peoples of all the Allies are with me in the sentiments that I have expressed' and that 'if necessary I can reach the peoples of Europe over the heads of their rulers'.[33]

In practice, of course, this proved not to be the case. The president's one attempt to act on this assumption, his appeal to the Italian people over the issue of Fiume and other parts of the Dalmatian coast, provoked such a hostile reaction in Italy that Americans were officially advised to keep their distance from the demonstrating crowds.[34] In the aftermath of war, nationalist antagonisms, fears and ambitions proved to be stronger than internationalist sentiment (as they had in 1914 when in all the belligerent countries Socialists had rallied to the patriotic cause). Wilson could not even rely on support for his principles at home. The Republicans had won majorities in both houses of Congress in the November 1918 elections after a campaign in which their leading spokesmen had denounced the Fourteen Points and demanded a dictated peace.[35] Nor did the Allies' indebtedness to the United States serve to give Wilson the diplomatic bargaining power that he had anticipated.[36]

Given that he lacked the means to impose his will on his negotiating partners at the peace conference, Wilson had to decide which of his foreign policy objectives was most important. He left little doubt as to what his priorities were. It was clear to those who dealt with him at the time that his overriding goal was the establishment of the League of Nations as an integral part of the peace treaty.[37] Wilson's determination to establish a credible league of nations in the form most acceptable to American opinion accounts for many of the compromises he made on other issues in Paris. For example, it seems that Wilson's early concession to Italy of a northern frontier incorporating a substantial German-speaking population was motivated by his desire for Prime Minister Vittorio Orlando's cooperation in the commission drafting the League of Nations Covenant.[38] The most dramatic instance was Wilson's reluctant assent to the takeover by the Japanese of the rights previously enjoyed by Germany in the Chinese province of Shantung. The president did not conceal from his associates that it was Japan's threat not to enter the League of Nations that had led him to yield (much to the disgust of the Secretary of State Robert Lansing).[39]

Wilson *did* fight for the principle of self-determination, not only in this instance but in several others – such as the Saar and the Italian claims in Dalmatia, particularly Fiume. More generally, with respect to the territorial settlement in Europe, he insisted that 'the consent of the governed' should be the basic criterion of legitimacy and he was largely successful in this, as the institution of plebiscites in disputed areas such as Upper Silesia, Schleswig and the Saar shows. His acceptance of South Africa's J. C. Smuts's three-tier mandate system for the colonies and other non-European territories taken from the defeated empires indicated that Wilson, in common with most Western opinion at the time, still thought of the capacity for self-government as something that had to be developed over time and saw different peoples as at different stages in that process. But mandatory authority was referred to in the League of Nations Covenant as 'tutelage'; the implication was that in due course it was expected to lead to the emergence of self-governing nations.

However, the way in which independent countries were governed was a matter for them. Even in the one case, that of Germany, where Wilson might be seen as having sought to promote democracy, concern for the standing of the new republic with German opinion was not a consideration to which Wilson paid any attention in the negotiations over the terms of the treaty. As a Burkean, Wilson might have been expected to realize that a newly planted government was inevitably fragile and that to force it to accept a settlement most Germans regarded as humiliating would hardly help it to establish legitimacy. But, in the end Wilson seems to have been concerned only with how the treaty would be regarded by Americans, and that it should not present a target for his Republican critics.[40]

In campaigning for the League at home, however, Wilson revived the claim that the new world order would be democratic. Blurring the distinction between independent sovereignty and democracy, he asserted that the treaty 'provides for the destruction of autocratic power' because 'no nation is admitted to the League of Nations that cannot show that it has the institutions which we call free': 'The League of Nations sends autocratic governments to Coventry'. In fact, the requirement was only that member states should be 'fully self-governing' and, as Tony Smith points out, 'of the thirty states that signed the original instrument creating the League in 1919, fewer than half were democracies. In 1938, when League membership had increased to fifty-seven states, the proportion was smaller still'.[41]

Conclusion

In its relationship to the United States' democratic values, as in other respects, Wilson's foreign policy followed a pattern that was to be persistent and recurrent in later years. Broadly speaking, democracy played a much larger part in his justifications of his policies than it did in determining the specific objectives he pursued in particular circumstances. And it came to the fore mostly when he was seeking support for strenuous and potentially costly undertakings, whether it was entering the war against Germany or joining the League of Nations. Generally speaking, the policies came first, their connection with democracy later.

A striking illustration of this is provided by the accounts Wilson gave at different times of the causes and ideological significance of the European war. From the beginning, American partisans of the Allies' cause, including Roosevelt and Robert Lansing saw the conflict both as one between democracy and autocracy, and as the product of German aggression. But while Wilson was following a neutral policy, he took a different view. As early as December 1914, he suggested that 'Germany is not alone responsible for the war', and in the autumn of 1916, as he was preparing to press for an early, compromise peace, he attributed its outbreak to the whole system of international power politics rather than to the character of any particular regime or regimes. 'Nothing in particular started it, but everything in general', he told an audience in 1916.

> There had been growing up in Europe a mutual suspicion, an interchange of conjectures about what this government and that government was going to do, an interlacing of alliances and understandings, a complex web of intrigue and spying, that presently was sure to entangle the whole of the family of mankind on that side of the water in its meshes.

But after the United States became a belligerent, the president declared that 'the war was started by Germany' and that it was 'the last decisive issue between the old principle of power and the new principle of freedom'.[42]

As we have seen, from at least 1916 Wilson was committed to the establishment of an international system that would prevent the recurrence of such a catastrophic conflict. Assessing the role of democracy promotion in his policy entails analysing its connection to that strategic goal. Some historians and analysts have seen its role as central and essential.[43] Leaving aside the distinction between national self-determination and constitutional democracy, the basic issue is the relationship between the establishment of an international system of collective security and the general acceptance of the principle of 'government by the consent of the governed' and other liberal values. Wilson suggested that these objectives were integrally related and mutually supportive. If a settlement was not based on the principle of government by the consent of the governed, he observed, 'the ferment of spirit of whole populations will fight subtly and constantly against it, and all the world will sympathize'.[44] Beyond this was the claim in his War Address that democratic governments are more pacific by nature. Conversely, Wilson argued as he made the case for the peace treaty in 1919, without the League of Nations small states could never be secure and frontiers would have to be fixed according to 'strategic considerations' rather than the principle of self-determination.[45]

Yet, as we have seen, Wilson's own experience at Paris demonstrated the difficulty of reconciling these objectives. Establishing a League of Nations that included all the great powers necessitated accommodating their interests in ways that compromised the principle of 'government by the consent of the governed'. And so long as such values as democracy, self-determination and human rights are not always and everywhere respected by governments, the tension between a commitment to promote them and adherence to a global compact for the conduct of international relations is likely to persist. Wilson's legacy thus includes a fundamental ambivalence over how far the United States should behave as a revisionist power in world politics. It is this ambivalence that enabled both sides in the debate over the Iraq war of 2003 to invoke his name in support.[46] And, of course, it is only one manifestation of a persistent dilemma for American policy-makers, in the Middle East and elsewhere.

The record of Wilson's presidency as a whole leaves little doubt as to where his own priority lay. In urging Americans to accept the limitations on unfettered freedom of action involved in cooperating with other nations to establish a system of collective security, he portrayed the alternative in these terms:

> We must be physically ready for anything to come. We must have a great standing army. [...] Not only the continuation of the present taxes but the increase of the present taxes. [...] But, what is much more serious than that is we have got to have the sort of organization that can handle armies of that sort. [...] You can't handle an armed nation by vote. You can't handle an armed nation if it is democratic. [...] You have got to have a concentrated, militaristic organization of government to run a nation of that sort.[47]

In the end, the animating purpose of Wilson's foreign policy was to enable the United States to live its own life in accordance with its own historic values and traditions, as undisturbed as possible by the turbulent and dangerous world of the twentieth century. The phrase most often taken to encapsulate it should be read literally. His strategy was designed to 'make the world *safe* for democracy', not to spread democracy to the ends of the earth.[48]

Notes

1 'The Modern Democratic State' (December 1885); 'Democracy and Efficiency', *Atlantic Monthly*, March 1901. Arthur S. Link *et al.* (eds), *The Papers of Woodrow Wilson* (hereafter *PWW*), (Princeton, NJ, Princeton University Press, 1966–94), vol. 5, pp. 54–92, vol. 12, pp. 6–20.

2 'The Modern Democratic State', *PWW*, vol. 5, pp. 62, 70–76. See also *The State* (c. June 1889). *PWW*, vol. 6, pp. 261, 310.

3 John Milton Cooper, Jr., *Woodrow Wilson: A Biography* (New York, 2009), p. 151.

4 This may be illustrated by the number of books by progressive publicists that had 'democracy' in their title or subtitle. For example, Herbert Croly, *Progressive Democracy* (New York, 1914); Frederic C. Howe, *The City: The Hope of Democracy* (New York, 1905), *Privilege and Democracy in America* (New York, 1910), *Wisconsin: An Experiment in Democracy* (New York, 1912); Lincoln Steffens, *The Struggle for Self-government* (New

York, 1906); Walter Weyl, *The New Democracy: An Essay on Certain Political and Economic Tendencies in the United States* (New York, 1912); William Allen White, *The Old Order Changeth: A View of American Democracy* (New York, 1910).

5 Ray Stannard Baker, *Woodrow Wilson: Life and Letters* (Garden City, NY, 1931), vol. 5, p. 55.

6 Address at Independence Hall, Philadelphia, 4 July 1914. *PWW*, vol. 30, p. 252.

7 Samuel G. Blythe, 'Mexico: The Record of a Conversation with President Wilson', *Saturday Evening Post*, 23 May 1914, p. 4.

8 For a full account of the complex evolution of Wilson's policy on Mexico, see Arthur S. Link, *Wilson: The Struggle for Neutrality* (Princeton, NJ, Princetown University Press, 1960), pp. 232–66, 456–94, and *Wilson: Confusions and Crises, 1915–1916* (Princeton, NJ, 1964), pp. 195–200.

9 Wilson to Lindley M. Garrison, 8 August 1914; After-lunch talk to the Democratic National Committee, 8 December 1915. *PWW*, vol. 30, p. 362, vol. 35, pp. 314–15.

10 Remarks to Foreign Correspondents, 8 April 1918. *PWW*, vol. 47, p. 288.

11 See, for example, Sir William Wiseman to Sir Eric Drummond, 14 June 1918. *PWW*, vol. 48, p. 315; Wilson's remarks at the Council of Four, 27 March 1919. Paul Mantoux (ed.), *The Deliberations of the Council of Four (March 24–June 28, 1919)*, vol. I (Princeton, NJ, 1992), p. 47. When Wilson did send US forces to Russia in 1918, he emphasized that this was solely 'to guard military stores which may subsequently be needed by Russian forces and to render such aid as may be acceptable to the Russians in the organization of their own self-defence' and that the American government contemplated 'no interference with the political sovereignty of Russia, no intervention in her internal affairs'. A Press Release (c. 3 August 1918). *PWW*, vol. 49, p. 171.

12 'An Appeal to the American People', 18 August 1914. *PWW*, vol. 30, pp. 393–94; Link, *Struggle for Neutrality*, pp. 54–55.

13 Annual Message to Congress, 8 December 1914. *PWW*, vol. 31, pp. 421–23.

14 A memorandum by Herbert Bruce Brougham, 14 December 1914. *PWW*, vol. 31, pp. 458–59. In an unpublished interview later, Wilson expressed the view 'that only governments initiate such wars as the present and that they are never brought on by peoples, and that, therefore, democracy is the best preventive of such jealousies and suspicions and secret intrigues as produce wars among nations where small groups control, rather than the great body of public opinion'. 'An Interview with Henry Noble Hall', 31 October 1916. *PWW*, vol. 38, p. 569. On the interpretations by American progressives of the war's causes, see John A. Thompson, *Reformers and War: American Progressive Publicists and the First World War* (Cambridge, 1987), pp. 91–103.

15 House diary, 10 February 1915. Charles Seymour, *The Intimate Papers of Colonel House* (London, 1926), vol. I, p. 375.

16 Wilson to Edith Galt, 19 August 1915. *PWW*, vol. 34, p. 261.

17 This was the initiative that led to the House–Grey Memorandum of February 1916. For more details on its connection with Wilson's commitment to a post-war league of nations, see John A. Thompson, *Woodrow Wilson* (London, 2002), pp. 106, 117–18, 122–23.

18 Address to the League to Enforce Peace, 27 May 1916; Address to the Senate, 22 January 1917; J. J. Jusserand to the French Foreign Ministry, 7 March 1917. *PWW*, vol. 37, pp. 113–16, vol. 40, pp. 533–39, vol. 41, pp. 356–57.

19 Address to Congress, 2 April 1917. *PWW*, vol. 41, pp. 519–27.

20 Address to Congress, 2 April 1917; Robert Lansing to W. H. Page, 27 August 1917; *PWW*, vol. 41, pp. 523, 526, vol. 44, pp. 57–59.

21 Thompson, *Woodrow Wilson*, pp. 173–77; Robert Lansing to F. Oederlin, October 23, 1918. *Foreign Relations of the United States, 1918*, Supplement 1, vol. 1 (Washington, DC, US Government Printing Office, 1933), pp. 381–83.

22 On this, see Arno J. Mayer, *Wilson vs. Lenin: Political Origins of the New Diplomacy* (Cleveland, OH, 1964), pp. 98–140.

23 Address to Congress, 8 January 1918. *PWW*, vol. 45, p. 539.

24 Address in Baltimore, 6 April 1918. *PWW*, vol. 47, pp. 267–70.

25 Speech to the League to Enforce Peace, 27 May 1916. *PWW*, vol. 37, p. 115. For an excellent analysis of this evolution, see Michla Pomerance, 'The United States and Self-determination: Perspectives on the Wilsonian Conception', *The American Journal of International Law*, 70 (1976), pp. 1–2, 16–19.

26 Betty Miller Unterberger, *The United States, Revolutionary Russia, and the Rise of Czechoslovakia* (Chapel Hill, NC, University of North Carolina Press, 1989), pp. 35, 62–63, 168, 233, 269–70, 284–86, 314–15.

27 Annual Message on the State of the Union, 4 December 1917. *PWW*, vol. 45, p. 197.

28 Addresses to Congress, 8 January 1918, 11 February 1918. *PWW*, vol. 45, pp. 537–38, vol. 46, p. 323.

29 Victor Mamatey has observed that a visitor to inter-war Prague 'would detrain at the Wilson station. Coming out of the station, he would face the Wilson Square and the Wilson Park, with a statue of President Woodrow Wilson in its center'. Victor S. Mamatey, *The United States and East Central Europe 1914–1918: A Study in Wilsonian Diplomacy and Propaganda* (Princeton, NJ, Princeton University Press, 1957), p. vii. On the wider impact of Wilson's rhetoric on self-determination, see Erez Manela, *The Wilsonian Moment: Self-determination and the International Origins of Anticolonial Nationalism* (New York: Oxford University Press, 2007).

30 As early as July 1917, Wilson had emphasized to House that 'England and France *have not the same views with regard to peace that we have* by any means'. Wilson to House, 21 July 1917, *PWW*, vol. 43, pp. 237–38. Emphasis in original.

31 Thompson, *Reformers and War*, pp. 193–212; Walter E. Weyl, *The End of the War* (New York, 1918), pp. 161–62, 167–68.

32 Address in the Metropolitan Opera House, 27 September 1918. *PWW*, vol. 51, p. 132.

33 T. W. Lamont Memorandum of Conversation with the President, 4 October 1918. *PWW*, vol. 51, pp. 222–26.

34 Wilson statement on the Adriatic question, 23 April 1919; Ambassador T. N. Page to American Mission in Paris, 24 April 1919. *PWW*, vol. 58, pp. 5–8, 91–93.

35 Thomas J. Knock, *To End All Wars: Woodrow Wilson and the Quest for a New World Order* (Princeton, NJ, 1992), pp. 176–77.

36 He had assured House that after the war, the United States would be able 'to force them [England and France] to our way of thinking, because by that time they will, among other things, be financially in our hands'. Wilson to House, 21 July 1917, *PWW*, vol. 43, p. 238. But Wilson would have been able to gain diplomatic leverage from America's financial power only if he had been able to offer either further credits or substantial relief on the repayment of the Allies' war debts, and neither was acceptable to the Treasury Department and Congress.

37 See, for example, Minutes of the Imperial War Cabinet, 30 December 1918. *PWW*, vol. 53, pp. 558–69.

38 Sterling J. Kernek, 'Woodrow Wilson and National Self-determination: A Study of the Manipulation of Principles in the Pursuit of Political Interests', *Proceedings of the American Philosophical Society*, 1982, vol. 126, pp. 255–62.

39 Lansing Memorandum, 28 April 1919; Diary of Ray Stannard Baker, 30 April, 1919. *PWW*, vol. 58, pp. 185, 270–71.

40 Klaus Schwabe, *Woodrow Wilson, Revolutionary Germany, and Peacemaking, 1918–1919* (Chapel Hill, NC, 1985), especially pp. 297, 321–24, 340, 390–91, 398. On Wilson's overriding concern with American opinion, see R. S. Baker diary, 23 May, 31 May 1919. *PWW*, vol. 59, pp. 447, 645–47.

41 Addresses at Minneapolis and St Paul, 9 September 1919. *PWW*, vol. 63, pp. 135, 144; Tony Smith, *America's Mission: The United States and the Worldwide Struggle for Democracy in the Twentieth Century* (Princeton, NJ, 1994), p. 94.

42 Brougham memorandum, 14 December 1914; Address to Women in Cincinnati, 26 October 1916; Address to the American Federation of Labor, 12 November 1917. *PWW*, vol. 31, pp. 458–59, vol. 38, p. 531, vol. 45, p. 12.

43 For example, Tony Smith, 'Wilsonianism after Iraq', G. John Ikenberry *et al.*, *The Crisis of American Foreign Policy: Wilsonianism in the Twenty-first Century* (Princeton, NJ, 2009), p. 58.

44 Address to the Senate, 22 January 1917. *PWW*, vol. 40, p. 537.

45 Address in Columbus, Ohio, 4 September 1919; Address in Sioux Falls, South Dakota, 8 September 1919. *PWW*, vol. 63, pp. 10–12, 112.

46 For example, Lawrence F. Kaplan, 'Regime Change', *The New Republic*, 3 March 2003, pp. 21–23, and John B. Judis, 'History Lesson', *The New Republic*, 9 June 2003, pp. 19–23.

47 Address at St Louis, 5 September 1919. *PWW*, vol. 63, pp. 46–47. This 'garrison state' argument was another that was used by Wilson's successors, particularly Harry S. Truman. See, for example, Special Message to Congress on the Mutual Security Program, 6 March 1952. *Public Papers of the Presidents of the United States: Harry S. Truman.* (Washington, DC, 1966), p. 189.

48 Address to Congress, 2 April 1917. *PWW*, vol. 41, p. 525. My emphasis.

4

FRANKLIN D. ROOSEVELT

Tony McCulloch

Franklin Roosevelt was no stranger to democracy promotion in its broadest sense. He was a member of Woodrow Wilson's two administrations from 1913 to 1921 as assistant secretary of the navy – a position that his distant cousin, former president Theodore Roosevelt, had occupied during the Spanish–American War of 1898. Needless to say, Franklin Roosevelt was a very proactive and ambitious assistant secretary who favoured a big navy and who, during the First World War, was an early advocate of aid to Britain and France. In 1920, helped by his illustrious name, he was chosen by the Democrats as their candidate for vice-president in the election of that year. A strong supporter of international cooperation, he campaigned vigorously for American membership of the League of Nations but went down to defeat in the Republican landslide associated with the United States' 'return to normalcy'. The Republicans remained in the ascendancy for the rest of the decade until the onset of the economic depression brought the Democrats back to power, led by Franklin Roosevelt.[1]

In February 1932, soon after declaring himself a candidate for the presidency, Roosevelt had been attacked by the Hearst press as an internationalist who would not stand up for American interests abroad. Fully aware of his political vulnerability during the upcoming election campaign as a member of the Wilsonian wing of the Democratic Party, he made it clear in a speech to the New York State Grange that he no longer supported American membership of the League. 'The League of Nations today is not the League conceived by Woodrow Wilson', he said. Instead of dealing with issues of world peace it had become 'a mere meeting place for the political discussion of strictly European national difficulties' in which 'the United States should have no part'. The League had not developed in the way that Wilson had hoped and therefore, he said, 'I do not favour American participation'. Roosevelt's disavowal of the League upset Wilsonians in the Democratic Party but it was an important step in his gaining the presidency.[2]

As president, Roosevelt – like Wilson and Bush – has had plenty of critics in terms of his contribution to democracy promotion. However, the most common criticism of Roosevelt has not been that he intervened abroad too much but rather that he did not intervene enough, especially to assist the democracies of Britain and France in countering the rise of the Axis powers of Germany, Italy and Japan in the 1930s. While few historians would deny Roosevelt's central role in the victory of the Allies over the Axis powers in the Second World War, his early foreign policy has been roundly criticized by many as lacking in international vision. A common view is that he pandered to isolationism during his first administration and that it was not until his Chicago speech in October 1937, in which he talked about a 'quarantine' of aggressor states, that he began to show some leadership in international affairs and even then rather fitfully.[3] In light of Roosevelt's Wilsonian credentials and his pivotal role in the emergence of the United States as the leader of the free world by 1945, his presidency clearly constitutes an important case study in terms of American democracy promotion and its place within the American foreign policy tradition.[4] In this respect, his 12 annual addresses on the State of the Union – together with his four Inaugural Addresses – comprise an authoritative source for the development of his thinking as president from the dawn of the New Deal in March 1933 to the twilight of his presidency in January 1945.

The Roosevelt Doctrine of 1936

When Roosevelt became president in March 1933 his focus was very much on the economic depression that had descended upon the United States and the rest of the world since 1929. In his Inaugural Address he mentioned the international dimension of the crisis but he said that he would deal with 'first things first' and that the emergency at home was his top priority.[5] In his now legendary One Hundred Days he launched the New Deal, which involved an unprecedented burst of detailed legislation aimed at dealing with the banking crisis and combating unemployment. In July 1933 he sent his infamous 'Bombshell' message to the World Economic Conference meeting in London, thereby torpedoing negotiations for an international currency agreement. John Maynard Keynes may have called the president's policy 'magnificently right' but, for the governments of Britain and France, Roosevelt's actions simply confirmed their views about American unreliability – views that had become commonplace following the Senate's rejection of the League of Nations in 1920.[6]

However, in a significant speech in honour of Wilson's birthday on 28 December 1933, he showed that he had not entirely forsaken his predecessor or the League. Addressing the Woodrow Wilson Foundation Dinner in Washington, he began with an amusing reference to his time as assistant secretary of the navy under Wilson. He also referred to Wilson's Mobile speech of March 1913 in which the president had said that 'the United States will never again seek one additional foot of territory by conquest'. Roosevelt himself went further still and declared that 'the definite policy of the United States from now on is one opposed to armed intervention', particularly in relation to Latin America. More generally, Roosevelt lamented the continuing threats to world peace and – in contrast to his New York Grange speech – he praised the League for providing at least a forum for peace and for the work of its social and economic agencies. 'We are not members and we do not contemplate membership', he continued, but 'we are giving cooperation to the League in every matter which is not primarily political'.[7]

Roosevelt's New Deal reforms continued to be the main focus of his presidency in his early years and formed the centrepiece of his State of the Union messages in 1934 and 1935.[8] But by the beginning of 1936 the international situation had become distinctly bleak and the reputation of Britain and France – the two leading European democracies and the backbone of the League of Nations – had fallen to its lowest ebb for many years. This was the context of Roosevelt's third State of the Union Address on 3 January 1936 in which, for the first time, he focused on the threat to democracy at home and abroad. Whereas his Inaugural Address in 1933 and his first two State of the Union Addresses in 1934 and 1935 – overshadowed by the great depression and focused on the New Deal – had said very little about world affairs, his 1936 address began with the international situation and devoted 20 paragraphs – almost half the speech – to this issue. The terms 'democracy' and 'democratic' were explicitly mentioned on five occasions, while their political opposites – 'autocracy' and 'autocratic' – were also referred to repeatedly.[9]

The reason for Roosevelt's new-found emphasis on democracy was not difficult to discern. As Roosevelt himself said at the start of his 1936 speech, when he had delivered his Inaugural Address in March 1933 the crisis facing the United States was seen as almost an entirely domestic one.

> The world picture was an image of substantial peace. International consultation and widespread hope for the betterment of relations between the nations gave to all of us a reasonable expectation that the barriers to mutual confidence, to increased trade, and to peaceful settlement of disputes could be progressively removed.
>
> However, since the summer of 1933 the international situation had deteriorated so that the people of the Americas must take cognizance of growing ill-will, of marked trends toward aggression, of increasing armaments, of shortening tempers – a situation which has in it many of the elements that lead to the tragedy of general war.[10]

Hitler's accession to power in Germany in January 1933 had led to a worsening of relations with France and had also accelerated the breakdown of the Disarmament Conference in Geneva in October 1933. This was followed by German withdrawal from the League of Nations and accelerated German rearmament in defiance of the Treaty of Versailles of 1919. At first the growing military threat from Hitler had at least been tempered by the fact that Germany appeared isolated in Europe and at odds with Japan, the other main threat to global security in the early 1930s. But

Japanese expansionism at the expense of China, following the invasion of Manchuria in 1931, was now matched by the desire of Mussolini to create an Italian empire in North Africa. By August 1935 Mussolini's designs on Ethiopia were clear for all to see and in October 1935 Italian forces launched an invasion of the country, which was a member of the League.[11]

Like many others, Roosevelt was greatly concerned by the Italian invasion of Ethiopia because it obviously increased the likelihood of a war in Europe that might eventually involve the United States, as had occurred in 1917. He was initially reassured when the British government appeared ready to stand up to Italian aggression and to lead the League of Nations in employing economic sanctions against it. In his Geneva speech in September 1935, Sir Samuel Hoare, the British foreign secretary, appeared to underline Britain's commitment to the League and to the principle of collective security. However, once war broke out the British government became increasingly alarmed at the prospect that sanctions against Italy might force Mussolini into a 'mad dog' act. It was in these circumstances that Hoare met Pierre Laval, his French opposite number, in Paris in December 1935 and agreed to a 'compromise' plan whereby Ethiopia would make large territorial concessions to Italy in return for peace. When news of the so-called 'Hoare–Laval pact' became public on 9 December there was a worldwide reaction against it and Hoare was forced to resign.[12]

In the wake of the worsening international situation Roosevelt used his State of the Union Address on 3 January 1936 to deliver an outspoken attack on the dictator nations of Italy, Germany and Japan. Making it clear that he believed the threat to world peace came from nations 'dominated by the twin spirits of autocracy and aggression', he said: 'I recognise that these words which I have chosen with deliberation will not prove popular in any nation that chooses to fit this shoe to its foot.' But he thought they would be welcomed by what he called the 'peace-loving nations' of the world who were caught up in 'the kaleidoscopic jockeying for position characteristic of European and Asiatic relations today'. Roosevelt then went on to say: 'The evidence before us clearly proves that *autocracy in world affairs endangers peace* and that *such threats do not spring from the nations devoted to the democratic ideal.*'[13]

Roosevelt's declaration on behalf of democracy did not cause any great surprise in the United States at the time because very few Americans disagreed with it as a statement of fact. The main issue was how far the president would try to seek powers from Congress to discriminate between belligerents in a conflict in order to favour the democracies of Britain and France against the dictator states. It was well known that Roosevelt wanted some degree of discretion in controlling the arms embargo introduced by Congress as a result of the resolution of August 1935 that sought to uphold US American neutrality by banning the export of 'arms, ammunition and the instruments of war' to any belligerent in an armed conflict. In the event, Roosevelt was persuaded by his allies in Congress that this would not be possible so he had to settle for a neutrality law passed in February 1936 that gave him very little discretion to discriminate against Italy.[14]

Unable to turn his rhetoric into reality, Roosevelt's State of the Union address in January 1936 has received relatively little attention from historians in terms of its significance for his foreign policy. This is despite the fact that he turned the event into an act of political theatre by delivering it in person in the evening surrounded by lights and microphones and much of the media. As one historian has written, 'Roosevelt transformed the usually dull occasion of the State of the Union message into a national spectacle'.[15] The only other occasion when a president had addressed Congress in the evening was on 2 April 1917, when Woodrow Wilson had asked for a declaration of war against Germany. Roosevelt's message contained obvious echoes of Wilson's assertion that 'the world must be made safe for democracy' but, unlike Wilson in 1917, he showed more understanding towards the European democracies in achieving this goal.[16]

Can Roosevelt's statement in January 1936 be regarded as a Roosevelt Doctrine on democracy promotion? Clearly, it has not been recognized as such by historians in the same way that, for example, the Monroe Doctrine of 1823 and the Truman Doctrine of 1947 have been recognized as presidential doctrines. Nor was Roosevelt's statement particularly original as it obviously owed much to the legacy of Wilson, among others. In fact, it could easily be referred to as the Wilson Doctrine except that historians have neglected to do so. It is also a classic statement of democratic peace theory, first championed by Immanuel Kant in 1795.[17] Notwithstanding these caveats, as an early declaration of the grand strategy that was to underpin the rest of his presidency, Roosevelt's 1936 statement deserves much more attention from historians and political scientists than it has generally received. Not only does his statement show that he was more concerned about the fate of democracy in Europe during the first term as president than is usually supposed but it also provided the basis for the development of his ideas on democracy promotion during the rest of his presidency.[18]

While not a great theorist, Roosevelt had a strong sense of history – and strategy. An examination of his annual messages to Congress and other key documents such as the Atlantic Charter reveals that democracy was a constant theme in his rhetoric, especially from 1936 onwards. In fact, it is possible to identify at least four main aspects of democracy promotion that grew out of his 1936 message and therefore constitute a fuller version of the 'Roosevelt Doctrine'. First, after 1936 he began to portray the Good Neighbour policy towards Latin America as an exercise in democracy promotion, in direct contrast to events in Europe and Asia. Second, he was not blind to the weaknesses of democracy and often referred to the need for economic and social reform at home as well as abroad, leading to his concept of the Four Freedoms. Third, from 1936 onwards, as well as stressing the danger to peace from the dictator states, Roosevelt increasingly implied the need for the United States to support the democracies of Europe who shared American values, especially Britain. The Atlantic Charter was an agreement between the two democracies on war aims but one that mainly reflected New Deal thinking. Finally, when the United States joined the war at the end of 1941 Roosevelt began to call for a democratic and permanent peace based on the cooperation of the wartime allies in the form of the United Nations (UN). In so doing he was very mindful of the fate of Wilson's League and determined that the lessons of the past would be learned.

Democracy and the Americas – the Good Neighbour policy

If there is one area of the world where American presidents have felt free to promote their own version of democracy, it is Latin America. But, at the very outset of his presidency, Roosevelt explicitly rejected interventionism in 'America's back yard'. In his 1933 Inaugural Address he said: 'I would dedicate this nation to the policy of the good neighbour – the neighbour who resolutely respects himself and, because he does so, respects the rights of others'.[19] Herbert Hoover had also talked about being a good neighbour, but during his presidency the United States had refused to commit to a declaration of non-intervention. In December 1933, at the Montevideo conference, Cordell Hull, Roosevelt's secretary of state, formally signed up to such a commitment in the Convention of Rights and Duties of States, albeit with a clarifying reservation. Thus in his 1934 address Roosevelt was able to say: 'We have, I hope, made it clear to our neighbours that we seek with them future avoidance of territorial expansion and of interference by one Nation in the internal affairs of others.'[20]

In his address on 3 January 1936 he went further and contrasted the state of the Americas with the rest of the world, especially Europe and Asia:

> At no time in the four and a half centuries of modern civilisation in the Americas has there existed – in any year, in any decade, in any generation in all that time – a greater spirit of mutual understanding, of common helpfulness and of devotion to the ideals of self-government than exists today in the twenty-one American Republics and their neighbour, the Dominion of Canada. There is neither war, nor rumour of war, nor desire for war. The inhabitants of this vast area, two hundred and fifty million strong, spreading more than eight thousand miles from the Arctic to the Antarctic, believe in, and propose to follow, the policy of the good neighbour.[21]

Shortly after his annual address Roosevelt wrote to the presidents of the Latin American republics suggesting a conference to discuss ways of preventing wars in the Western hemisphere. The conference was held in Buenos Aires in December 1936 and Roosevelt, who had been greeted by rapturous crowds in Latin America, gave the opening address. The delegates adopted 'the Convention for the Maintenance, Preservation and Reestablishment of Peace' as well as a protocol that broadened the meaning of non-intervention beyond the 1933 convention.[22] Roosevelt's 1937 address explicitly linked the happy state of the Americas with the democratic spirit he discerned during his Latin American trip. 'The very cordial receptions with which I was greeted were in tribute to democracy', he declared.

In a very real sense, the Conference in Buenos Aires sent forth a message on behalf of all the democracies of the world to those nations which live otherwise. Because such other governments are perhaps more spectacular, it was high time for democracy to exert itself.[23]

Of course, the republics of Latin America were by no means all model democracies living in peace with each other, as liberal critics of Roosevelt's Good Neighbour policy such as Carleton Beals were quick to mention. To Beals, the policy of the Roosevelt administration towards Latin America was both hypocritical and patronizing as at least some of its leaders, such as Rafael Trujillo in the Dominican Republic, were as much tyrants and dictators, albeit on a smaller scale, as Mussolini or Hitler. Nor were the American republics slow to resort to arms against each other, as Beals pointed out. There was obviously much truth in such criticisms of the Good Neighbour policy and Roosevelt's lauding of the American republics no doubt owed a great deal to security concerns and the fear of Nazi or Fascist propaganda turning one or more of them against the United States.[24]

'Fortunate it is', Roosevelt declared in his 1939 address, 'that in this Western Hemisphere we have, under a common ideal of democratic government, a rich diversity of resources and of peoples functioning together in mutual respect and peace.' Then, referring directly to the security aspect of American policy in the Americas, he said: 'That Hemisphere, that peace and that ideal we propose to do our share in protecting against storms from any quarter.'[25] Similarly, in his 1940 address he said

> Twenty-one American Republics, expressing the will of 250 million people to preserve peace and freedom in this Hemisphere, are displaying a unanimity of ideals and practical relationships which gives hope that what is being done here can be done on other continents.[26]

In his 1941 address he stressed the danger to the Western hemisphere from Axis agents, many of whom, he argued, were already in Latin America preparing for an invasion. 'That is why the future of all the American Republics is today in serious danger', he said.[27]

Security concerns were clearly a major factor in Roosevelt's policy towards Latin America and these increased yet further after the United States formally joined the world war in December 1941. Democracy promotion was an important element in the Good Neighbour policy but it took the form of promoting regional agreements among the American republics and accepting the principle of non-intervention by the United States in the government of individual states. Roosevelt maintained this principle throughout his presidency, unlike many American presidents before and since. The declaration he made against armed intervention in his Woodrow Wilson speech in December 1933 was a direct rejection of the Roosevelt corollary put forward by his namesake in 1908.[28] Thus the evidence of the Good Neighbour policy clearly suggests that Roosevelt was opposed to military intervention in the affairs of the Latin American republics and preferred instead to focus on democratic cooperation between them.[29]

Democracy and reform – the Four Freedoms

Although a great advocate of democracy in the Americas, Roosevelt was certainly not blind to its weaknesses in practice, not least in the United States where he was engaged in a constant struggle during his presidency to realize the aspirations of his New Deal programme of reform. He was also very conscious of the view – common in the 1930s – that liberal democracy could not cope with a major crisis such as the economic depression and that a dictatorship of the right or left was the most efficient method of government in such circumstances. He confronted these doubts in his first Inaugural Address when he famously said to his fellow citizens that 'the only thing we have to fear is fear itself'. With the American political system seemingly on trial he declared: 'We do not distrust the future of essential democracy.' The people of the United States had not failed, according to Roosevelt, but their politicians had been found wanting and new leadership was required.[30] The need for reform at home was also a major theme in Roosevelt's 1934 and 1935 addresses.[31]

In his landmark 1936 address Roosevelt went further still by explicitly linking the situation in Europe and Asia with the need to embrace New Deal reforms at home in order to avoid the economic and social inequalities that led to the rise of dictators pledged to change the status quo, by force if necessary. In particular, the battle against autocracy abroad was linked to the struggle against economic autocracy at home. 'Within democratic nations the chief concern of the people is to prevent the continuance or the rise of autocratic institutions that beget slavery at home and aggression abroad', said Roosevelt. 'Within our borders, as in the world at large, popular opinion is at war with a power-seeking minority.' This was no new thing, according to Roosevelt. Rather it was the continuation of battles fought by previous presidents such as Theodore Roosevelt and Woodrow Wilson.[32]

Roosevelt's address in January 1937, after his landslide re-election, continued this theme. Mentioning the word 'democracy' or 'democratic' no fewer than 20 times in a relatively short speech, he argued that social and constitutional reform was required at home. Referring to the crisis of 1933 he said: 'Ours was the task to prove that democracy could be made to function in the world of today as effectively as in the simpler world of a hundred years ago.' And, echoing Abraham Lincoln, he declared that: 'The United States of America, within itself, must continue the task of making democracy succeed.'[33] He continued to stress the domestic threat to democracy shortly afterwards in his Second Inaugural Address when he referred to 'one third of a nation' being 'ill-housed, ill-clad and ill-fed'.[34] His 1938 address also restated the need to move ahead with the New Deal agenda.[35]

Roosevelt's 1939 address again included numerous references to the threat to democracy in the United States from abroad, which he now linked directly with American freedoms:

Where freedom of religion has been attacked, the attack has come from sources opposed to democracy. Where democracy has been overthrown, the spirit of free worship has disappeared. And where religion and democracy has vanished, good faith and reason in international affairs have given way to strident ambition and brute force.

Roosevelt also linked this external threat to the need for internal reform in order to produce a united nation:

A dictatorship may command the full strength of a regimented nation. But the united strength of a democratic nation can be mustered only when its people, educated by modern standards to know what is going on and where they are going, have conviction that they are receiving as large a share of opportunity for development, as large a share of material success, and of human dignity, as they have a right to receive.[36]

In his 1940 address Roosevelt continued to stress the link between foreign and domestic policies. 'The social and economic forces which have been mismanaged abroad until they have resulted in revolution, dictatorship and war are the same as those which we here are struggling to adjust peacefully at home', he said. 'Dictatorships', he argued, 'have originated in almost every case in the necessity for drastic action to improve internal conditions in places where democratic action for one reason or another has failed to respond to modern needs and modern demands.' The peoples of other nations had the right to choose their own form of government, he continued. 'But we in this nation still believe that such choice should be predicated on certain freedoms which we think are essential everywhere.' Then, adding what could be seen as a corollary to his 1936 statement that associated democracy with peace and autocracy with war, he said: 'We know that we ourselves shall never be safe at home unless other governments recognise such freedoms.'[37]

Roosevelt's 1941 address has become known as the Four Freedoms speech. Declaring that the foundations of a healthy and strong democracy included economic and social rights such as employment for those who were able to work, he then linked those rights to 'a world founded upon four essential human freedoms' – freedom of speech, freedom of religion, freedom from want and freedom from fear.[38] He also referred to these Four Freedoms in 1943. 'The blessings of two of them,' he said, 'freedom of speech and freedom of religion [...] are an essential part of the very life of this nation; and we hope that these blessings will be granted to all men everywhere.' He then referred to the third freedom – freedom from want – which in domestic terms he equated with full employment after the war. He also said that it was necessary to strive for the fourth freedom – freedom from fear – which he said meant achieving a just and lasting peace through the UN.[39]

Roosevelt's concept of the Four Freedoms was an important part of his contribution to the promotion of democracy in its broadest sense. As with his Good Neighbour policy, it evolved gradually during his presidency, especially after his

1936 address. Although regarded as a statement of international policy, applicable 'everywhere in the world', it obviously had its roots in the New Deal and Roosevelt's view that economic and social reform was a prerequisite to the health of democracy at home as well as abroad. After Roosevelt's death the concept of the Four Freedoms was championed by Eleanor Roosevelt and was incorporated into the preamble of the Universal Declaration of Human Rights in 1948. No doubt with Roosevelt's 1941 annual address in mind, this stated that 'the advent of a world in which human beings shall enjoy freedom of speech and belief and freedom from fear and want has been proclaimed the highest aspiration of the common people'.[40]

Democracy abroad – the Atlantic Charter

When Roosevelt became president in 1933 few could have foreseen the emergence within less than a decade of an Atlantic alliance under his leadership. Such was the strength of isolationism at that time that any American involvement in the political affairs of Europe was out of the question, as Roosevelt acknowledged in his Woodrow Wilson speech in December 1933. Moreover, Britain and France, the two leading European democracies, had fallen out with the United States over financial policy at the London Economic Conference in July 1933 and had defaulted on their war debts.[41] However, in his 1934 annual address Roosevelt made it clear that, although the United States could not take part in any political arrangements in Europe, participation in economic and disarmament negotiations would be welcomed.[42] Later, in his 1935 address, mindful of German rearmament and Japanese expansion and anxious for regime change, he said he hoped for 'the coming of new and more practical forms of representative government throughout the world'.[43]

Roosevelt's 1936 address went much further and made a clear distinction between what he termed the 'peace loving' democracies of Britain and France and the autocracies of Germany, Italy and Japan. It also implied a willingness to support the former against the latter as far as this was possible given the constraints of American isolationism.[44] With his re-election safely achieved, Roosevelt followed up his moral support for the democracies in his 1937 address, pointing out that 'in oligarchies, militarism has leapt forward, while in those nations which have retained democracy, militarism has waned'.[45] In his 1938 address he stressed the need for increased American defence spending and again attached the blame for worsening international relations to the autocracies. 'Disregard for treaty obligations seems to have followed the surface trend away from the democratic representative form of government', he said.

> It would seem, therefore, that world peace through international agreements is most safe in the hands of democratic representative governments – or, in other words peace is most greatly jeopardized in and by those nations where democracy has been discarded or has never developed.[46]

During 1938 the democracies of Britain and France, desperate to avoid a European war, continued their policy of appeasement, resulting in the notorious Munich agreement that ceded the Czech Sudetenland to Germany. Roosevelt, like many other observers, suspected that the respite obtained from Munich would not last long. 'A war which threatened to envelope the world in flames has been averted', he said at the start of his 1939 address, 'but it has become increasingly clear that world peace is not assured.' Still constrained by the American Neutrality Law he stressed the danger to American security posed by events in Europe. 'We have learned that God-fearing democracies of the world which observe the sanctity of treaties and good faith in their dealings with other nations cannot safely be indifferent to international lawlessness anywhere.' He then declared that: 'There are many methods short of war, but stronger and more effective than mere words, of bringing home to aggressor governments the aggregate sentiments of our people.'[47]

Among these methods short of war Roosevelt no doubt had in mind the repeal of the American Neutrality Law that prevented the belligerents in a conflict from obtaining 'arms, ammunition and the implements of war' from the United States. If a European war was to break out this would greatly handicap the democracies of Britain and France against Germany and Italy. He was unable to secure the repeal before war began but shortly after, in November 1939, the arms embargo was replaced by 'cash and carry', which favoured Britain in particular.[48] However, there remained a strong body of isolationist opinion in and out of Congress, and it was this group that Roosevelt challenged in his 1940 address. 'There is a vast difference between keeping out of war and pretending that this war is none of our business', he said. 'It is not good for the ultimate health of ostriches to bury their head in the sand.'[49]

Following the German blitzkrieg in May 1940 and the fall of France the following month, Roosevelt agreed to the destroyer-bases deal that gave Britain 50 over-age destroyers in return for the use of bases in the West Indies and Newfoundland.[50] Roosevelt was taking a political risk in agreeing to this deal in a presidential election year but he went on to be re-elected for an unprecedented third term. In his 1941 address he argued that the democracies of Europe – primarily Britain – were the first line of defence for the United States and should therefore be supplied with the materials of war even when they had run out of money to pay for them.[51] This was a follow-up to his 'arsenal of democracy' Fireside Chat a few days earlier and led to the Lend Lease Act in March 1941. This allowed the flow of military aid to Britain and, subsequently, to the Soviet Union when it too was attacked by Germany in June 1941. In August 1941, before the United States had officially joined the war, Roosevelt and Winston Churchill met on the USS *Augusta*, in Placentia Bay off the coast of Newfoundland, and produced a statement of democratic war aims that became known as the Atlantic Charter.[52]

In his remaining annual addresses Roosevelt spoke in glowing terms of the role of Churchill and Britain in defending democracy, making specific mention of the Atlantic Charter in his last address in 1945. Referring to the incorporation of the principles of the Atlantic Charter into the Declaration of the United Nations in January 1942, he said: 'It is a good and useful thing – an essential thing – to have principles toward which we can aim.'[53] Historians have rightly attached great importance to the Atlantic Charter in the development of liberal internationalism after Woodrow Wilson. But the principles it advanced – such as 'the right of all peoples to choose the government under which they will live' and 'assurance that all the men in all the lands may live out their lives in freedom from fear and want' – had evolved out of the New Deal domestic and foreign policies of the 1930s and had been set out in Roosevelt's State of the Union addresses since 1936.[54]

Democracy and peace – the UN

When Roosevelt delivered his ninth State of the Union address in January 1942 the United States was at war with Germany, Italy and Japan and in alliance with Britain, Canada, the other countries of the British Commonwealth and also the Soviet Union. In the remaining annual addresses of his presidency he therefore referred less to American support for the democracies and focused more on international cooperation in general, especially among what had already become known as the United Nations. In his 1942 address Roosevelt referred to the recent UN declaration. 'Gone forever are the days when the aggressors could attack and destroy their victims one by one without unity of resistance', he said. 'We of the United Nations will so dispose our forces that we can strike at the common enemy wherever the greatest damage can be done him.' The ultimate result, Roosevelt declared, would be a victory for democracy, freedom and religion and for all of the values that Americans held dear.[55]

In his 1943 address Roosevelt, encouraged by the military progress of the UN during the previous year, looked forward to a peace settlement that would be informed by the lessons of the past, especially those associated with the League of Nations. 'After the first World War we tried to achieve a formula for permanent peace, based on a magnificent idealism', he said. 'We failed. But, by our failure, we have learned that we cannot maintain peace at this stage of human development by good intentions alone.' It was therefore vital that the UN remained united in order to prevent the rearmament of the Axis powers and to ensure that they abandoned their militaristic philosophy. To underline the need for regime change Roosevelt returned to the theme of democracy versus dictatorship that he had first highlighted in his 1936 address:

> The issue of this war is the basic issue between those who believe in mankind and those who do not – the ancient issue between those who put their faith in the people and those who put their faith in dictators and tyrants.[56]

The need for Americans to enjoy a lasting peace after the sacrifices of the war was also highlighted by Roosevelt in his 1944 address:

> We are united in determination that this war shall not be followed by another interim which leads to new disaster – that we shall not repeat the

tragic errors of ostrich isolationism – that we shall not repeat the excesses of the wild twenties when this Nation went for a joy ride on a roller coaster which ended in a tragic crash.

The mistakes of the last war had to be avoided, he said, including the mistake of not discussing the peace with leaders of other countries until the war was over. This was a major purpose of the recent wartime conferences with Churchill and Stalin. 'The one supreme objective for the future, which we discussed for each nation individually, and for all the United Nations, can be summed up in one word: Security.' To achieve this security, said Roosevelt, a 'just and durable system of peace' was required.[57]

Roosevelt returned to this issue in his 1945 address, shortly after his re-election to a fourth term. He talked of creating a 'people's peace' and said that the recent Dumbarton Oaks conference had gone some way towards developing a 'democratic and fully integrated world security system'. He then looked forward to the year ahead. 'This new year of 1945 can be the greatest year of achievement in human history', he said. Not only could it witness the final defeat of Nazi Germany and Imperial Japan, but:

> Most important of all – 1945 can and must see the substantial beginning of the organization of world peace. This organization must be the fulfilment of the promise for which men have fought and died in this war. It must be the justification of all the sacrifices that have been made – of all the dreadful misery that this world has endured.[58]

Thus Roosevelt, like Wilson, staked American democracy promotion and his own legacy in international affairs on the establishment of an international organization dedicated to upholding world peace. As many writers have observed, the UN owed much to the League of Nations that Roosevelt – like Wilson – had championed at the end of the First World War but that the United States failed to join. Its structure and machinery were indeed similar but Roosevelt enjoyed the benefit of hindsight and sought to avoid the mistakes made by Wilson and his contemporaries in setting up the League. His determination to do so was shown by his establishment of a group in the State Department under Cordell Hull to begin the process of planning a post-war peace organization as early as September 1939, just a few days after the outbreak of war in Europe. Roosevelt called Hull the father of the UN and Hull was later awarded a Nobel Peace Prize for his efforts. But Franklin Roosevelt was in a very real sense the UN's godfather.[59]

Conclusions – Roosevelt's legacy for democracy promotion

In January 1945, at the end of his twelfth and last annual message, Franklin Roosevelt concluded with the words: 'We Americans of today, together with our allies, are making history – and I hope it will be better history than ever has been made before.'[60] Few historians or political scientists would doubt the contribution that Franklin Roosevelt made to America's standing as a global super power or to the promotion of American democracy. Since his death in April 1945 he has regularly been rated by American scholars as one of the top three American presidents, alongside Lincoln and Washington. In a recent poll of British academics specializing in American history and politics he came first, doubtless because of his international reputation, especially in the field of transatlantic relations.[61]

Not the least of Roosevelt's strengths was his ability to communicate with the American people, whether on great state occasions or in his 'fireside chats'. Of particular significance for American democracy promotion is his annual message of 3 January 1936 when his presidency symbolically changed gear and moved from one primarily focused on the New Deal and domestic concerns to one that became increasingly influenced by events in Europe and Asia and their potential impact on the Americas. The choice for American diplomacy identified in that speech between aiding democracy or dictatorship constituted the basis of a Roosevelt Doctrine that was directly descended from the Wilson presidency, under which he served.

Roosevelt elaborated upon this doctrine in his subsequent annual messages in four main ways. First, his Good Neighbour policy was based upon the conviction that it was in the economic and security interests of the United States to avoid any semblance of military intervention against the countries of Latin America. He may have exaggerated the democratic credentials of his southern neighbours from 1936 as part of his rhetoric aimed at the dictators in Europe and Asia, but under his leadership the United States was a better neighbour than it had ever been before. Second, he never abandoned his own liberal convictions and his belief that democracies, not least the United States, had to reform in order to survive. Hence the Four Freedoms that he advanced in January 1941 and championed at home and abroad during his wartime presidency. Third, while he may have been slow to aid the democracies of Britain and France in the 1930s, as has been alleged, he began to develop the principles that were to underpin the Atlantic Charter long before August 1941. Finally, like Wilson, he put his faith in an international organization to keep the peace and, rather fittingly, the UN emerged from the Second World War as a reformed League under American leadership and based in New York.

Roosevelt died before the onset of the Cold War that led to the Truman Doctrine of March 1947, advocating the containment of the Soviet Union and aid to countries threatened by Soviet communism.[62] Therefore we cannot know how far he would have modified his views on democracy promotion under the pressure of post-war realities, although he was certainly aware of the difficulties that lay ahead, especially over the future of eastern Europe and he referred to these in his wartime addresses. But he also cautioned that international cooperation was 'not a one-way street' and pointed out that no nation could assume that it had 'a monopoly of wisdom or of virtue'. 'In a democratic world, as in a democratic nation,' he said, 'power must be linked with responsibility, and obliged to defend and justify itself within the framework of the general good.' It was therefore necessary to achieve international cooperation through compromise with nations that 'did not see and think exactly as we do'.[63]

What then would Franklin Roosevelt have made of the recent American policy of democracy promotion in Iraq and Afghanistan, and its putative links with Wilsonian internationalism? Does the Roosevelt Doctrine of 1936, based on a significant Wilsonian heritage but subsequently elaborated under the very different circumstances of the Second World War, have anything in common with the democracy promotion advanced in the Bush Doctrine of 2002? Clearly there are similarities, not least Roosevelt's view, often repeated in his annual addresses, that democracy in the United States would never be safe while there were powerful enemies abroad that did not subscribe to this ideology. Furthermore, no American president could have refrained from action against the government of Afghanistan after 9/11. But given Roosevelt's adherence to the non-intervention principle of the Good Neighbour policy, together with his authorship of the Atlantic Charter and the Four Freedoms, it is difficult to believe that he would have supported a doctrine of pre-emptive action, especially in the case of Iraq – a war that was based on incomplete intelligence and that proceeded without a clear resolution of approval from the UN organization that Roosevelt had done so much to establish.

Notes

1 David Kennedy, *Freedom From Fear: The American People in Depression and War, 1929–1945* (New York and Oxford: Oxford University Press, 1999), pp. 1–130; Frank Freidel, *Roosevelt: A Rendezvous with Destiny* (Boston: Little, Brown and Company, 1990), pp. 3–78; Robert Dallek, *Franklin D. Roosevelt and American Foreign Policy, 1932–1945* (New York and Oxford: Oxford University Press, 1979), pp. 3–20.

2 Robert Dallek, *FDR and American Foreign Policy*, pp. 18–19.

3 ibid., 23–168. For the 'Quarantine' speech, on 5 October 1937, see Richard Heffner, *A Documentary History of the United States*, 8th edition (New York: Signet, 2009), pp. 391–96.

4 Tony McCulloch, 'Franklin Roosevelt as Founding Father of the Transatlantic Alliance', *Journal of Transatlantic Studies*, 8:3 (September 2010), pp. 224–35 includes a brief historiography of Roosevelt's foreign policy in the 1930s.

5 Franklin D. Roosevelt, First Inaugural Address, 4 March 1933, paragraph 13, www.presidency.ucsb.edu

6 For the London Economic Conference see Dallek, *FDR and American Foreign Policy*, pp. 35–58; Kennedy, *Freedom From Fear*, pp. 155–57; and Anthony J. Badger, *FDR: The First Hundred Days* (New York: Hill and Wang, 2008), pp. 135–50.

7 Speech at Woodrow Wilson Foundation Dinner, Washington, 28 December 1933, in Edgar B. Nixon (ed.), *Franklin D. Roosevelt and Foreign Affairs*, Volume 1 (Cambridge, MA: Harvard University Press, 1969), pp. 558–63.

8 Franklin D. Roosevelt, Annual Messages, 3 January 1934 and 4 January 1935, www.presidency.ucsb.edu

9 ibid., FDR, Annual Message, 3 January 1936, paragraphs 3–22.

10 ibid., 3 January 1936, paragraphs 4–7.

11 McCulloch, 'Franklin Roosevelt as Founding Father', pp. 224–35; Dallek, *FDR and American Foreign Policy*, pp. 59–97; B. J. C. McKercher, *Transition of Power: Britain's Loss of Pre-eminence to the United States, 1930–1945* (Cambridge: Cambridge University Press, 1999), pp. 216–23; George Herring, *From Colony to Superpower: US Foreign Relations since 1776* (New York and Oxford: Oxford University Press, 2008), pp. 505–8.

12 ibid., pp. 98–117.
13 Franklin D. Roosevelt, Annual Message, 3 January 1936, paragraph 22, www.presidency. ucsb.edu; emphasis added.
14 Dallek, *FDR and American Foreign Policy*, pp. 117–21.
15 Freidel, *FDR*, pp. 195–96.
16 Woodrow Wilson, War Message to Congress, 2 April 1917, www.ourdocuments.gov
17 Immanuel Kant, *Perpetual Peace* (New York: Cosimo Classics, 2005); Steven W. Hook (ed.) *Democratic Peace Theory in Theory and Practice* (Kent, OH: Kent State University Press, 2010).
18 For American presidential doctrines see Cecil V. Crabb, *The Doctrines of American Foreign Policy: Their Meaning, Role and Future* (Baton Rouge, LA: Louisiana State University Press, 1982).
19 Roosevelt, First Inaugural Address, 4 March 1933, paragraph 15, www.presidency.ucsb.edu.
20 ibid., Franklin D. Roosevelt, Annual Address, 3 January 1934, paragraph 19; see also Robert Holden and Eric Zolov (eds) *Latin America and the United States: A Documentary History* (New York: Oxford University Press, 2000), pp. 130–48.
21 ibid., Franklin D. Roosevelt, Annual Address, 3 January 1936, paragraph 5.
22 Holden and Zolov, *Latin America and the United States*, pp. 149–50.
23 ibid., Franklin D. Roosevelt, Annual Address, 6 January 1937, paragraphs 33–36.
24 Holden and Zolov, *Latin America and the United States*, pp. 156–58; see also David Haglund, *Latin America and the Transformation of US Strategic Thought, 1936–1940* (Albuquerque, NM: University of New Mexico Press, 1984)
25 Roosevelt, Annual Address, 4 January 1939, paragraphs 13 and 14, www.presidency. ucsb.edu
26 ibid., Franklin Roosevelt's Annual Address, 3 January 1940, paragraph 32.
27 ibid., Roosevelt, Annual Address, 6 January 1941, paragraph 27.
28 Roosevelt, Speech at Woodrow Wilson Foundation Dinner.
29 For Frank F. Roosevelt and Latin America see Haglund, *Transformation*; Holden and Zolov, *Latin America*; Frederick Pike, *FDR's Good Neighbour Policy* (Austin, TX: University of Texas Press, 1995); Irwin Gellman, *Good Neighbour Diplomacy: United States Policies in Latin America, 1933–1945* (John Hopkins University Press, 1979); Paul Drake, 'From Good Men to Good Neighbours, 1912–32' in Abraham Lowenthal (ed.), *Exporting Democracy: The United States and Latin America* (1991).
30 Roosevelt, First Inaugural Address, 4 March 1933, paragraphs 4 and 52.
31 ibid., Roosevelt, Annual Addresses, 3 January 1934 and 4 January 1935.
32 ibid., Roosevelt, Annual Address, 3 January 1936, paragraphs 23 and 24.
33 ibid., Roosevelt, Annual Address, 6 January 1937, paragraphs 6 and 38.
34 ibid., Roosevelt, Second Inaugural Address, 20 January 1937, paragraph 28.
35 ibid., Roosevelt, Annual Address, 3 January 1938, paragraph 73.
36 ibid., Roosevelt, Annual Address, 4 January 1939, paragraphs 10 and 31.
37 ibid., Roosevelt, Annual Address, 3 January 1940, paragraphs 5, 6 and 31.
38 ibid., Roosevelt, Annual Address, 6 January 1941, paragraphs 64 and 81–85.
39 ibid., Roosevelt, Annual Address, 7 January 1943, paragraphs 66–87.
40 For the legacy of Four Freedoms, see David Woolner, Warren Kimball and David Reynolds (eds) *FDR's World: War, Peace and Legacies* (New York: Palgrave Macmillan, 2008); for the UN declaration of human rights, see www.un.org/en/documents/udhr
41 Dallek, *FDR and American Foreign Policy*, pp. 48–58; McKercher, *Transition of Power*, pp. 169–76.
42 Roosevelt, Annual Address, 3 January 1934, paragraph 20, www.presidency.ucsb.edu
43 ibid., Roosevelt, Annual Address, 4 January 1935, paragraph 48.
44 ibid., Roosevelt, Annual Address, 3 January 1936, paragraph 13.
45 ibid., Roosevelt, Annual Address, 6 January 1937, paragraph 32.
46 ibid., Roosevelt, Annual Address, 3 January 1938, paragraphs 9 and 10.
47 ibid., Roosevelt, Annual Address, 3 January 1939, paragraphs 3, 22 and 23.

48 Dallek, *FDR and American Foreign Policy*, pp. 199–205; McKercher, *Transition of Power*, 282–83.

49 Roosevelt, Annual Address, 3 January 1940, paragraphs 15 and 29, www.presidency. ucsb.edu.

50 Dallek, *FDR and American Foreign Policy*, pp. 243–47; McKercher, *Transition of Power*, 296–98.

51 Roosevelt, Annual Address, 6 January 1941, paragraph 54, www.presidency.ucsb.edu.

52 Dallek, *FDR and American Foreign Policy*, pp. 281–86; McKercher, *Transition of Power*, 299–300.

53 Roosevelt, Annual Address, 6 January 1945, paragraph 121, www.presidency.ucsb.edu

54 G. John Ikenberry, 'Woodrow Wilson, the Bush Administration and the Future of Liberal Internationalism', pp.14–20, in Ikenberry *et al.*, *Crisis of American Foreign Policy*; Elizabeth Borgward, *A New Deal for the World: America's Vision for Human Rights* (Cambridge, MA: Harvard University Press, 2005). For the text of the Atlantic Charter, see Heffner, *Documentary History of USA*, 405–6.

55 ibid., Roosevelt, Annual Address, 6 January 1942, paragraphs 20–24, www.presidency. ucsb.edu.

56 ibid., Roosevelt, Annual Address, 7 January 1943, paragraphs 86 and 90.

57 ibid., Roosevelt, Annual Address, 11 January 1944, paragraphs 5 and 13.

58 ibid., Roosevelt, Annual Address, 6 January 1945, paragraphs 133 and 177–80.

59 Stephen Schlesinger, *Act of Creation: The Founding of the United Nations* (Cambridge, MA: Westview Press, 2003); Townsend Hoopes and Douglas Brinkley, *FDR and the Creation of the United Nations* (New Haven, CT: Yale University Press, 1997); Robert Hildebrand, *Dumbarton Oaks: The Origins of the United Nations and the Search for Postwar Security* (Chapel Hill, NC: University of North Carolina Press, 1990).

60 FDR's Annual Address, 6 January 1945, paragraph 181, www.presidency.ucsb.edu.

61 www.americas.sas.ac.uk/digital-resources-for-researchers/us-presidency-centre.

62 Harry Truman, Address to Congress, 12 March 1947, www.ourdocuments.gov.

63 Roosevelt, Annual Address, 6 January 1945, paragraphs 113 and 114.

5

HARRY S. TRUMAN

Martin H. Folly

'Democracy is based on the conviction that man has the moral and intellectual
capacity, as well as the inalienable right, to govern himself with reason and justice.'

Harry S. Truman

The presidency of Harry S. Truman has been, and remains, the subject of widely
divergent opinions among scholars. To some, he was a successful president who
responded with courage and skill to the tough challenges he faced. To them,
notably biographer David McCullough, Truman was an honest, direct and gutsy
man who led the United States to victory in the Second World War and then
steered the country through difficult post-war years. He recognized the threat from
expansionist Soviet communism and marshalled both domestic opinion and other
like-minded nations in an effective response to it that saved democracy. In the
1947 Truman Doctrine, the president committed the United States to the defence
of freedom wherever it was threatened. This was a landmark event that established
that, for reasons of both idealism and national security, the United States would
be active in the spreading of, and if necessary the defence of, democracy around
the world.[1]

To others, Truman was a man out of his depth, offering a poor comparison to
the man who was president before him, Franklin D. Roosevelt. Arnold Offner
describes Truman as a 'parochial nationalist'.[2] To such scholars, his visceral anti-
communism and hostility to the Soviet Union led Truman to reverse Roosevelt's
policy of cooperation and initiated the Cold War. Some claim he authorized the
use of the atom bomb in order to intimidate the USSR and force it to accom-
modate American wishes, rather than to end the war with Japan with as few
casualties as possible, as he subsequently claimed.[3] Truman is seen by these critics as
having been inflexible and stubborn, initiating anti-communist witch-hunts at
home with the federal loyalty programme and advancing American hegemony

under the guise of protecting freedom. Some see the motivations behind the 1947 Marshall Plan, which followed the Truman Doctrine, as 'dollar imperialism' – designed to draw Europe into an American-dominated trading bloc and isolate and ultimately squeeze the USSR out of existence.[4] Truman's rhetoric concerning the defence of democracy and freedom was therefore a mere smokescreen for the expansion of American power. Truman presided over massive rearmament in the second term of his presidency (1949–53) and therefore bore heavy responsibility for the creation of the military-industrial complex at home and for the United States' association with, and arming of, unsavoury dictators abroad.[5]

On Truman's commitment to democratic enlargement there is therefore a broad consensus, if much disagreement on the motivations for it and the implications thereof, both in the short and long term. In Truman's presidency some fundamental issues of definition were at stake – though it should be noted that many of these were issues that were ongoing, having been central to the United States' relationship with its Latin American neighbours for a long time. These continuities need to be acknowledged when considering the Truman policies: even though the Truman Doctrine was on the face of it a revolutionary step for American peace-time policy, it can be seen as actually a globalization of existing American paradigms.

Elizabeth Edwards Spalding makes the case most forcefully that Truman was guided by a firm commitment to the promotion of democracy. She sees him as a liberal internationalist. Unlike Woodrow Wilson (1913–21), the earlier internationalist president, whom she characterizes as principally concerned with advancing international justice, Spalding sees Truman as concerned with liberty. Truman's internationalism meant American leadership – an active role in promoting democracy – rather than a commitment to any specific form of international organization. It was, she argues, free governments and free peoples that mattered to him.[6] Organizations and arrangements like the Bretton Woods agreements were to the president not universal institutions, but means by which states could combine their efforts to prevent or stop conflict and promote free markets. Far more than Wilson, Spalding argues, Truman saw the promotion of democratic principles as a central American goal. The United States should promote principles of liberal, constitutional democracy and help maintain them against the threat of despotism. To him, peace, justice and order were meaningless if not grounded in free peoples, institutions and countries.[7]

One of Spalding's central arguments is that Truman derived his liberal internationalism not from Wilson, but from more generic American values. In that sense, she sees Truman to be part of an American tradition.[8] Certainly, Truman had a strong belief that American history was the story of the advance and defence of liberty, as conceived by the founding fathers. He seems to have had an uncritically Whig understanding of that history. To Truman, freedom was vested in the republican system of Thomas Jefferson and the Hamiltonian economic system of liberal capitalism that had accompanied it. His reading of American history underpinned his sense of what democracy was, and how it was linked to a particular economic system, which was therefore a vital prerequisite for its achievement.

The events of the 1930s and the Second World War gave a clear indication of the major barriers to this: totalitarian dictatorship linked to autarkic or state-monopolized economies. This binary was to define his approach to the issues of freedom and unfreedom during his presidency.

Truman, democracy and anti-communism

To understand the administration's goals, and the ways in which they conflicted and hamstrung the attempt to spread democracy and development, it is necessary to track back to the early years of Truman's presidency. It is a period that has been the subject of divergent interpretations. Truman was responsible for the establishment of a series of landmark statements and institutions that shaped American foreign policy up to at least the end of the Cold War, and arguably beyond. Depending often on the ideological perspectives brought to the question, Truman is either lauded for his timely and appropriate responses to the threat of Joseph Stalin's totalitarian expansionism, or else castigated for aggressive policies and posturing that initiated the Cold War, led the United States into interventionism in the name of the containment of communism and created the institutions of American imperial overreach and repressive domestic anti-communism. Close examination of the Truman presidency presents a more complex picture than this overdrawn dichotomy, and in particular reveals a defining ambivalence in Truman's attitudes. This derived from two of his fundamental principles that, when operationalized in the post-Second World War context, produced a foreign policy that at its heart enshrined contradictory impulses.

These two principles, put simply, were a strong attachment to the internationalist approach identified with Wilson, and an equally strong belief that American national security was threatened by the expansion of Soviet communism. This mixture of attitudes could be described as an uneasy mix of idealism and realism, though such labels do not fully capture the particular thrust of Truman's ideas. Truman's internationalism was more fully formed and consistently held than that of Franklin D. Roosevelt, as Spalding has argued. He believed that the United States had a mission in the world to advance its values of democracy and liberal capitalism. It should do so through active membership of international organizations and through other interventionist policies. He had little sympathy with the isolationist ideas often identified with his native Mid-West: in this sense he was closer to the traditions of the South – which his home state, Missouri, borders.

Truman was also staunchly anti-communist. He had never shown any sympathy for the USSR, and indeed in the summer of 1941, before Washington and Moscow were allies, he publicly stated that he hoped that Germany and the USSR would fight each other to exhaustion.[9] This underlying attitude did not lead to his immediately breaking with Roosevelt's wartime policy of accommodation with Stalin on becoming president.[10] Although some have seen an immediate shift to an anti-Soviet attitude when he took office, it is more accurate to say that Truman followed an inconsistent and uncertain course.[11] Signs of increasing distrust of the

Soviets can be seen, but so can a reluctance to accept that relations were irrevocably broken down, and to break finally with the policy of his greatly esteemed predecessor. However, he did have a more rigid set of criteria for judging the acceptability of Soviet actions than did Roosevelt. Typical of a man who tended to be straightforward, direct and somewhat literal, they hinged on the Soviets keeping to what they had agreed, or at least to what Truman and the United States believed they had agreed. Soviet attempts to manoeuvre within the meanings of agreements met with short shrift from Truman and tended to lead to the confirmation of his underlying belief that Soviet aims were antithetical to those of the United States.[12] One consequence of the growing distrust of Soviet motives and intentions throughout the second half of 1945 and 1946 was a sharpening definition of Truman's commitment to democratization. In as much as the Soviets were seen as not only geopolitically expansionist, but also as seeking to expand their influence by installing communist regimes under their own control, so Truman's commitment to democracy came to merge with his anti-communism to produce what came to be the classic Cold War binary mindset that identified all anti-communist forces as 'free', and to see 'free' and 'democratic' as synonymous.[13]

The Truman Doctrine

Gradual development of this merging of Truman's attitudes – or, to put it another way, the distortion of his commitment to democratic values, or at least the overlaying of it with the imperatives of anti-communism – took place throughout 1946 to reach a culmination in the Truman Doctrine of 12 March 1947. It is worth noting, however, that Truman did not entirely submerge the contradiction within these attitudes, and showed through the rest of his presidency periodic signs of discomfort with the implications, notably with regard to the domestic anti-communism that he somewhat thoughtlessly unleashed.

That notwithstanding, the Truman Doctrine speech stands as an undisputed landmark in the history of American engagement in world affairs and set down a clear, and as it turned out, irreversible, commitment to the idea of American intervention on the side of democracy. Moreover, democracy was defined a certain way: as a default position for nations and peoples that had not fallen under totalitarianism. Truman outlined how American aid to help solve Greece's economic problems was linked to its political future; aid would directly promote democracy, which was threatened by external and internal subversive forces:

> Greece must have assistance if it is to become a self-supporting and self-respecting democracy. ... There is no other country to which democratic Greece can turn. No other nation is willing and able to provide the necessary support for a democratic Greek government.

Truman conceded that Greece was not yet fully democratic, but in the worldview that he projected the principal difference between the two types of regimes was that one of them allowed correction of flaws: 'No government is perfect. One of the chief virtues of a democracy, however, is that its defects are always visible and under democratic processes can be pointed out and corrected.' While conceding this, Truman maintained that the Greek government was based on majority support in a fair election.[14] American aid would not imply approval of everything the Greek government did. The important thing was to create the conditions wherein democracy could develop, which were, Truman implied, prosperity and political stability.[15]

The most significant part of the speech was where Truman justified the request to aid Greece and Turkey by presenting a stark view of the present state of the world and its implications for the United States' own security and prosperity:

> One of the primary objectives of the foreign policy of the United States is the creation of conditions in which we and other nations will be able to work out a way of life free from coercion. This was a fundamental issue in the war with Germany and Japan. ...
>
> We shall not realize our objectives, however, unless we are willing to help free peoples to maintain their free institutions and their national integrity against aggressive movements that seek to impose upon them totalitarian regimes. This is no more than a frank recognition that totalitarian regimes imposed on free peoples, by direct or indirect aggression, undermine the foundations of international peace and hence the security of the United States.
>
> ... At the present moment in world history nearly every nation must choose between alternative ways of life. The choice is too often not a free one.
>
> One way of life is based upon the will of the majority, and is distinguished by free institutions, representative government, free elections, guarantees of individual liberty, freedom of speech and religion, and freedom from political oppression.
>
> The second way of life is based upon the will of a minority forcibly imposed upon the majority. It relies upon terror and oppression, a controlled press and radio; fixed elections, and the suppression of personal freedoms.

Truman asserted that American interests required active help to those resisting attempts to impose the 'second way':

> I believe that we must assist free peoples to work out their own destinies in their own way. I believe that our help should be primarily through economic and financial aid which is essential to economic stability and orderly political processes.[16]

The speech is worth quoting at such length for it states principles that became enshrined at the heart of American attitudes towards the establishment and spread of democracy, in particular in the principle that this would follow naturally from the act of the containment of communism and the extirpation of internal subversion.[17] Truman asserted that the American role in ensuring this would be largely economic, but the implications even then were that other actions might be necessary, so that the subsequent developments of containment into military and other arrangements did not require a revision of the basic precept nor did they call into question the principle that there was a natural progression from containment to the development of democratic practices in those countries thus protected from communist penetration, such that the act of containment itself could be seen as the promotion of democracy.[18]

The *New York Times* hailed Truman's speech as replacing isolation with 'the epoch of American responsibility', but critics emerged immediately.[19] They pointed to the flaw at the heart of the argument.[20] The Greek and Turkish regimes might well have firm anti-communist credentials, but that did not mean they were of themselves free or democratic.[21] Truman defended his position in a letter to Eleanor Roosevelt, who had made this point directly to him. Mrs Roosevelt pointedly wrote that she did not believe that 'taking over Mr Churchill's policies in the Near East, in the name of democracy, is the way to really create a barrier to communism or promote democracy'.[22] Although drafted by the State Department, the president's reply represents a clear and direct statement by Truman of how he saw the mission of American foreign policy at this crucial point. He argued that the Greek–Turkish situation had 'caused me more worry and soul-searching than any matter in these past two years', but nevertheless brought him, when a decision was made, to a growing sense of certainty about the correctness of the direction the United States was taking. Mrs Roosevelt had argued that communism could not be stopped by throwing American economic resources into areas of strategic importance but deficient in the practice of democracy. Truman responded that if the United States could stop communism on the Greek–Turkish frontier, then that was the place to do it, regardless of whether or not the terrain (that is, the depth of commitment to the practice of democracy) was good.[23]

But it was not true that the United States would just be strengthening autocracy. Truman went on that he thought it had made great strides in establishing a democratic peace, but to a certain extent it had been reticent in stating the democratic processes it had in mind. He accepted that the United States must not overlook the need for social progress at home: he was not in favour of shifting resources away from domestic programmes to fund containment of communism:

> I will continue to do all in my power to see the country has a progressive domestic policy that will deserve the confidence of the world and will serve as a sound foundation for our international policy. ... Nor does it seem to me that we can overlook the fact that as much as the world needs a progressive America, the American way of life cannot survive unless other peoples who want to adopt that pattern of life throughout the world can do so without fear and in hope of success. If this is to be possible, we cannot allow the forces of disintegration to go unchecked.[24]

The State Department was equally sensitive to the need to identify the fight for democracy with the mission of halting communism and advanced the key concept of containment by arguing that it was not simply a matter of democracy in the country being aided; it was about holding communism back from other areas. Doubts about the democratic credentials of the Greek government were widely aired – but the attitude within the Truman administration as well as in its outward-facing information policy was to define the issue in different terms. In doing so, they both confirmed the direction that official attitudes had moved and set a clear marker for the whole issue of democratic enlargement in the future. Under-secretary of State Dean Acheson told the Senate Foreign Relations Committee that the programme would promote stability in Greece, Turkey and the Middle East generally, and thereby 'pave the way for peaceful and democratic development', while reiterating Truman's caveat that this was not a blanket endorsement of the Greek government. The question, claimed Acheson, was not a choice between a perfect democracy in Greece and an imperfect democracy, but whether there would be any democracy there at all.[25]

Internal discussions, in particular the urgent messages from American representatives MacVeagh and Porter in Greece, prior to the British appeal for help, emphasized the prime goal must be to create a functioning Greek economy. Failure to do so would open the door to totalitarianism: success was seen as the vital prerequisite for the establishment of democratic practices.[26] The implication therefore was that democracy could be defined in terms of negatives: it would appear provided totalitarianism was successfully excluded – or 'contained' – and economic reforms activated to bring prosperity, or at least the free flow of capital. American policy should be oriented towards these goals: democracy would follow. Notably absent were specific schemes of reforming political practices or setting up definitions of democracy that regimes would have to meet to qualify for American support, beyond resistance to totalitarianism and a readiness to follow American advice on economic reforms.

In a bulletin dated 3 April, the State Department stated that aid would encourage 'constructive, democratic forces in other areas' and there would then be less chance of similar crises of freedom happening elsewhere. Thus, non-democratic forces could be supported and strengthened as part of the defence of democracy elsewhere, or as a general concept. In any case, argued the State Department, aware of the weaknesses of this argument, Greece and Turkey were essentially democratic and were progressing along the road of democracy.[27] In the interest of creating an independent Greece, the United States was quite prepared to supply economic and financial aid that made it dependent on Washington, and to intervene directly in the course of Greek politics – for example in August 1947 when Konstantinos Tsaldaris tried to form an overtly right-wing government in Greece and American pressure was applied to ensure it had a broader base. The Chief of the American Mission for Aid to Greece, Dwight Griswold, reported that the Greek people approved of such intervention. Thus interventionist, and not strictly democratic, methods were applied and justified in terms of the long-term goal.[28]

The State Department continued to set out the issues for the general public in such a way that states like Greece were identified as inherently democratic – independent of specific contemporary circumstances – so that protection of their integrity as states was the same as advancing the cause of democracy. Thus, on 5 May 1947, Henry S. Villard, Deputy Director of the Department of Near Eastern Affairs in the State Department, said: 'by long-standing tradition and by their heroic resistance to Axis aggression the Greek people have earned the right to be classed among those who prefer our way of life to any other'. This neatly ignored the fact that the same thing could be said of the people of the USSR itself. It was in line with the constantly reiterated theme that nations like Greece were part of a 'Western tradition' and therefore by definition democratic, without need for further proof.[29]

Truman had made clear in the 12 March speech that American aid would be administered with discrimination to ensure the desired outcome, stating that it was 'of the utmost importance that we supervise the use of any funds made available to Greece; in such a manner that each dollar spent will count towards making Greece self-supporting, and will help to build an economy in which a healthy democracy can flourish'. Truman reiterated the underlying position frequently over the next few years. For example, in his address to Congress on 19 December 1947, he said:

> Our deepest concern with European recovery, however, is that it is essential to the maintenance of the civilization in which the American way of life is rooted. It is the only assurance of the continued independence and integrity of a group of nations who constitute a bulwark for the principles of freedom, justice and the dignity of the individual. ... The economic plight in which Europe now finds itself has intensified a political struggle between those who wish to remain free men living under the rule of law and those who would use economic distress as a pretext for the establishment of a totalitarian state.[30]

Truman and administration representatives forcibly stated this view to Congress and the public: economic aid in the Marshall Plan would restore prosperity in Europe, thereby ensuring the Europeans did not succumb to the lure of totalitarianism; they would be saved for liberty.[31] This suggests that we should see stability and order as more central to Truman's foreign policy goals than Spalding would allow, for they were seen as a means to the end of achieving democratic proliferation.[32] In the dichotomy enshrined in the Truman Doctrine and perpetuated in Marshall Aid, any state that was not a communist totalitarian one was regarded as having the potential to move to democracy, provided the right economic conditions were provided. This was modified in the face of successive Cold War crises in 1948 over Czechoslovakia and Berlin to include the right conditions of security as well. This movement to regard the issue as being tied up with military measures was made permanent with the formation of the North Atlantic Treaty Organization (NATO) in 1949, followed later in the year by the Soviet atom bomb test and the communist victory in China's civil war.

The conflation of 'anti-communist' with 'democratic' set a significant marker for the future. The Truman administration's firm belief was that the greatest menace to democracy where it was already practised, and to the possibility of it developing where it did not, was Soviet expansionism.[33] Its commitment to democratic proliferation was therefore increasingly focused on the containment of that expansionism to the exclusion of others. The implication, sometimes made explicit, was that any state that remained outside the Soviet bloc, under the influence of the prosperity and security underwritten by the United States, would in time move towards democracy. That was the natural development of human institutions, as long as they were not impeded by malicious minorities; that is, communists. This Whiggish view of human development justified the inclusion of imperial powers and authoritarian regimes among the ranks of the free. Thus NATO included Great Britain, France, Belgium and the Netherlands, all colonial powers, and Portugal, ruled at the time by the authoritarian Antonio Salazar. Relations with Francisco Franco's Spain and even with Josip Tito's Yugoslavia slowly improved, without any obvious attempts to make American support, aid or investment contingent on democratization.[34] Likewise, in Asia, Chiang Kai-Shek and South Korea's Synghman Rhee received American backing. If it was reduced for Chiang it was not because of his democratic failings, but because he came to be seen as a lost cause – and it was anyway increased again after his ejection from mainland China. The domestic furore that attached itself to Truman after Chiang's final defeat in October 1949 only underlined the political advantages of placing anti-communist credentials above democratic ones, or rather regarding them as essentially synonymous. The consequence was soon apparent, with Truman's rapid decision to go to the aid of Rhee's South Korea when invaded by the communist North in June 1950.[35]

Thus, the Truman presidency committed the United States firmly to the principle of actively supporting democracy overseas. This embraced not only the processes of denazification in Germany and the re-education of Japan, but also the adoption of a strategy of containment that prioritized anti-communism as a defining characteristic of a commitment to American values. Simultaneously, therefore, the Truman administration set the United States along the road of the altruistic propagation of democracy. It also prefigured American interventions that stultified democratic movements and narrowed the definition of democracy to the extent that the very actions that the United States did take to advance democracy were regarded with suspicion and mistrust in many parts of the world.

Truman and democracy in Latin America

The part of the world where American actions with regard to democracy had been most controversial was Latin America. During the 1930s, the Roosevelt administration had made dramatic public declarations at Inter-American conferences that the United States would no longer directly intervene in the internal affairs of states in the region.[36] Some, however, have argued that the so-called 'Good Neighbor' policy was simply a different form of intervention, in that American economic and commercial influence was increasingly used to ensure regimes were established whose credentials were based on their acceptance of American economic interests rather than their democratic practices. By the end of the Second World War, it was more of a 'rich neighbor policy'.[37] In addition, the American focus shifted to organizing a common security front against penetration from outside, most strongly demonstrated in the Act of Havana (1940), the Rio Conference (1942) and the Act of Chapultepec (1945). This policy was continued by Truman, reaching its culmination in the 1947 Rio Treaty. The established view among historians is that the administration supported right-wing, often anti-democratic, forces in the region in furtherance of a policy based on stability and order and defence coordination. Latin America was thus the first, and in many ways archetypal, area for the practice of American 'dollar imperialism'.[38] This predated the rise of anti-communism as the predominant driver of American foreign policy. However, an alternative view has been proposed that emphasizes the 'civility' of American imperialism. Steven Schwartzberg, in particular, has argued that American officials, who were given considerable autonomy because the administration was preoccupied with the post-war issues in Europe and East Asia, acted on the side of social democratic forces. Diplomats like Spruille Braden in Argentina and Adolf Berle in Brazil favoured leftist and democratic movements. Moreover, it is argued that Truman himself was idealist in this regard. Democratic movements were genuinely seen as the best barrier to communism, Schwartzberg argues.[39] However, when two such regimes collapsed in 1948, in Peru and Venezuela, conservatives were able to increase their influence. They were supported by conservative cold warriors in the United States, using the principle of non-intervention in a selective manner to secure the success of dictators who were strong on anti-communism and who upheld the interests of American business, but who were less committed to maintaining civil liberties.

Thus the global cold war distorted the idealistic commitment of the administration to the advance of democracy in the region.[40] It has been argued in response to this approach that even before 1948 American support for social democrats and leftists was distinctly muted in many Central and South American states, such as Costa Rica and Venezuela, and there was always anxiety about their potential connections to communists.[41] It may well be correct, as Schwartzberg's work implies, that American positions depended on the individual perceptions of diplomats on the spot. In Washington there was a prolonged struggle for influence between two schools of thought that left some space for such autonomy.[42] By 1948 there was more coherence and the Truman Doctrine provided a blueprint (albeit a crude one) for assessing issues of regime change and regime maintenance in Latin America as elsewhere.

For Truman the core matter was his understanding of a fundamental dichotomy between liberal democracy and communist totalitarianism. This ran strongly through the Truman Doctrine and was central to the subsequent policies of the administration. Moreover, Truman later emphasized that he believed the best political structure was republican, not democratic. He said:

> I am not for a democracy ... I have never felt that a democracy would be a
> success in government. A republic is a government of elected officials with

responsibility, and there's a difference between a democracy and a republic. The New England town meeting is the idea of democracy, and all they do is talk. ... A republic is one that has checks and balances in it, as ours is set up for that purpose ... there can be a continuing form of government carried out by men who are responsible to the people and yet who can't be thrown out every fifteen minutes if something goes wrong.[43]

Thus it can be argued that indeed Truman attached great importance to order and stability, both within a nation and in economic and political relations between states. These themes were reiterated endlessly by his administration with reference to conditions in Europe, but the principles transferred elsewhere also into what became essentially a globalized policy. Despite the focus of the 'civility' school with regard to American policy to Latin America, it applied there equally to elsewhere.

The Point Four initiative

On 20 January 1949, Truman delivered his inaugural address, following his surprise victory in the 1948 election. Truman was now president in his own right. It was the high point of his career and a vindication of his determination and campaigning skill. In his address, Truman outlined what he saw as four main points in American foreign policy. These were a commitment to the United Nations, economic aid to Western Europe in the Marshall Plan (European Recovery Programme), a commitment to collective regional security with European allies in the negotiations for a North Atlantic Treaty, which were soon to come to fruition, and finally a 'bold new programme' to provide technical assistance to peoples in backward and undeveloped parts of the world. This latter idea, which was the only entirely new one of the points outlined, became known as 'Point Four'. On the face of it, it was an extension of the other three points, and indeed drew upon the original Truman Doctrine that the president had stated in March 1947. It drew a direct connection between economic hardship and backwardness and susceptibility to communism and other forces that, as Truman had outlined in that earlier speech, represented a threat to the security of the United States. Point Four was presented as a commitment to spread prosperity, capitalism and democracy, for the good of the United States and the good of the peoples involved. The Point Four initiative, and its fate, encapsulates the Truman administration's equivocal and ambivalent attachment to the principles of democratic proliferation.

The idea had originated with *Atlantic Journal* reporter Benjamin J. Hardy, who at the time was a minor official in the office of public affairs in the State Department. While in Brazil in 1944, Hardy had witnessed projects sharing scientific knowledge and advice in underdeveloped areas. He had the idea that such activities could be broadened and coordinated in a central government programme, making technical assistance an instrument for preventing the spread of communism in poorer countries. Clark Clifford, who was looking for new ideas for Truman's speech, liked the scheme and it was therefore included among the courses of action to achieve 'peace and freedom'.[44] In the speech, Truman described American aims as being to help 'the free peoples of the world through their own efforts, to produce more food, more clothing, more materials for housing and more mechanical power to lighten their burdens'.[45]

Point Four was, however, more a statement of broad intent than a plan. There was no firm bureaucratic backing for the scheme, and lack of enthusiasm from Republicans in Congress meant that no appropriation was given until May 1950. It was part of the Foreign Economic Assistance Act, which established economic development of poorer areas in the world as national policy, but assigned only \$26.9 million to the scheme.[46] It was thus dwarfed by the existing European Recovery Programme, and even more by the military aid programme envisioned in NSC-68 and activated once the Korean War broke out in June 1950.

Indeed, although Point Four can be seen as an antecedent for policies implemented by the Kennedy administration in the 1960s, it was NSC-68 that offered a more lasting legacy from the Truman administration with regard to the nature of American international action to promote democracy. NSC-68 was produced by Paul Nitze and Dean Acheson in the State Department in response to a query from Truman in January 1950.[47] This was a time when, despite the foundation of NATO and the victory over the Berlin blockade, communism appeared to be making gains, with the Soviet detonation of an atomic bomb and the triumph of the communists in China. The paper was presented to Truman in April but he refused to act upon it at first because of the costs and the implications for American society and programmes for social reform of the massive rearmament the paper advocated.[48] This changed after the outbreak of war in Korea with fears that it was only the first stage of further aggressive communist expansion. The important issue here about NSC-68 is that it reflected accurately Truman's core belief that the Cold War was a clash of two cultures. Containing the Kremlin was a crucial prerequisite for preserving and indeed proliferating free democratic institutions and market capitalism. It reiterated that the potential for these developments existed in the world outside communist domination – thus these areas were the 'free world' even if at present under imperialist or authoritarian rule. NSC-68 therefore confirmed the binary at the heart of the Truman Doctrine speech and which had informed the actions of the administration since 1947.[49] It had been used to justify covert interference in the elections in Italy in 1948, and would continue to be used to support even more undemocratic actions, such as the coup against Mohammed Mossadeq in Iran authorized by Dwight Eisenhower, Truman's successor.[50] This was a plan that the Truman administration, to its credit, had shied away from, but while Truman cannot be blamed directly for what was done in Iran, he had set a weighty precedent, and indeed had framed the terms of engagement of the United States with democracy in the developing world: the key criterion for 'democracy' being now firmly established as active opposition to the Soviet Union and to domestic communism.

Conclusion

Truman's legacy is a mixed one. He committed the United States firmly to the principle that it had a vital interest in democratic enlargement. This interest justified the commitment of large amounts of national resources to the cause. He committed the United States to doing so through international organizations, multilateral, bilateral and unilateral actions. However, his attachment to simple binaries led to a crude and flawed definition of democracy. Moreover, the essence of NSC-68 and other policy formulations had become primarily negative: American security, as Melvyn Leffler has demonstrated, had become identified with the spread of liberty and free enterprise, but this had become reduced to a concentration on the defeat of those regimes most opposed to those ideals, as an end in itself.[51] American commitments had become stretched beyond areas of vital strategic or economic interest – and would carry on being so – accompanied by support for corrupt, sometimes anti-democratic, leaders. In his defence, many scholars have pointed to the serious domestic political constraints in which he operated: constructing a public and congressional consensus for the break with the United States' past traditions that was involved in peacetime international intervention outside the Western hemisphere required an oversimplification and an appeal to baser prejudices.[52]

The lesson of the Second World War widely drawn across the political spectrum was that American security was irrevocably tied up with the ideological orientation of states in other continents: no longer could the country afford to tolerate the rise of a totalitarian enemy on the far shores of the Atlantic or Pacific oceans. Cold War institutions were growing in the United States, embracing government, the military, business and the media for whom this was both their great concern and their *raison d'être*.[53] To his credit, at times Truman showed awareness of the bind that he had got into, but his own ambiguity as well as his political position contributed to his remaining trapped within it.[54] The result was a contradiction in terms: in John Lewis Gaddis's words, the legacy was a 'democratic empire' reflecting the conflicting ideas at the heart of much that Truman did.[55] He left the presidency with an upbeat message, declaring in his farewell address, '[B]ut when history says that my term of office saw the beginning of the cold war, it will also say that in those eight years we have set the course that can win it.' Truman's legacy was a commitment to democratic enlargement, but in the context of the maintenance of American power and shaped by overriding threat perception that saw the enemy of all American values to be Soviet-orchestrated totalitarianism. The defence of democracy had become subsumed in a heavily armed response to communism that was increasingly, in the years that followed Truman's presidency, to see the United States privileging order and stability and economic prosperity, linked to American free enterprise, above the application of concepts of political or social liberty.

Notes

1 David McCullough, *Truman* (New York: Simon and Schuster, 1992); Wilson Miscamble, *From Roosevelt to Truman: Potsdam, Hiroshima, and the Cold War* (Cambridge: Cambridge

University Press, 2007); Alonzo Hamby, *Man of the People: A Life of Harry S. Truman* (New York: Oxford University Press, 1995), p. 57.

2 Arnold Offner, *Another Such Victory: President Truman and the Cold War, 1945–1953* (Stanford: Stanford University Press, 2002), p. 5.

3 Tsuyoshi Hasegawa, *Racing the Enemy: Stalin, Truman and the Surrender of Japan* (Cambridge: Harvard University Press, 2005), p. 296; Gar Alperovitz, *The Decision to Use the Atomic Bomb* (New York: Knopf, 1995), pp. 643–68; cf. Robert H. Ferrell, *Harry S. Truman and the Cold War Revisionists* (Columbia: University of Missouri Press, 2006), pp. 37–43.

4 The phrase 'dollar imperialism' was coined by Soviet Foreign Minister Vyacheslav Molotov. Walter LaFeber, *America, Russia and the Cold War* (9th edition, London: McGraw-Hill, 2002), pp. 64–68; William Appleman Williams, *The Tragedy of American Diplomacy* (revised edition, New York: Norton, 1972), pp. 269–73.

5 Offner, *Another Such Victory*, pp. 148, 154, 383, 459, 468.

6 Elizabeth Edwards Spalding, *The First Cold Warrior: Harry Truman, Containment, and the Remaking of Liberal Internationalism* (Lexington: Kentucky University Press, 2006), p. 2.

7 ibid., p. 224.

8 ibid., p. 223.

9 *New York Times*, 24 June 1941; McCullough, *Truman*, p. 262.

10 Mary E. Glantz, *FDR and the Soviet Union: The President's Battles over Foreign Policy* (Lawrence: Kansas University Press, 2005), pp. 143, 179–81; John Lewis Gaddis, *Strategies of Containment* (revised edition, New York: Oxford University Press, 2005), pp. 16–18.

11 Dianne S. Clemens, 'Averell Harriman, John Deane, the Joint Chiefs of Staff and the "Reversal of Cooperation" with the Soviet Union in April 1945', *International History Review*, 14 (1992), 277–306.

12 Robert J. Donovan, *Tumultuous Years: The Presidency of Harry S. Truman, 1949–1953* (New York: Norton, 1982), pp. 26–27.

13 Lloyd C. Gardner, *Architects of Illusion: Men and Ideas in American Foreign Policy, 1941–1949* (Chicago: Quadrangle, 1970), pp. 83, 105; Randall B. Woods and Howard Jones, *Dawning of the Cold War: The United States Quest for Order* (Athens: University of Georgia Press, 1991), p. 144.

14 American observers reported the 1946 elections to have been generally fair, and, although the communists and their allies boycotted them, to have produced a result representative of the wishes of the majority of Greeks. Paul Porter, who headed a two-month mission to Greece to examine the economic, financial and political position at the start of 1947, reported to Truman, however, that the chance of vital economic reforms taking place was poor, because the Greek government was 'completely reactionary … incredibly weak stupid and venal'. See Woods and Jones, *Dawning of the Cold War*, p. 140. Haris Vlavianos questions the legitimacy of the election and American assumptions of majority support for the government, in his 'The Greek Communist Party' in Tony Judt (ed.), *Resistance and Revolution in Mediterranean Europe, 1939–1948* (New York: Routledge, 1989), p. 195.

15 Howard Jones, *'A New Kind of War': America's Global Strategy and the Truman Doctrine in Greece* (New York: Oxford University Press, 1989), pp. 126, 226, 236, cf. Lawrence S. Wittner, *American Intervention in Greece, 1943–49* (New York: Columbia University Press, 1982), p. xi.

16 Truman address to joint session of Congress, 12 March 1947 available online from the Truman Library at www.trumanlibrary.org/publicpapers/index.php?pid=2189&st=&st1=

17 Jones, *A New Kind of War*, p. 45.

18 Lawrence S. Wittner, 'The Truman Doctrine and the Defense of Freedom', *Diplomatic History*, 4 (1980), pp. 161–87.

19 Woods and Jones, *Dawning of the Cold War*, p. 146.

20 Digest on public and press reactions, late March 1947, Dennis Merrill (ed.), *Documentary History of the Truman Presidency, volume 8: The Truman Doctrine and the Beginning of the Cold War 1947–49* (hereafter cited as *Truman Papers*), p. 131.

21 Walter L. Hixson, 'Orthodoxy or Objectivity? The Truman Doctrine and the Noble Dream', *Diplomatic History*, 15 (1991), p. 128.

22 Eleanor Roosevelt to Truman, 17 April 1947, *Truman Papers*, p. 255.

23 Porter told the House Committee on Foreign Affairs on 28 March that the majority of Greeks were eager to perfect their democratic institutions: 'they need material assistance and technical guidance if they are to function as a free, self-sustaining democracy', *Truman Papers*, pp. 175–76.

24 Truman to Eleanor Roosevelt, 7 May 1947, *Truman Papers*, pp. 251–54.

25 Dean Acheson statement to Senate Committee on Foreign Relations, 24 March 1947, *Truman Papers*, p. 183.

26 MacVeagh (ambassador to Greece) to Marshall, 20 February 1947, *Foreign Relations of the United States 1947*, vol. 5, pp. 28–29.

27 State Department Bulletin, 3 April 1947, *Truman Papers*, p. 203.

28 Griswold report, 20 September 1947, *Truman Papers*, p. 379.

29 Villlard speech to 194th Rotary District, Charlotte, North Carolina, 5 May 1947, *Truman Papers*, p. 245; and for a forceful statement of the overarching concept, see Dean Acheson memorandum to George Marshall, 21 February 1947, and Mark Ethridge report from Athens, 21 February 1947, *Foreign Relations of the United States 1947*, vol. 5, pp. 29–31, 37–39.

30 Truman address to Congress, 19 December 1947, US Department of State, *A Decade of American Foreign Policy, Basic Documents 1941–1949* (Washington: Department of State Printing Office, 1985), p. 969.

31 Woods and Jones, *Dawning of the Cold War*, pp. 165, 172; Spalding, *First Cold Warrior*, p. 223.

32 William Burr, 'Marshall Planners and the Politics of Empire: The United States and French Financial Policy, 1948', *Diplomatic History*, 15 (1991), pp. 521–22.

33 Denise Bostdorff, *Proclaiming the Truman Doctrine: The Cold War Call to Arms* (College Station: Texas A&M University Press, 2008), p. 13.

34 H. W. Brands, *The Specter of Neutralism: the United States and the Emergence of the Third World, 1947–1960* (New York: Columbia University Press, 1989), pp. 143–65; Lorraine M. Lees, 'The American Decision to Assist Tito, 1948–49', *Diplomatic History*, 2, (1978), pp. 407–22.

35 James Hershberg, 'Where the Buck Stopped: Harry S Truman and the Cold War', *Diplomatic History*, 27 (2003), p. 736.

36 Frank Niess, *A Hemisphere to Itself: A History of U.S.–Latin American Relations* (London, 1990), pp. 100–23.

37 Fredrick B. Pike, *FDR's Good Neighbor Policy: Sixty Years Of Generally Gentle Chaos* (Austin: University of Texas, 1995), p. 264; Bryce Wood, *The Dismantling of the Good Neighbor Policy* (Austin: University of Texas, 1985), p. 47; Elizabeth Cobbs Hoffman, *The Rich Neighbor Policy: Rockefeller and Kaiser in Brazil* (New Haven: Yale University Press, 1992).

38 See Leslie Bethell and Ian Roxborough (eds), *Latin America between the Second World War and the Cold War 1944–1948* (Cambridge: Cambridge University Press, 1992); Lars Schoultz, *Beneath the United States: A History of U.S. Policy toward Latin America* (Cambridge, Harvard University Press, 1998).

39 Steven Schwartzberg, *Democracy and U.S. Policy in Latin America during the Truman Years* (Gainesville: University Press of Florida, 2003), p. 189.

40 ibid., pp xii–xiii.

41 Piero Gleijeses, *Shattered Hope: The Guatemalan Revolution and the United States, 1944–1954* (Princeton: Princeton University Press, 1991); David F. Schmitz, *Thank God They're On Our Side: the United States and Right-Wing Dictatorships, 1921–1965* (Chapel Hill: University of North Carolina Press, 1999); Kyle Longley, *The Sparrow and the Hawk: Costa Rica During the Rise of José Figueres* (Tuscaloosa: University of Alabama Press, 1997).

42 Roger R. Trask, 'Spruille Braden versus George Messersmith: World War II, the Cold War, and Argentine Policy, 1945–47', *Journal of Interamerican Studies and World Affairs*, 26 (1984), pp. 70–75.

43 Ralph Weber (ed.), *Talking with Harry: Candid Conversations with Harry S. Truman* (Wilmington, DE: Scholarly Resources, 2001), pp. 105–6.

44 Robert Schlesinger, *White House Ghosts: Presidents and Their Speechwriters* (New York: Simon & Schuster, 2008), pp. 60–63.

45 Truman inaugural address, 20 January 1949, www.trumanlibrary.org/whistlestop/50yr_archive/inagural20jan1949.htm

46 'Foreign Economic Assistance Act of 1950: an Act to provide foreign economic assistance', *Volume 7797 of Public Law 535, Congress 81, Chapter 220-Sess. 2. H.R Issue 2117 of Report*, United States Congress; 'Truman Orders to Implement Point IV Plan', *New York Times*, 9 September 1950.

47 'A report to the National Security Council (NSC-68)', *Foreign Relations of the United States: 1950*, vol. I, pp. 235–92, www.fas.org/irp/offdocs/nsc-hst/nsc-68.htm; Truman to Lay, 12 April 1950, President's Secretary's Files, Truman Papers, Truman Library, Independence, Missouri.

48 Michael J. Hogan, *A Cross of Iron: Harry S. Truman and the Origins of the National Security State, 1945–1954* (New York: Cambridge University Press, 1998), pp. 302–4.

49 Spalding, *First Cold Warrior*, pp. 223–25.

50 Effie Pedalieu, *Britain, Italy, and the Origins of the Cold War* (London: Palgrave, 2003), p. 58.

51 Melvyn Leffler, *A Preponderance of Power: National Security, the Truman Administration, and the Cold War* (Stanford: Stanford University Press, 1992), p. 13.

52 John Lewis Gaddis, *The United States and the Origins of the Cold War, 1941–1947* (New York: Columbia University Press, 1972), pp. 356–61.

53 Hogan, *Cross of Iron*, p. 66.

54 An observation of a number of critics is that Truman was given to strong decisive statements and bold and defiant words but they were often followed either by half-hearted actions, or by none at all; see Norman A. Graebner, *Cold War Diplomacy 1945–1960* (New York: Van Nostrand, 1962), p. 7.

55 John Lewis Gaddis, *We Now Know: Rethinking Cold War History* (New York: Oxford University Press, 1997), p. 287.

6

JOHN F. KENNEDY AND LYNDON JOHNSON

Jon Roper

In 1917, the year that John F. Kennedy was born, Woodrow Wilson asked Congress to support military intervention in the First World War and to send American troops to the battlefields of Europe in order 'to keep the world safe for democracy'. Three decades later, shortly after Kennedy first entered Congress, and when 'Cold War' was becoming the popular term to describe the contemporary state of American–Soviet relations, Harry Truman, the only president to have served with the American forces that Wilson sent to France, requested funding from the legislature to combat the spread of communism in Greece and Turkey. The Truman Doctrine, with its accompanying commitment to containment, defined the United States' Cold War foreign policy. Later in 1947, in a further effort to forestall the development of the political conditions in which communism was thought to thrive, the Marshall Plan invested American aid to support those Western European economies that were struggling to recover from the impact of the Second World War.

Throughout the 1950s, during Dwight Eisenhower's administration, Cold War tensions and domestic anti-communist sentiments ebbed and flowed. In 1960, Kennedy was elected to the White House with a slim mandate for change. His administration embraced a new sense of activism, seeing the promotion of democracy abroad not simply as an end in itself, but also as vital to the preservation of the United States' national security in the contemporary context of intensifying superpower rivalry.

In the five decades that have elapsed since Kennedy's presidency, historical assessments of his stature as a world leader and evaluations of his foreign policy have veered between extremes. Initially, the 'Camelot historians', principally Theodore Sorensen and Arthur Schlesinger Jr., reacted to his assassination by seeking to establish an idealistic image of Kennedy in the public mind. They focused on his rare abilities, not only in steering the nation through moments of extreme international crisis, but also in empathizing with the nationalistic aspirations of the post-colonial world.[1]

By the 1970s revisionists were taking a radically different view. Surveying the literature on Kennedy's foreign policy, Burton Kaufman points out that, a decade after Dallas, Kennedy was being seen as 'a person of style rather than substance, of profile rather than courage, driven by ambition rather than commitment, physically handsome but intellectually and morally unattractive'.[2] In 1989 Thomas Paterson's introduction to his edited collection of essays, *Kennedy's Quest for Victory*, concluded that 'Arrogance, ignorance, and impatience combined with familiar exaggerations of the Communist threat to deny Kennedy his objectives – especially the winning of the Third World. ... Actually, he had his chance, and he failed'.[3]

Such damning indictments reflected a contemporary mood in the aftermath of the Vietnam War. By the 1990s, assessing Kennedy's national security policy, Anna Kasten Nelson suggested indeed that it was 'the disillusionment and frustration with the Kennedy promise that seems to be stimulating the recent research. There is an undertone of anger at being misled, of succumbing to the vision, that characterizes the first stages of revisionism'.[4] Kennedy's critics were sceptical of the flattering portraits drawn in the immediate aftermath of his assassination, which had sought to absolve him from the contemporary failures of American foreign policy. Following revelations about his private life, these less favourable assessments of Kennedy saw him as fatally flawed.[5]

The conflicting strands of historiography have been woven together. Kaufman concluded that assessments of Kennedy 'suggested a person with two very different sides torn by contradictory impulses'. The 'Kennedy of Camelot' coexisted with a traditional Cold Warrior and 'the most recent literature suggests a more complex figure whose personality embraced elements of both images, but more of the latter than the former'.[6] This is still the consensus verdict. In *John F. Kennedy: World Leader*, Stephen Rabe acknowledges that 'Kennedy showed sensitivity to anti-colonial, nationalistic aspirations of Third World people'. Nevertheless, quoting Kaufman's earlier judgement, he endorses the dominant thrust of the historical literature that has cast Kennedy as 'an inveterate Cold Warrior whose dogmatic anticommunism often blinded him to the very forces he championed'.[7]

Such characterizations miss an important point that an exploration of Kennedy's approach to democracy promotion in the Third World helps to illustrate. As president at a time of intense Cold War competition, Kennedy was staunchly anti-communist; indeed, he could not be anything else and expect to retain the support of the American people. This did not prevent him understanding and sympathizing with nationalist movements in the developing world. What he wanted was to channel that nationalism towards democracy rather than communism. Moreover, he thought he had found the means to this end in the ideas of those modernization theorists whose academic research convinced them that democracy could be encouraged through 'nation-building'.

Kennedy did not simply abandon these ambitions as reflexive anti-communism came to dominate his foreign policy decision-making. Rather, it was the economic and military tool-kit that he thought could be used for democracy promotion that proved unfit for its purpose. Kennedy's faith in modernization theory, some of whose advocates he appointed to positions within his administration, together with his fascination with the potential of counter-insurgency to combat indigenous communist guerrilla movements in the developing world, ultimately proved to be profoundly misplaced.

Kennedy accepted the premises of Wilson's internationalism and Truman's conviction that a combination of American military power and economic aid could advance democracy and contain communism. He also recognized that the post-colonial world was the new Cold War battlefield. Throughout the decade prior to his election in 1960, he repeatedly tried to encourage public debate on the issue of how the United States should engage with those European colonies that had either achieved their freedom from imperial control or were fighting for their independence. At the same time, he established links with the academic commu-nity, particularly in his native Massachusetts, to help formulate new approaches to democracy promotion in the developing world.

As a senator, therefore, Kennedy consistently challenged the United States' prevailing Cold War policies. In 1951, in a radio address, he outlined the lessons he had learned from a fact-finding visit overseas that year. He rejected an American presence in the Middle East predicated merely on arms supplies and shows of military force. Instead it should be based upon 'the export of ideas, of techniques, and the rebirth of our traditional sympathy for and understanding of the desires of men to be free'. During the seven-week trip, Kennedy noted significantly that in Indochina Americans had: 'allied [themselves] to the desperate effort of a French regime to hang on to the remnants of empire'. He believed it was a self-defeating approach: to ignore a country's 'innately nationalistic aims spells foredoomed failure'.[8]

France's continuing involvement in Vietnam neatly encapsulated some of the dilemmas the United States would face in approaching the problem of political change in the Third World. Following the Second World War, Ho Chi Minh's resistance to French attempts to re-establish its colonial presence in Indochina was easily characterized by the fading European imperial power as inspired by communism as much as by nationalism. Once persuaded by that argument, the United States instinctively sided with the French. Yet, as Kennedy appreciated, in supporting France in Vietnam, the United States was distancing itself from its own revolutionary heritage and placing itself on the wrong side of historical progress. Following the French defeat at Dien Bien Phu in 1954, he opposed American unilateral military action in Southeast Asia to forestall a communist takeover. In the Senate, he warned that 'to pour money, materiel, and men into the jungles of Indochina without at least a remote prospect of victory would be dangerously futile and self-destructive'.[9]

Kennedy was not alone in advocating the need for the United States to develop better policies that addressed the political and economic problems of the Third World. At the Massachusetts Institute of Technology (MIT), the Center for International Studies, established in 1952, brought together a group of academics described by its first director, the economist Max Millikan, as 'social science entrepreneurs'. Their academic agenda was heavily influenced by the ideological priorities of the Cold War (Millikan had worked for the Central Intelligence Agency (CIA) and the centre initially received funding from the agency). Research programmes were established in areas such as economic and political development, and communist studies. Walt Rostow, Millikan's fellow economist, was another founding member.[10]

Research at MIT and elsewhere started from the Truman administration's initial Cold War premise that communist subversion was most likely to occur where there was economic deprivation and social unrest. In his speech at Harvard on 5 June 1947, announcing the plan that bears his name, Truman's Secretary of State George Marshall had argued that:

> Our policy is directed not against any country or doctrine but against hunger, poverty, desperation and chaos. Its purpose should be the revival of a working economy in the world so as to permit the emergence of political and social conditions in which free institutions can exist.[11]

In the aftermath of war in Western Europe American aid had helped to restore health to economies in established nation states with a tradition of representative government. The challenge of promoting democracy in countries that had only recently achieved independence or that were still fighting against imperial control was very different. Yet American modernization theorists assumed that if the appropriate economic conditions could be established then, just as in Europe, countries in the developing world would be more inclined to support democratic institutions than turn to communist governments.

Rostow later observed, therefore, that 'the central, distinctive feature of our approach' to the issue of Third World development 'was that we placed economic growth and foreign aid systematically within the framework of the process of the modernization of societies as a whole'. Modernization was equated with achieving the economic preconditions to sustain democratic systems of government. Moreover, for Rostow,

> in its widest sense, economic development is seen as a potentially constructive outlet for nationalism, a social solvent, a matrix for the development of new leadership, a means for generating at the grass roots confidence in the demo-cratic process and for imparting a strain of reality to the concept of international solidarity.[12]

Rostow joined an informal group of Kennedy advisers, principally from MIT and Harvard, who during the 1950s developed policy statements supporting this kind of 'nation-building', an approach to democracy promotion in the Third World that they would later seek to implement as members of his presidential administration.

In his influential 1960 work, *The Stages of Economic Growth*, Rostow argued that targeted American aid could provide necessary capital investment, particularly when a country was undergoing the transition from traditional to modern society. The aim was to help it reach the vital stage of 'take-off' into a period of sustained economic growth. Successful 'nation-building' depended on establishing an economic infrastructure that would encourage political elites in emerging Third World countries to see capitalist democracy as a more attractive model for development than communism, which for Rostow remained 'a disease of the transition'.[13]

Inoculating the developing world against ideological contagion was the single most important task then facing American policy-makers. According to Rostow, 'the central challenge of our time' was to forge relationships with 'non-Communist politicians and peoples' in those countries where modernization was taking place that 'will see them through into sustained growth on a political and social basis which keeps open the possibilities of progressive, democratic development'.[14] Yet economic growth could not occur in a political vacuum. In the Third World, armed struggle either to achieve independence or in opposition to entrenched and undemocratic post-colonial political elites was an endemic problem. The entrepreneurial social scientists at MIT recognized that economic aid and investment was a necessary but not a sufficient precondition for progress towards democratization. Modernization was a challenging process that could itself spark economic, social and political conflict, potentially inflamed by communists who opposed the precepts of democratic nation-building.

The threat from communist-backed insurgencies was acute. In 1955, Rostow co-authored *An American Policy in Asia* and drew attention to the

> possibility that new territories will fall to the enemy by a combination of subversion and guerilla warfare. ... In Vietnam, Laos, Cambodia, Thailand and possibly Indonesia as well, the enemy is now conducting targetless warfare in which he is a professional and we are amateurs.[15]

Rostow was convinced that guerrilla activity in the developing world necessitated a new form of American military response. Counter-insurgency doctrine joined economic development as the means by which communist insurgencies in Third World countries could be defeated.

In 1957, as a member of the Senate foreign relations committee, Kennedy made a controversial speech supporting a negotiated settlement to bring about Algeria's independence from France. For Kennedy, it was plain that

> No amount of mutual politeness, wishful thinking, nostalgia, or regret should blind either France or the United States to the fact that, if France and the West at large are to have a continuing influence in North Africa ... the essential first step is the independence of Algeria.

Observing that 'most political revolutions – including our own – have been buoyed by outside aid in men, weapons, and ideas', Kennedy argued that:

> Instead of abandoning African nationalism to the anti-Western agitators and Soviet agents who hope to capture its leadership, the United States, a

product of political revolution, must redouble its efforts to earn the respect and friendship of nationalist leaders.[16]

Ronald Nurse points out that 'while in the Senate, Kennedy often expressed his belief that … a flexible anti-colonial policy in Washington was essential to combat the spread of communism in the Third World nations'.[17] Kennedy's critique was consistent with the arguments he had been making throughout the decade: the United States should accept that in the post-colonial world the political problems of emerging nations could not be viewed entirely through the prism of Cold War containment. Nevertheless, a contemporary article in *Time* magazine saw the political motive behind Kennedy's argument: 'to Administration ears, Kennedy's Algeria speech sounded like troublesome meddling, possibly part of the build-up of his stock as a Democratic presidential nominee in 1960'. Both John Foster Dulles and Eisenhower were highly critical of an intervention that caused diplomatic protest on both sides of the Atlantic.[18]

With the 1960 election approaching *Time*'s suspicion of Kennedy's motives appeared well-founded. He took advantage of any opportunity that might help to burnish his credentials as the candidate who offered a fresh, creative approach to leadership. In 1958, William Lederer and Eugene Burdick's polemic, *The Ugly American*, became an instant national best-seller. It was a powerful endorsement of Kennedy's critique of the Eisenhower administration's approach to Third World diplomacy. Kennedy sent a copy of the book to every member of the Senate. Its concluding paragraph might have been taken from one of his speeches:

> All over Asia we have found that the basic American ethic is revered and honoured and imitated when possible. We must, while helping Asia toward self-sufficiency, show by example that America is still the America of freedom and hope and knowledge and law. If we succeed, we cannot lose the struggle.[19]

In a series of vignettes and caricatures, *The Ugly American* portrayed an American foreign service staffed by incompetent political appointees and bureaucrats, more interested in the generous benefits and luxury lifestyle they enjoyed than in fighting the spread of communist influence in the Third World. The heroes of the book were those whose common decency and belief in core American values enabled them to offer constructive help to the developing world, along with those prepared to study and if necessary adopt the enemy's tactics in order to combat communism.

On 2 November 1960, in San Francisco, in one of his final campaign speeches, Kennedy referred directly to the *The Ugly American*'s critique of the foreign service, suggesting that 'the United States is going to have to do much better in this area if we are going to defend freedom and peace in the 1960s'. He then called for 'a peace corps of talented young men and women, willing and able to serve their country … well qualified through rigorous standards, well trained in the languages, skills, and customs they will need to know'.[20]

This initiative would be financed through the foreign aid budget. Less than two months after he had entered the White House, on 1 March 1961, the new president had signed the executive order establishing the Peace Corps: a potent symbol of his new approach to democracy promotion in the developing world. The Peace Corps would become one of Kennedy's most enduring and successful contributions to the diffusion of American democratic values overseas: a means of promoting cross-cultural understanding that has transcended the Cold War era in which it was established. It dramatized his desire to engage with the developing world, embracing *The Ugly American*'s argument that a small-scale investment of human resources could pay large dividends in terms of promoting a positive image of the United States abroad.

Kennedy's presidency began with a flurry of activism as campaign promises and the ideas developed in the academic research centres of Massachusetts during the previous decade were implemented. The principal theatre for superpower rivalry had shifted from Europe to those areas of the world where former European colonies were now struggling for, or had recently achieved, independence. The United States also had to confront the potential impact of the Cuban revolution in Latin America, which Kennedy described as 'the most dangerous area in the world'.[21] The Kennedy administration approached this post-colonial world convinced of the potential of 'nation-building' as a means of spreading American democratic values abroad and containing communism. In Latin America, as Stephen Rabe observes, the president and his advisers: 'acted confidently, certain they knew how to "modernize" societies and build sturdy, self-reliant democracies'.[22] The core belief of nation-builders was that the strategic targeting of economic aid would encourage the development of democracy overseas.

Thomas Carothers points out that:

> when foreign aid became a major component of U.S. policy towards the developing world in the 1950s, democracy promotion was not a priority. ... It was only with the arrival of the Kennedy administration and some new thinking about the relationship of development and democracy that the idea of giving aid to promote democracy caught on among policy makers.[23]

Twelve days after the Peace Corps had been established, therefore, Kennedy formally announced his vision for the future of Latin America in a White House speech. The 'Alliance for Progress' reflected Rostow's argument: economic growth was the key to encouraging democratization in the developing world. The new president called for 'a vast cooperative effort, unparalleled in magnitude and nobility of purpose, to satisfy the basic needs of the American people for homes, work and land, health and schools'. Kennedy proposed that 'the American Republics begin on a vast new 10-year plan for the Americas, a plan to transform the 1960s into an historic decade of democratic progress'.[24] The United States pledged $20 billion that was to be invested during the decade alongside a further $80 billion contributed by Latin American countries with the aim of promoting economic growth across the continent.

The new administration also acted quickly and dramatically to reorganize the American foreign aid budget to invest it more effectively in the strategic ambition of building democracy in the developing world. In his Special Message to Congress on Foreign Aid on 22 March 1961, Kennedy announced that the 1960s would be a 'crucial decade of development' in which the United States would help other nations on the path to economic growth and stability. He again echoed Rostow's analysis in arguing that:

> the fundamental task of our foreign aid program in the 1960s is not negatively to fight Communism: its fundamental task is to help make a historical demonstration that in the twentieth century, as in the nineteenth – in the southern half of the globe as in the north – economic growth and political democracy can develop hand in hand.[25]

There were sceptics, some within the administration itself. At the State Department George Ball saw that this 'Kennedy doctrine' aligned the United States' past as a nation born of revolution with contemporary political struggles in the post-colonial world. The Alliance for Progress was an ambitious attempt to modernize a continent. However, for Ball it encapsulated the Cold War dilemma raised by Kennedy's approach to the Third World. The United States might be prepared to tolerate: 'the risk of transient instability; but since the Soviets regularly exploited instability, rhetoric did not answer the hard questions. How much instability could we accept without risking a shift in the power balance?'[26]

In an attempt to answer this question, democracy promotion during the Kennedy years had to be underpinned where necessary by a new military approach that was designed to combat communist insurgencies in the developing world. Rostow joined the administration as deputy national security adviser. As his earlier work had shown, he was an influential advocate for counter-insurgency. The president was easily persuaded, rapidly adopting it as his military tactic of choice. He was fascinated with its potential. Soon after he took office, at a meeting of the National Security Council on 1 February 1961, the president, who reportedly had read the works of Che Guevara and Mao Tse Tung on how to conduct guerrilla warfare, requested that Secretary of Defence Robert McNamara 'in consultation with other interested agencies, should examine means for placing more emphasis on the development of counter-guerilla forces'.[27]

Kennedy's sense of urgency was a reaction to a perceived change in the communist approach to the Third World. During the interval between Kennedy's election and inauguration, Nikita Khrushchev had made it clear that as leader of the Soviet Union he too was intent on redrawing the battle lines of the Cold War. In a Kremlin speech that was subsequently leaked to the American media, he pledged support for 'national liberation wars' of the kind that were continuing in Vietnam and Algeria. These guerrilla wars were 'revolutionary' and 'inevitable' because colonial 'freedom and independence' could be achieved 'only by struggle, including armed struggle'.[28]

For the incoming American president, already aware of the Eisenhower administration's plans to invade Cuba to counter the potential influence of its revolution spreading across Latin America, the challenge was clear. Whatever efforts Kennedy might make to deliver on democracy promotion in implementing the new foreign policy agenda he had framed during the 1950s, he could neither afford to appear 'soft on communism' nor risk losing countries from the American sphere of influence. Counter-insurgency was an attractive way of meeting the heightened threat of Soviet-backed communist subversion in the developing world without committing conventional forces overseas.

In April 1961, the attempted invasion of Cuba at the Bay of Pigs went ahead. The new president's public commitment to the Alliance for Progress in Latin America was immediately undercut by his decision to endorse military action against a neighbouring Caribbean country. To his critics, this action alone illustrates the contradictory sides of his character: the Camelot idealist giving way to the Cold War enthusiast. Yet it is worth reflecting on Kennedy's inaction when it soon became obvious that the invasion plan was not going to succeed. Conventional American forces were not sent to Cuba to support the attempt to overthrow Castro. The president preferred to face the domestic political repercussions of the failure rather than risk a military commitment to a prolonged conflict with an uncertain outcome. Popular opinion quickly rallied to Kennedy. When a Gallup poll showed 82 per cent support for the administration, according to Arthur Schlesinger Jr., the President saw the irony: 'it's just like Eisenhower. The worse I do the more popular I get'.[29] He might also have drawn the conclusion that, with memories of Truman's intervention in Korea no more than a decade old, Americans had no wish to see a new president start another war against a communist country; this time much closer to home.

In May 1961, Kennedy's Special Message to Congress on Urgent National Needs requested funding for an ambitious set of policy proposals, including the goal of a manned lunar landing. The president outlined what he considered to be at stake in the Third World during the time that he envisaged the space programme succeeding:

> the adversaries of freedom plan to consolidate their territory – to exploit, to control, and finally to destroy the hopes of the world's newest nations; and they have ambition to do it before the end of this decade. It is a contest of will and purpose as well as force and violence – a battle for minds and souls as well as lives and territory. And in that contest, we cannot stand aside.[30]

Five months later Congress passed the Foreign Assistance Act, separating budgets for military and non-military aid and paved the way for the establishment of the United States Agency for International Development (USAID).

Despite his alarmist and bellicose rhetoric, Kennedy's reluctance to commit American troops to fight communism overseas, evident at the Bay of Pigs, tempers the characterization of him as an aggressive Cold Warrior. His caution was evident in his prevarications over increasing American military involvement in Vietnam, despite the advice of some of his aides. The *Pentagon Papers* note that as early as June 1961, 'someone or other is frequently promoting the idea of sending US combat units' to support Ngo Dinh Diem's regime in South Vietnam. However: 'Kennedy never makes a clear-cut decision but some way or other action is always deferred on any move that would probably lead to engagements on the ground between American units and the Viet Cong.'[31] Instead the president remained confident that counter-insurgency would succeed in defeating communism: American Special Forces could intervene in the developing world, training and assisting local populations to fight indigenous guerrilla forces.

The Green Berets were the elite unit that the president believed could win wars of national liberation. By October 1961, when Kennedy toured the Army Special Warfare Center at Fort Bragg in North Carolina, members of these Special Forces were already on active service in Southeast Asia. An article in *Life* magazine, published to coincide with the president's visit, gave a public relations gloss to the administration's new approach to meeting the communist challenge in Third World conflicts. Under the headline 'Tough Men and Terrain for an Ugly War', *Life* portrayed the American advisers in Vietnam as 'expert in guerrilla psychology and tactics'. Trainees at Fort Bragg were profiled as archetypes from the United States' past. Among them was 'Ace Richardson' who was 'one-half Sioux Indian, and he is now learning all the warrior qualities his ancestors knew: cunning, stealth, mastery of terrain, an ability to live off the land for weeks without shelter or rest'.[32]

Like their Peace Corps counterparts, recruits such as Richardson were also emissaries for American democracy. As Russell Weigley observes,

> With the Green Berets trained not only in unconventional warfare but also in community organization and leadership, preventive medicine, and construction techniques, the Special Forces could engage in nation building as well, both physically and through inspirational leadership, contributing to the remedy for the underlying national incohesiveness that exposed underdeveloped countries to subversion and guerrilla war.[33]

Yet the fallacy that lay at the heart of the Kennedy administration's embrace of counter-insurgency as the means to combat communist forces in the Third World was similar to that which was undermining the efforts of nation-builders to promote democracy through strategic economic aid and investment. Developing nations often lacked the political culture in which democratic institutions could be established. American military advisers and economic aid supported non-communist governments that were themselves profoundly undemocratic and unpopular. As Douglas Blaufarb points out, the United States had to convince its non-communist allies in the Third World

> first to improve and strengthen their administration of government, notably in security and counterguerilla military operations, but also in other relevant

fields; and secondly, to carry out reforms to satisfy popular needs and undercut Communist appeals.[34]

Frequently those governments refused to be persuaded, remaining obstinately unaccountable to their people. As a result they lacked political legitimacy and were resistant to American imprecations to adopt democratic reforms if that risked compromising their hold on power. Ngo Dinh Diem in South Vietnam was one such notorious example.

The initial optimism and activism that characterized the Kennedy administration's attempts at nation-building and democracy promotion did not result in many immediate or significant gains. Moreover it was the collapse of Diem's regime in South Vietnam in the November 1963 coup in which he was assassinated that was the most dramatic illustration of the United States' failure to help build a viable democratic government in a developing country. Nevertheless later that month Kennedy planned a speech in which he would offer a robust defence of his approach to Third World development as a means of containing communist expansion. The president remained convinced that: 'our military and economic assistance plays ... a key role in enabling those who live on the periphery of the Communist world to maintain their independence of choice'. Moreover,

> About 70 percent of our military assistance goes to nine key countries located on or near the borders of the Communist-bloc – nine countries confronted directly or indirectly with the threat of Communistic aggression – Viet-Nam, Free China, Korea, India, Pakistan, Thailand, Greece, Turkey, and Iran. ... Reducing our efforts to train, equip, and assist their armies can only encourage Communist penetration and require in time the increased overseas deployment of American combat forces. And reducing the economic help needed to bolster these nations that undertake to help defend freedom can have the same disastrous result. In short, the $50 billion we spend each year on our own defense could well be ineffective without the $4 billion required for military and economic assistance.[35]

Kennedy did not live to deliver these remarks which were scheduled to be given at the Dallas Trade Mart at lunchtime on 22 November 1963.

From Kennedy to Johnson

Lyndon Johnson was born in 1908, the last full year of Theodore Roosevelt's administration. More so than Kennedy, he was a child of that progressive era. He entered national politics during Franklin Roosevelt's presidency and as Senate majority leader during the 1950s he was instrumental in forging a bipartisan approach to Cold War foreign policy. Nevertheless contemporaries saw his strengths as primarily focused on domestic politics. Prior to the 1960 Democrat convention, the journalist

Walter Lippmann considered Johnson as 'not a genuine alternative to Kennedy. For Johnson knows little of the outer world'.[36]

Johnson was consistently marginalized by 'the best and the brightest' who joined the new administration. After Kennedy's assassination, it was easy for those who wanted to preserve his memory untarnished by the events that followed to accept Lippmann's conclusion and to suggest that because Johnson did not share his predecessor's sophisticated understanding of international affairs, it led him to entangle the nation in the Vietnam War. Johnson's lack of involvement in policy-making during the Kennedy administration was taken to imply that he had little to contribute to the new agenda of Third World nation-building.

Historical assessments of Johnson, like those of Kennedy, focus on his contra-dictions. On the one hand, his domestic achievements, notably his advocacy of civil rights and shaping of the 'Great Society', demonstrate unique political talents which, in terms of his legislative abilities, put him in the premier league of twentieth-century presidents. On the other hand, because of the failure of the Vietnam War, Johnson's foreign policy is easily caricatured as a product of his parochialism and lack of understanding of the wider world. Moreover, his decision to go to war and the disastrous consequences of it places him alongside Richard Nixon as an archi-tect of the 'Imperial Presidency'. His fiercest critics, not least the Camelot historian Arthur Schlesinger Jr., even suggest that Johnson's overweening ego collapsed into paranoia as domestic opposition to the conflict in Southeast Asia increased and the war became an intractable stalemate.[37]

While the United States' appetite for nation-building and democracy promotion abroad would be diminished as a result of the Vietnam War, Johnson's achieve-ment of the Great Society and civil rights legislation at home remains the positive legacy of a president whose understanding of the relationship between domestic and foreign policy was more subtle than some of his critics have been prepared to admit. As vice-president, Johnson supported Kennedy's conviction that democracy promotion in the Third World was a critical element in the United States' Cold War strategy of containment. Moreover, he went further than Kennedy in appreciating that by extending democracy at home the United States would have greater moral authority and political leverage abroad.

Johnson's experience as vice-president involved him in a crash course in foreign travel. Senator George Smathers is credited for suggesting to Kennedy that one way of avoiding Johnson's morose and taciturn presence at White House meetings would be to send him abroad as an 'ambassador-at-large'. Between 1961 and 1963 Johnson spent almost a third of his time overseas, making 11 visits to 33 separate countries. His roots in rural Texas had given him first-hand experience of the benefits of economic investment, the cornerstone of Kennedy's democracy promotion strategy. During the 1930s he had witnessed how Franklin Roosevelt's policies helped to improve living standards in his region of the country. As Robert Dallek therefore observes,

> in Africa and Asia his trips partly became a crusade for the New Deal reforms that had transformed America. Eager to combat Communist appeals to poor

developing nations, Johnson pointed to economic change in his native South as a model for Third World advance.[38]

Johnson's support for the administration's ambitious attempts at democracy promotion abroad was genuine and visceral, sincere and personal.

Moreover, the vice-president recognized that advancing democracy was a domestic issue as well as a foreign policy one. His impromptu remarks at the commencement ceremony at Southwest Texas State College – his *alma mater* – in May 1961 echoed Kennedy's rhetoric in announcing the Alliance for Progress. Johnson argued that 'the three greatest friends that communism has are illiteracy, poverty and disease'. But he also pointed out that low educational achievement, lack of economic self-sufficiency and inadequate healthcare were problems for the United States as well as for the developing world. Indeed, for Johnson they were: 'the three greatest enemies that our democratic system has'.[39]

More so than Kennedy, Johnson was willing to make a powerful rhetorical connection between the fight for freedom against communism abroad and the struggle for civil rights at home. In May 1963, he spoke at Gettysburg. In language that at times borrowed from Lincoln, he pledged that

> Until the world knows no aggressors, until the arms of tyranny have been laid down, until freedom has risen up in every land, we shall maintain our vigil to make sure our sons who died on foreign fields shall not have died in vain. As we maintain the vigil of peace, we must remember that justice is a vigil, too – a vigil we must keep in our own streets and schools and among the lives of all our people – so that those who died here on their native soil shall not have died in vain.[40]

Johnson's remarks reflected his awareness of the significant challenge then facing the United States in promoting its democratic values abroad, particularly in the developing nations of Asia and Africa, at a time when the Soviet Union could point to the United States' continuing tolerance of racial segregation in its southern states as a symbol of its failure to live up to the ideals expressed in its Declaration of Independence.

As president, Johnson's immediate priorities were focused on encouraging economic development and the extension of civil liberties at home rather than abroad. In so doing, his approach to domestic democracy promotion borrowed from the Kennedy administration's policies towards the Third World. In his first State of the Union Address, Johnson declared 'unconditional war on poverty in America', and proposed the creation of 'a National Service Corps to help the economically handicapped of our own country as the Peace Corps now helps those abroad'.[41] He persuaded Sargent Shriver, Kennedy's brother-in-law who had set up the Peace Corps, to become Director of his newly established Office of Economic Opportunity and to help create its domestic equivalent as the Volunteers in Service to America (VISTA) programme.

Mary Dudziak points out that outside the United States some had seen Kennedy's assassination as 'retaliation for his support of civil rights'. In this context, Johnson's success in persuading Congress to pass the Civil Rights Act in 1964 was a landmark achievement in domestic politics that also paid a significant foreign policy dividend in bringing about a significant improvement in the United States' standing on the world stage. Developing nations, particularly in Africa, welcomed Johnson's commitment to this legislation. So, as Dudziak observes: 'as President Johnson moved forward on civil rights, the Cold War/civil rights conundrum, seemed, for a moment, to be resolved'.[42] Yet at the same time that Johnson was extending democracy at home, so the United States' nation-building effort in South Vietnam was rapidly disintegrating.

The coup there and Diem's assassination meant that Johnson entered the White House at a pivotal moment in the history of American involvement in Southeast Asia. It became apparent that, during the year following Diem's death, the South Vietnamese generals who succeeded him were either unwilling or incapable of establishing a more viable democratic government there. Johnson was forced to confront the political consequences of that failure as it impacted on the United States' Cold War foreign policy. Advocates of nation-building began to rethink their theories in relation to the collapse of South Vietnam's political structures. The problem lay with the Hanoi government. In August 1964, Walt Rostow provided the president with a rationale for bombing North Vietnam. Implicit in it was an admission that counter-insurgency, which he had championed in the Kennedy White House, was proving ineffective as a military tactic. To sever the connection between the Viet Cong in the South and the government in Hanoi, Rostow now argued that

> By applying limited, graduated military actions reinforced by political and economic pressures on a nation providing external support for insurgency, we should be able to cause that nation to decide to reduce greatly or eliminate altogether support for the insurgency. ... the threat that is implicit in initial US actions would be more important than the military effect of the actions themselves.[43]

As he gained influence in Johnson's administration – he eventually became the National Security Adviser – Rostow moved from promoting counter-insurgency to advocating bombing of North Vietnam and finally to supporting the increasing commitment of American conventional forces to fight the war in South Vietnam.

Even before Rolling Thunder, the sustained bombing campaign against North Vietnam, commenced in March 1965, the president had acceded to a request from General William Westmoreland, commanding the 23,000 American military advisers then in South Vietnam, for additional troops to be sent to Southeast Asia. It was the beginning of the build-up of conventional forces that would transform the conflict there into an American war. The critical decisions Johnson made in 1965: to begin bombing North Vietnam, to accede to his generals' requests for more troops and ultimately to agree their deployment in a combat role, graphically illustrate the limitations of Kennedy's approach to nation-building and democracy promotion in the developing world. Economic aid and counter-insurgency tactics had failed to create a political culture in South Vietnam that could enable a viable democratic government to be established there.

Nevertheless, Johnson did not entirely abandon the hope that the promise of economic assistance might give him political leverage in the worsening military situation in Vietnam. In April 1965, in a speech at Johns Hopkins University, the president drew once more on his experience of the New Deal in his native South in an attempt to find a solution to the problems of Southeast Asia. Johnson struck a familiar rhetorical chord in lamenting that

> This war, like most wars, is filled with terrible irony. For what do the people of North Viet-Nam want? They want what their neighbors also desire: food for their hunger; health for their bodies; a chance to learn; progress for their country; and an end to the bondage of material misery. And they would find all these things far more readily in peaceful association with others than in the endless course of battle.

He proposed a United Nations sponsored cooperative international initiative that would include North Vietnam and the Soviet Union in an 'effort to replace despair with hope, and terror with progress'. The United States would contribute a billion dollars in aid to develop the region in the same way that its southern states had been transformed three decades previously. Reminiscing about what the New Deal had achieved in the United States of his youth, Johnson was convinced that

> The vast Mekong River can provide food and water and power on a scale to dwarf even our own TVA ... A dam built across a great river is impressive. In the countryside where I was born, and where I live, I have seen the night illuminated, and the kitchens warmed, and the homes heated, where once the cheerless night and the ceaseless cold held sway. And all this happened because electricity came to our area along the humming wires of the REA. Electrification of the countryside − yes, that, too, is impressive.[44]

Brian de Mark suggests that the Hanoi government rejected Johnson's attempt to negotiate a political settlement in Southeast Asia for one of a number of reasons: 'disdain for Johnson's aid-for-peace proposal', its lack of control over the insurgent Vietcong forces in the South or its confidence that its military campaign would be successful. Johnson's recourse was to continue the bombing. As De Mark observes, 'the destruction would persist. America would keep punishing North Vietnam, even as LBJ offered to help it'.[45]

The Kennedy administration's approach to democracy promotion had been exposed as simply a proving ground for academic theories that proved untenable when applied to the developing world. In his memoirs, George Ball observed that the prospect of leading the Third World into the twentieth century offered almost unlimited scope for experimentation ... It was the golden age of development theorists. ... But the most presumptuous undertaking of all was 'nation-building', which suggested that American professors could make bricks without the straw of experience and with indifferent and infinitely various kinds of clay.[46]

The essential problem, as Tony Smith points out, was that 'armed with academic thinking on "development", "modernization," and "nation building" in the early 1960s, Washington was relying on intellectual arguments long on self-confidence but short on practical understanding'.[47]

Similarly, Stephen Rabe argues that those involved in planning the Alliance for Progress 'placed too much faith in their development theories and misapplied the lessons of history'.[48] As far as nation-building in Latin America was concerned, therefore, as John and Richard Toye conclude, 'the original rhetoric of the promotion of democracy became somewhat tarnished. The firm anti-communism of the new administration led the US government to shore up repressive regimes ... with foreign aid and to destabilize several democratic ones'.[49]

American economic aid did not act to spur democratic nation-building in the Third World as its advocates in the Kennedy and Johnson administrations anticipated. As the experience of South Vietnam illustrated, the problems of Third World development in a Cold War context did not admit to easy academic solutions. Contemporaries recognized the problem. In 1966, Donald Fraser, a leading Democrat supporter of USAID, argued in Congress that: 'a basic reorientation in our thinking is required to put social and political evolution as the first concern of our foreign assistance program rather than the other way around'.[50] Fraser joined forces with the Republican Bradford Morse to put forward Title IX as an addendum to Kennedy's 1961 Foreign Assistance Act. It required the Agency to ensure: 'maximum participation in the task of economic development on the part of the people of the developing countries, through the encouragement of democratic private and local government institutions'.[51] However, as Thomas Carothers points out, despite its sponsors' hopes, Title IX did not immediately lead to a fundamental reorientation in USAID's approach to targeting foreign assistance.[52]

One reason for this was the continuing war in Southeast Asia. As Fraser himself admitted in 1967, despite all its efforts, neither the government nor USAID were able to find: 'the key to the social and political side of ... (the Vietnam) conflict'. Moreover, in an indictment of the approach of Rostow and others, he acknowledged that

> Those who talk with confidence about our capacity to intervene in these societies have their heads stuck firmly in the sand. We know very little about nation-building. Few of us even understand how our own nation developed, much less how other nations are likely to develop. We operate on simplistic, almost pious assumptions which have failed repeatedly.[53]

Ironically it was only after the Vietnam War had played its part in discrediting modernization theory that USAID, which, along with the Peace Corps, survived as part of Kennedy's foreign policy legacy, began to be seen more positively as a potential channel for democracy promotion overseas.

The Kennedy and Johnson administrations attempted to establish a viable democratic government in South Vietnam. They failed. Modernization theory had suggested a way in which the United States could combat communism in the developing world without committing conventional military forces overseas. Kennedy did not live to witness the collapse of the United States' nation-building efforts in Southeast Asia, yet Vietnam is still a salutary reminder of his misplaced confidence in the ideas put forward by the 'action-intellectuals' who accompanied him to the White House.[54] After Kennedy's assassination some remained as influential voices, eventually persuading Lyndon Johnson to go to war there. The repercussions of his decision continue to reverberate in the nation's democratic politics, society and culture and to impact not least on the institution of the American presidency itself.[55]

Notes

1 Theodore Sorensen, *Kennedy* (New York: Harper & Row, 1965), and Arthur Schlesinger Jr., *A Thousand Days: John F. Kennedy in the White House* (New York: Houghton Mifflin Company, 1965).

2 Burton Kaufman, 'John F. Kennedy as World Leader: A Perspective on the Literature', in M. Hogan, ed., *America in the World: The Historiography of American Foreign Relations Since 1941* (Cambridge: Cambridge University Press, 1995), p. 326.

3 Thomas Paterson, ed., *Kennedy's Quest for Victory* (New York: Oxford University Press, 1989), p. 23.

4 Anna Kasten Nelson, 'President Kennedy's National Security Policy: A Reconsideration', *Reviews in American History*, 19, 1 (1991), pp. 1–14.

5 See for example, Thomas Reeves, A *Question of Character: A Life of John F. Kennedy* (New York: Macmillan Press, 1991).

6 Kaufman, 'John F. Kennedy as World Leader', p. 357.

7 Stephen Rabe, *John F. Kennedy: World Leader* (Dulles: Potomac Books, 2010), p. 11.

8 Quoted in Robert Dallek, *An Unfinished Life: John F. Kennedy, 1917–1963* (Boston: Little, Brown & Co., 1963), p. 167.

9 Quoted in William Conrad Gibbons, *The US Government and the Vietnam War* (Princeton: Princeton University Press, 1986), part 1: 1945–60, p. 204.

10 See http://web.mit.edu/cis/pdf/Panel_ORIGINS.pdf for details of the centre's history.

11 George C. Marshall, 'The Marshall Plan Speech', 5 June 1947, http://www.marshallfoundation.org/documents/MarshallPlan.pdf

12 Walt Rostow, *Concept and Controversy: Sixty Years of Taking Ideas to Market* (Austin: University of Texas Press, 1973), pp. 98, 199.

13 Walt W. Rostow, *The Stages of Economic Growth* (Cambridge: Cambridge University Press, 1960), p. 162.

14 ibid., p. 164.

15 Quoted in Douglas Blaufarb, *The Counterinsurgency Era* (New York: The Free Press, 1977), p. 50.

16 John F. Kennedy, 'Imperialism – The Enemy of Freedom', *Congressional Record*, part 8, vol. 103, 2 July 1957, 85th Congress 1st Session (Washington DC: Government Printing Office, 1957), pp. 10780–83.

17 Ronald Nurse, 'Critic of Colonialism: JFK and Algerian Independence', *The Historian*, 39, 2, 1977, pp. 307–26, 324.

18 'Foreign Relations: Burned Hands Across the Sea', *Time*, 15 July 1957, http://www.time.com/time/magazine/article/0,9171,809643–1,00.html

19 William Lederer and Eugene Burdick, *The Ugly American* (London: Victor Gollancz Ltd, 1966 edition), p. 285.

20 John F. Kennedy, 'Speech at Cow Place, San Francisco', 2 November 1960, http://www.jfklink.com/speeches/jfk/nov60/jfk021160_cow02.html

21 Quoted in Stephen Rabe, *The Most Dangerous Area in the World* (Chapel Hill: University of North Carolina Press, 1999), p. 7.

22 ibid., p. 9.

23 Thomas Carothers, *Aiding Democracy Abroad* (Washington DC: Carnegie Endowment for International Peace, 1999), p. 19.

24 John F. Kennedy, 'Address at a White House Reception for Members of Congress and for the Diplomatic Corps of the Latin American Republics', 13 March 1961, *Public Papers of the Presidents of the United States, John F. Kennedy, 1961* (Washington DC: US Government Printing Office, 1962), p. 172.

25 Kennedy, 'Special Message to the Congress on Foreign Aid', 22 March 1961, ibid., p. 205.

26 George Ball, *The Past Has Another Pattern* (New York: W.W. Norton & Co., 1982), p. 181.

27 National Security Action Memorandum no. 2, 3 February 1961, http://www.jfklibrary.org/Asset-Viewer/B3leMaWRSkOnvMDbjd00Cw.aspx

28 Khrushchev made his speech on 6 January 1961. For a transcript, see http://www.osaarchivum.org/files/holdings/300/8/3/text/58_4-307.shtml

29 Schlesinger, *A Thousand Days*, p. 292.

30 Kennedy, 'Special Message to the Congress on Urgent National Needs', 25 May 1961, *Public Papers of the Presidents of the United States, John F. Kennedy, 1961*, p. 397.

31 The Pentagon Papers IV.B.1 Evolution of the War 1, The Kennedy Commitments and Programs, 1961, p. 68, http://www.archives.gov/research/pentagon-papers/.

32 *Life*, 27 October 1961, pp. 44–46.

33 Russell Weigley, *The American Way of War* (Bloomington: Indiana University Press, 1973), p. 457.

34 Douglas Blaufarb, *The Counterinsurgency Era* (New York: The Free Press, 1977), p. 86.

35 John F. Kennedy, 'Remarks Prepared for Delivery at the Trade Mart in Dallas', 22 November 1963, http://www.jfklibrary.org/Research/Ready-Reference/JFK-Speeches/Remarks-Prepared-for-Delivery-at-the-Trade-Mart-in-Dallas-November-22_1963.aspx

36 Quoted in Philip Walker, 'Lyndon B. Johnson's Senate Foreign Policy Activism: The Suez Canal Crisis, A Reappraisal', *Presidential Studies Quarterly*, 26, 4, 1996, pp. 996–1008.

37 See for example, Kent Germany, 'The Many Lyndon Johnsons: A Review Essay', *Journal of Southern History*, LXXV, 4, 2009, pp. 1001–28, and Jon Roper, 'The Politics of Sanity: Vietnam, Watergate and the Psychological Afflictions of Presidents', *EurAmerica*, 30, 2, 2000, pp. 31–69, http://www.ea.sinica.edu.tw/eu_file/12015971454.pdf.

38 Robert Dallek, *Flawed Giant: Lyndon Johnson and His Times 1961–1973* (New York: Oxford University Press, 1998), p. 12.

39 Quoted in Randall Woods, *LBJ: Architect of American Ambition* (Boston: Harvard University Press, 2007), p. 390.

40 'Remarks of Vice President Lyndon B. Johnson Memorial Day, Gettysburg, Pennsylvania', 30 May 1963, http://www.lbjlib.utexas.edu/johnson/archives.hom/speeches.hom/630530.asp.

41 'President Lyndon B. Johnson's Annual Message to the Congress on the State of the Union', 8 January 1964, http://www.lbjlib.utexas.edu/johnson/archives.hom/speeches.hom/640108.asp

42 Mary Dudziak, *Cold War Civil Rights: Race and the Image of American Democracy* (Princeton: Princeton University Press, 2000), pp. 205, 208.

43 Gibbons, *The US Government and the Vietnam War*, part III, p. 118.

44 President Lyndon B. Johnson, 'Peace Without Conquest', Johns Hopkins University, 7 April 1965, http://www.lbjlib.utexas.edu/johnson/archives.hom/speeches.hom/650407.asp.

45 Brian Van De Mark, *Into the Quagmire: Lyndon Johnson and the Escalation of the Vietnam War* (New York: Oxford University Press, 1991), p. 124.

46 Ball, *The Past Has Another Pattern*, p. 183.

47 Tony Smith, *America's Mission: The United States and the Worldwide Struggle for Democracy in the Twentieth Century* (Princeton: Princeton University Press, 1994), p. 222.

48 Stephen Rabe, *The Most Dangerous Area in the World*, p. 196.

49 John and Richard Toye, *The UN and Global Political Economy* (Bloomington: Indiana University Press, 2004), p. 176.

50 Fraser's 15 March 1966 speech in Congress is reprinted as 'New Directions in Foreign Aid', *World Affairs*, 129, 4, 1967. Extracts are reproduced in AID's *Primer on Title IX of the United States Foreign Assistance Act* (Washington DC: AID, 1970), http://pdf.usaid.gov/pdf_docs/PNABR894.pdf

51 *Legislation on Foreign Relations Through 2008* (Washington DC: US Government Printing Office, 2010), vol. I-A, p. 167, http://frwebgate.access.gpo.gov/cgibin/getdoc.cgi?dbname=111_cong_senate_committee_prints& docid = f:51120.pdf

52 See Carothers, *Aiding Democracy Abroad*, pp. 22–26.

53 Quoted in Brian Butler, 'Title IX of the Foreign Assistance Act: Foreign Aid and Political Development', *Law & Society Review*, 3, 1 (1968), pp. 115–52, 129.

54 'Action-intellectual' was a term used by Theodore White in a series of articles in *Life* in June 1967 in which he profiled a number of the American academics who left Universities to become influential policy-makers in the Kennedy and Johnson administrations. See also Smith, *America's Mission*, p. 222.

55 For a further discussion see Jon Roper, *The American Presidents: Heroic Leadership from Kennedy to Clinton* (Edinburgh: Edinburgh University Press, 2000), and 'George W. Bush and the Myth of Heroic Leadership', *Presidential Studies Quarterly*, 34, 1, 2004, pp. 132–42.

7

JIMMY CARTER

John Dumbrell

President Jimmy Carter is frequently remembered as a foreign policy leader who sought to reintroduce morality into American foreign relations following the years of Henry Kissinger-led *Realpolitik*. Carter's Inaugural Address of January 1977 promised a new commitment to the interpenetration of moral idealism and national self-interest. Wilsonian themes of moralistic internationalism undergirded many of Carter's major foreign policy speeches. One strand in academic writing explicitly links the contradictions of the Wilsonian tradition – the cloaking of expansionist, market-oriented and imperialist goals in the language of democracy-oriented moralism – to parallel tendencies under Carter.[1] However, Carter's version of exportable democracy was structured around a strong and particular commitment to human rights. It was influenced not only by the reaction to Kissinger's *Realpolitik*, but also by Carter's desire to transcend the quasi-imperialist hubris of the moralistic foreign policy that had ensnared the United States into the Vietnam War. This chapter assesses the degree to which the Carter administration managed to further the agenda of a post-imperialist, human rights-oriented commitment to the international promotion of democracy.

President Carter has found his academic defenders in recent years, several of whom stress his post-White House commitment to the promotion of human rights, peace and free democratic institutions. Yet the general verdict on Carter's foreign policy is still generally negative. He is seen by some on the right as the naive idealist who came belatedly to embrace a more coherent anti-communism after 1978. More left-leaning commentators commend the early foreign policy and deplore the proto-Reaganism of his reaction to the Soviet invasion of Afghanistan in 1979. Many commentators across the political spectrum see Carter's foreign policy leadership as fundamentally confused – both in terms of its goals and its internal management.[2] On the narrower theme of democracy, Carter's stance and record are difficult to assess. His position on democracy promotion was structured around the prior commitment to 'human rights' as the guiding principle (especially early in his presidency) of foreign engagement. The commitment to democracy promotion was also profoundly affected by the underlying dynamic of the administration – the move towards more orthodox policies of containment of communism in the later period – and by the intense bureaucratic and personal rivalries between White House and State Department.

This chapter begins with a consideration of the administration's general commitment to human rights, focusing particularly on President Carter's own understanding of the concept and its links to democracy promotion. It discusses the operationalization of the policy, especially in the context of the bureaucratic politics of the administration. How far did the human rights policy succeed in its goals? To what extent did it help or hinder the cause of global democracy? There follows a section on policy towards the Soviet Union. What was Carter's contribution to the unravelling of Soviet communism?

The policy

Jimmy Carter's commitment to human rights in foreign policy was developed in a rather *ad hoc* fashion on the campaign trail in 1976. However, its roots were evident in Carter's own beliefs, in his reactions to the Vietnam War and the Kissinger years, and in what he saw as the possibility of restoring internationalist foreign policy consensus to the Democratic Party.

Carter imbibed and reflected an ideological commitment to American global leadership, rooted in moral purpose. More profound even than his identification with an American historic mission to spread democratic rights, however, was his religious belief. Carter's religious sense may be understood as a kind of optimistic Nieburhism. He recognized Reinhold Niebuhr as perhaps the major influence on his political outlook. For Carter, the evangelical Christian, human perfectibility was not possible on earth, even in a 'city on a hill': 'The perfect standard is one that human beings don't quite reach, but we try to.'[3] His foreign policy would *try* – though, by the highest standards, inevitably fail – to achieve justice in a fallen world in which real progress towards justice is possible. Any tendency towards messianism in Carter's thinking was held back not only by deep appreciation of limits to human perfectibility, it was also tempered by his enthusiasm, presented in his 1976 campaign autobiography, for managerial or technocratic 'solutions' to political questions. Equally influential in Carter's thinking was his commitment to the exigencies of the 'age of limits', as expressed in the Inaugural Address: 'We have learned that "more" is not necessarily "better", that even our great nation has its recognized limits, and that we can neither answer all questions nor solve all problems.'[4]

In foreign policy terms, recognition of limits meant learning the lessons of the Vietnam War. The recent conflict had come to be seen by the Democratic mainstream in the mid-1970s as having been driven by a combination of hubris and what Carter called in 1977 'that inordinate fear of communism which had once led the US to embrace dictators'.[5] The human rights initiatives had their immediate genesis in this reaction to the Vietnam War, and in the various initiatives undertaken by Members of Congress such as Tom Harkin and Donald Fraser in the early 1970s. Far from promoting democracy in Vietnam, Presidents Lyndon Johnson and Richard Nixon had supported illiberal leaders in Saigon in the name of democratic freedoms. The various initiatives of Nixon and Kissinger had extended a kind of power-oriented amorality to American policy across the globe, even as they ignored democratic checks on executive authority within the United States itself. The Helsinki Accords of 1975 had begun to involve the United States in some commitment to promoting democratic rights in the Soviet Union, but for Carter the Nixon–Kissinger–Ford legacy was primarily a negative one – 'policy by manipulation' rather than internationalism grounded in respect for personal liberties.[6] Part of any successful post-Vietnam War foreign policy involved the restoration of an internationalist consensus, and a commitment to 'human rights' presented itself as a way to glue together opposing wings of the Democratic Party. One wing had long demanded an end to policies of supporting dictators, notably military governments in Latin America, in the name of freedom. Human rights advocacy could also, however, appeal to the wing of the party (led by Senator Henry Jackson and including Senator Daniel Patrick Moynihan) that urged action in support of democratic freedoms in the Soviet Union. Carter praised Jackson's efforts in 1976 to tie trade with the USSR to a liberalization of restrictions on Jewish emigration. Moynihan remarked to Sam Brown (the former anti-Vietnam War activist and leftist Democrat) at the 1976 nominating convention: 'We'll be against the dictators you don't like the most … if you'll be against the dictators we don't like the most.'[7]

Carter's embrace of 'human rights' raised major problems of definition, including the extent to which human rights advocacy was more or less coterminous with the promotion of democratic freedoms. The best-known effort to define 'human rights' in the context of Carter's foreign policy was that made by Secretary of State Cyrus Vance in April 1977. For Vance, 'human rights' included 'integrity of the person' rights, notably in respect of torture and arbitrary arrest; the 'right to fulfilment of such vital needs as food, shelter, health care and education'; and 'civil and political liberties', notably in respect of voting, free speech and travel. Vance's definition clearly indicated the possibility that 'human rights' could extend beyond common definitions of democracy promotion, including economic rights. Carter himself sometimes included economic rights as part of his commitment to 'human rights', while Andrew Young (Ambassador to the United Nations until his sacking in 1979) described poverty as 'the basic obstacle to the realisation of human rights for most people'. Besides political and even economic rights – what White House staffer Jessica Tuchman called the right to '800 calories a day' – senior administration figures also sometimes appealed to the simple right to live in peace. Carter declared in December 1978 that 'the most basic right' was 'to be free of arbitrary violence – whether that violence comes from governments, from terrorists, from criminals, or from self-appointed messiahs operating under the cover of politics or religion'.[8]

The administration's tendency to move beyond a simple identification of 'human rights' with democracy promotion reflected contemporary philosophical debates associated with the late twentieth-century 'rights revolution'.[9] It also derived from administration discomfort about charges of cultural and attitudinal imperialism – the advancement, or even imposition, of narrowly based political and civil liberties in respect of countries with differing cultures and economic conditions. Moving beyond democratic liberties as a working definition of 'human rights', however, opened Washington to the charge that it was flinging stones from a glasshouse. Andrew Young famously referred to 'hundreds, perhaps even thousands' of people 'I would call political prisoners in the US' during a discussion of the treatment of Soviet dissidents.[10] The administration never achieved a reliable definition of 'human rights'. A working definition effectively emerged from domestic legislation, notably the 1974 Foreign Assistance Act, which proscribed aid to countries with a 'consistent pattern of gross violations' of 'internationally recognised human rights', including torture, arbitrary detention and 'flagrant denials of the right to life, liberty and the security of the person'. The administration also sought to evade charges of imperialism, by appealing (as in Vance's three-part definition of 1977) to the 1948 Universal Declaration of Human Rights.

Bureaucratic politics

The human rights agenda was compromised by definitional ambiguities, always tending to expose tensions between rights, interests and the principle of state sovereignty. Presidential Directive 30, issued in February 1978, announced the intention to pursue human rights on a global basis, though in accord both 'with the cultural, political and historical characteristics of each nation' and with 'fundamental US interest'. A White House staffer described intra-administration debates about human rights in 1977:

> It's pretty easy to say torture, political imprisonment, arbitrary murder violate human rights. Beyond that, you start getting into important political areas. Some say it begins at breakfast, it's having jobs. Then you get into arguments about trade-offs: liberty versus having a job ... Even if you could establish a natural law of human rights – and there *is* a bit of natural law – there are other considerations of value to us: a country whose security is at issue.[11]

Anthony Lake, who served in the Carter administration as head of policy planning in the State Department, wrote:

> Unhappily, in a complicated world ... any but the most simple of political philosophies – when put into practice – may collide as often as they coincide. So it was with the principles of respect for the sovereignty of other nations and support for human rights.[12]

Beyond these clashes of principles, the human rights policy consistently encountered problems of uneven leverage. If a rights-abusing nation was in receipt of foreign aid from Washington, the way forward was reasonably clear: the executive should recommend to Congress that aid be cut off or possibly made contingent on improvements. In the case of countries not in receipt of American aid, Washington could only exhort, publicize misbehaviour and perhaps urge international sanctions. In respect of recipients, the administration often had to run the gauntlet of lobbies in Congress that favoured the continuance of aid. Even if aid were suspended, there was every likelihood that this would impact negatively on general populations rather than their rights-abusing governments.

The job of effectuating human rights policy in a way that overcame these dangers fell to former Mississippi civil rights activist Patricia Derian, who was appointed head of the Human Rights Bureau at the State Department. She told Warren Christopher, the Deputy Secretary of State: 'If you want a magnolia to decorate foreign policy, I'm the wrong person. I expect to get things done.'[13] Along with her deputy Mark Schneider, Derian declared war on State Department traditions of clientelism and professionalism shading into cynicism. Resistance from the career bureaucracy took subtle forms, including the under-reporting of abuses by regional bureaus. The East Asia Bureau (headed by Richard Holbrooke) consistently argued that the aid cuts to the regime of Ferdinand Marcos in the Philippines would risk the United States losing vital basing facilities there. Holbrooke and Derian were openly antagonistic.[14] Beyond resistance from the bureaucracy at State, Derian's initiatives were undermined by simple uncertainty about the extent to which Carter was in fact committed to human rights as a cause that would transcend all others. Joyce Starr, a White House aide who dealt with human rights issues, wrote in 1978 that 'Derian is not perceived within the Department as a spokesperson for the President. Her wins and losses are essentially dependent on the consensus and support of Secretary Vance and Warren Christopher.'[15] D. C. McGaffney, a diplomat, put the problem as follows:

> No-one in the Foreign Service assumed that President Carter was politically naive, or totally cynical. Unfortunately, the human rights policy as enunciated did not give sufficient guidance or definition to determine exactly where between these extremes the real, desired policy would fall.[16]

Crucially, Vance and Christopher declined to support Derian's efforts to include military assistance under the bureaucratic aegis of the Human Rights Bureau. They effectively sided with Undersecretary of State Lucy Benson, who wished to keep such assistance outside the control of the inter-agency group (chaired by Christopher) that adjudicated on human rights issues across the administration. By 1978, the Christopher Group was primarily concerned with American policy concerning funding from the multilateral development banks (such as the Inter-American and African Development Banks) rather than with security assistance.[17] It did not deal directly with decisions relating to the International Monetary Fund either. Within the foreign policy bureaucracy, security assistance came under the aegis of an inter-agency group chaired by Benson instead. The Human Rights Bureau did have representation on the Benson Group, however, and sometimes appealed decisions directly to Christopher. The Christopher Group adjudicated private arms sales to countries identified by the State Department as transgressing international human rights norms. Its approach was consciously a case-by-case one. This prioritized flexibility and the integration of human rights and security concerns, but it also further exposed the administration to charges of inconsistency and left private arms contractors with little guidance about which sales were likely to be approved. Caleb Rossiter, a staffer in Congress who was concerned with arms sales, commented that it made the United States 'look silly when' it 'blocks a loan to South Korea but gives them a thousand military helmets'.[18] The Christopher Group developed its own guidelines for weighing security against human rights concerns. These included a preference for 'quiet diplomacy' over formal sanctions and an awareness that human rights norms would vary from country to country. The Group also gave particular priority to 'integrity of the person' violations, and relatively little to less drastic questions of procedural democracy. Derian later commented: 'I never really understood Christopher's mode of decision.'[19]

Beyond the State Department, the institutionalization of human rights met even stiffer resistance. The Department of Defence during the Carter years saw no significant efforts to institutionalize human rights concerns. At the National Security Council (NSC), it is tempting simply to assert that everything came under the sway of anti-communist *Realpolitik* as represented in the person of National Security Adviser Zbigniew Brzezinski. In broad terms, the rivalry between the NSC and the State Department came to define and compromise Carter's entire foreign policy. President Carter saw Vance and Brzezinski as representing those wings of the Democratic Party and the foreign policy establishment that would have to be accommodated if the United States was to achieve a viable post-Vietnam War internationalism. The two men, however, clashed personally, stylistically and ideologically. Vance's collegial approach was utterly removed from the confrontational style of Brzezinski. The two foreign policy principals also differed in how they understood the world: Vance's post-Vietnam War caution and serious commitment to post-Soviet containment agendas vied with Brzezinski's traditional Cold War commitments. As early as February 1977, Brzezinski informed Carter that the 'primary task' of the United States was 'to inhibit disruptive Soviet acts […] Our policies in every region must be related to an overarching coherent strategy for gradually transforming the nature of the Soviet challenge'.[20] From such a perspective, democracy promotion was always likely to be regarded by the National Security Adviser as best effected through the containment (and indeed ultimate defeat) of Soviet communism, rather than via the kind of internationalist human rights activism represented by Derian and generally backed by Vance. In his memoir, *Power and Principle*, Brzezinski recalled that Carter 'thirsted for the Wilsonian mantle'. He apparently cautioned the president: 'before you are a President Wilson you have to be for a few years a President Truman'. Regarding Carter's human rights initiatives, Brzezinski 'put stronger emphasis' on 'the notion that strengthening American power was the necessary point of departure'. He 'saw in human rights an opportunity to put the Soviet Union ideologically on the defensive'. For Brzezinski, it was Carter's return to clear support for democracy in the context of post-1978 anti-Sovietism, rather than in the context of broadly defined human rights, which underpinned the administration's claim to represent moral virtue: 'It was Carter's major accomplishment that, by the time he left office, there was more widespread appreciation worldwide that America stood again for principle and identified itself with the movement for more social and political justice'.[21]

The Vance–Brzezinski split was deeply damaging to the coherence of Carter's foreign policy. The president's unwillingness to adjudicate clearly the rivalry, even as the National Security Adviser outflanked the Secretary of State in bureaucratic influence, was a key Carter failure. However, from the viewpoint of human rights and democracy promotion, a few qualifications can be made to this rather stark, received view of the inner workings of the Carter administration. For one thing, Brzezinski was not *simply* an anti-communist ideologue. It is difficult to reduce his approach to simple formulae. However, his general views about the centrality of Soviet aggression may be said to have combined elements of traditional, moralistic anti-communism with strong elements of Kissingerian *Realpolitik* – both rooted in a strong appreciation of how the world had changed since the era of the Vietnam War. Brzezinski's academic background had included work on totalitarian systems, but also on global interdependence and north–south conceptions of global relations. A major policy statement produced for Carter in April 1977 described 'an unstable world organised almost entirely on the principle of national sovereignty and yet increasingly interdependent socially and economically'. The paper espoused the cause (promoted by the Rockefeller-backed Trilateral Commission, the forum where Brzezinski and Carter first came together) of inter-capitalist – notably American–Japanese–West European – cooperation. It called for a prioritization of north–south relations and enhancement of 'global sensitivity' regarding human rights. Regarding democracy promotion, Brzezinski's paper looked in contradictory directions: towards normalizing relations with the Peoples' Republic of China, and towards moving South Africa towards multi-racial democracy, along with a majority-rule, democratic settlement in Rhodesia-Zimbabwe. Deterrence and containment of the Soviet Union were emphasized, but not to the exclusion of other agendas.[22]

Brzezinski's staff included a human rights officer within its 'global issues cluster'. Between 1977 and 1979, the human rights officer at the NSC, Jessica Tuchman, worked assiduously on Soviet-related human rights issues, notably as they related to Jewish emigration and to congressional efforts to pass legislation in this area. She also saw her job as encompassing the raising of the profile of American support for human rights internationally, including the promotion of democracy in the developing world. In January 1978, she described the raising of human rights as 'the major accomplishment' of the administration. World leaders, she said, 'know that their human rights image is a significant factor in their standing in the international community – as well as in their relationship to the US'.[23] It would certainly be wrong to see Brzezinski and his staff as opposed in any blanket fashion to democracy promotion (essentially as an aspect of human rights) as understood in Derian's State Department bureau. However, the ground rules became fairly clear. Non-security 'global issues' were not at the forefront of NSC concerns; indeed they were referred to on occasion as 'globaloney'. Tensions between Derian and the NSC are evident from the archival record. In March 1977, Brzezinski warned Carter of human rights initiatives in Latin America leading to simultaneous bad relations with Brazil, Argentina and Chile. A 1979 NSC staff memo described 'a considerable amount of history' between Derian and Brzezinski 'on the subject of Argentina'.[24]

The record

It should be emphasized that the human rights policy in general, and its links to democracy promotion in particular, varied greatly across regions. Issues of uneven leverage, perceptions of national security interest and specialized bureaucratic focus militated against consistency. Various efforts have been made to measure the impact of Carter's human rights agenda across the globe. A Congressional Research Service study of 1981 concluded that the policy affected the behaviour of rights-abusing governments only marginally. Efforts to establish correlations between aid levels and human rights conditions – as measured by organizations such as Amnesty International and Freedom House, or indeed by the State Department itself – are very inconclusive. Scholarship in this area is complicated by the fact that in the Carter years some countries (such as Brazil and Uruguay) sometimes rejected aid in protest against what they regarded as improper American interference in their affairs.[25] It can also be argued that the real impact of the Carter policies occurred over the long term: that Carter contributed to the wave of democratization associated with the end of the Cold War; indeed that Carter (as is considered below) contributed significantly to ending the Cold War; that (as Jessica Tuchman maintained in 1978) Carter put human rights and democratic freedoms at the top of the international agenda in a way that no other government could ignore; and that human rights became institutionalized within the foreign policy bureaucracy.

Given the incidence of military dictatorship in Latin America, it was probably in the Western hemisphere that human rights joined most closely to democracy promotion. Carter later wrote:

> Most South American countries had military governments when I became president, and we actively encouraged movements to democracy, using our aggressive human rights policy as a lever. Most of the governments began changing before I left office, and all nations in Latin America ultimately developed democracies, except Cuba, which has clung to a dictatorship.[26]

In Latin America, Washington had far more leverage to effect change than elsewhere. Even there, however, the administration did not see itself as embarking on a crusade for democracy. Rather, human rights initiatives were to be part of a 'post-imperial' foreign policy, sensitive to local cultures and with renegotiation of the Panama Canal Treaty at its centre. Interpretation of Carter's Latin American policies veers between neoconservative condemnation of excessive accommodation to communist influence and inability to escape the logic of American hemispheric imperialism.[27] For current purposes, it is important to emphasize that experiences in Latin America stand at the centre of efforts to judge Carter's democracy promotion record. As Tom Harkin put it:

> We always hear it said, 'Well, we don't want to interfere in those countries. We don't want to go in there and mess in their internal affairs'. I don't see why not. We have been doing it for a hundred years anyway ... We are going to influence Latin America ... The question is how.[28]

The Carter administration certainly developed a public attitude towards the big South American dictatorships that was far more critical than that inherited from the Republican years. Carter's personal trips to Brazil, Argentina and Chile involved direct discussion of human rights abuses. His diary entries (published in 2010) record his genuine concerns, even if in a slightly unfortunately naive tone. In 1977, Carter 'informed' General Augusto Pinochet of Chile 'about the serious problem of human rights deprivation'. Carter writes: 'He seems to be a very strong leader, sure of himself, beginning to be more worried about outside condemnation on human rights issues, and defensive of their attitudes (sic) because of instability in Chile.'[29] Significant cuts in aid were made in respect of South America's military governments, despite the power of relevant supporting lobbies in Congress. The impact of American pressure, however, was blunted by scepticism (for example, among staff at the American Embassy in Buenos Aires) about the efficacy of human rights initiatives. Though military and non-military aid to the dictatorships was cut, the administration tended merely to abstain in multilateral bank loan voting, effectively allowing loans to proceed. Derian's agency worked closely with Argentinean groups protesting about the huge numbers of 'disappeared' democratic oppositionists.[30] Jacobo Timerman, a jailed Argentinean editor, wrote in 1981: 'Those of us who were imprisoned, those of us who are in prison still, will never forget President Carter and his contribution to the battle for human rights.'[31] Claims have been made that American pressure caused the dictatorships at least to modify their behaviour. Repression in Argentina tailed off a little in 1979, though arguably as much in response to the effective elimination of opposition as a reaction to American pressure. In the case of Brazil, American pressure for demo-cratization became complicated by issues relating to nuclear arms proliferation. It can, however, be argued plausibly that Carter's policies contributed directly to the fall from power of the military dictatorship in Ecuador.[32] Despite this, Carter's South American democratization record is not particularly impressive, at least not in any way that is directly measurable in cause-and-effect terms. Moreover, pressure to democratize was noticeably lessened in 1980, as the administration turned more directly to a policy of opposing communist influence in the Western hemisphere. The American Embassy in Buenos Aires reported in March 1980 that the Argentinean regime believed Washington was now 'in retreat from its human rights concerns'.[33]

The switch towards more direct anti-communism in the region was associated with events in Nicaragua, where Carter's policies bore the imprint of severe bureaucratic battles and contradictory pressures. The cause of applying pressure on the Nicaraguan dictator, Anastasio Somoza, was advanced clearly on Capitol Hill (notably by Congressman Ed Koch of New York), as well as by Derian's bureau. It was opposed by strongly anti-communist sections of Congress, notably on the House Appropriations Committee, and by influential elements within the State Department and the NSC. The resulting policy was a kind of carrot-and-stick process, which left the administration open to the charge that it had opened the way to the leftist Sandinista revolution of 1979. Administration reactions to the revolution were confused. In terms of democracy promotion, Carter achieved little in Central America. Enhanced support for repressive regimes, notably in El Salvador, earlier the subject of security aid termination, was evident by 1980.[34]

If human rights policy in Latin America was preoccupied by efforts to ameliorate abuses conducted by dictatorial regimes, set within debates about the relevance of traditional anti-communist policy, African democracy promotion focused on issues of race. A State Department Africanist interviewed in 1977 declared that 'our first priority in Africa is elimination of racism, and human rights deprivations are second'.[35] 'Regionalists' in the administration, led by Andrew Young, sought to promote 'progressive' policies in Africa with little reference to Soviet and Cuban involvement in the continent, while putting opposition to the apartheid regime in South Africa at the centre of attention. Policy towards South Africa involved moving away from the containment-oriented stance of the Kissinger years, and towards much clearer condemnation of the apartheid regime. Indeed, Betty Glad argues,

> The administration ... upheld UN sanctions to maintain pressure on the South African government to dismantle the apartheid system. These and other external pressures led to the release of Nelson Mandela from prison ten years later, and the subsequent negotiations with Afrikaaner President F. W. de Klerk issued in a new postapartheid regime.[36]

The drift of Carter's policy, however, was not unequivocally to isolate Pretoria. Thus, Andrew Young supported American corporate investment under the terms of the Sullivan Code, which committed investors to fair employment practices. South Africa policy also became bound up in efforts to secure a majority-rule settlement in Rhodesia/Zimbabwe, as well as recognition by Pretoria of Namibian independence. Elsewhere in Africa, aid was cut to Tunisia, Ethiopia and the Central African Empire in response to State Department-identified human rights abuses. Carter personally pressed Zaire's ruler, Joseph Mobutu, to make democratic reforms. As in some other regions, some cosmetic changes were made – in this case, competitive local elections. However, Zaire – a major source of cobalt – remained in receipt of substantial American aid despite continuing human rights abuses.[37]

Zaire was one of several countries – Guinea, Haiti, Somalia and Liberia were others – specifically exempted from human rights-related aid cuts because these were deemed more likely to damage the general population than to move the regimes towards democracy.[38] Such considerations were real, at least in the case of non-military aid, and one should be careful not automatically to assume that perceived security interests trumped human rights. However, especially looking beyond Latin America and Africa, it is difficult to find much evidence of concerted and consistent application of democracy promotion, at least in the context of the human rights policy. Carter's greatest diplomatic triumph, the Camp David agreement between Egypt and Israel, qualifies as successful 'peace promotion' rather than 'democracy promotion' in any meaningful sense. In fact, it is very easy to identify countries that 'escaped' any serious application of human rights-oriented democracy promotion. Carter attempted to move the Shah of Iran towards some kind of democratic opening, but was met by cosmetic gestures and invocations of the dangers posed by Iranian communists. In May 1977, Vance promised the Shah that all arms contracts from the Republican years would be honoured. Washington tried to encourage a parliamentarist solution following the upheavals of 1978–79, and prior to the takeover by radical Islamists. No regional democratic progress was made.[39] Normalization of relations with China proceeded without concern for democratic rights. The administration repeatedly supported the granting of most-favoured-nation trading status to Romania, seen by Washington in this period as prepared rather courageously to resist complete Soviet domination. In Pakistan, the regime of General Zia Ul Haq was initially criticized and sanctioned as a result of the arrest and execution of former Prime Minister Zulfikar Ali Bhutto. But following the Soviet invasion of Afghanistan, Zia was welcomed in Washington with an offer of enhanced aid.[40]

Carter, the Soviet Union and the end of the Cold War

Rather than human rights and democracy promotion, Carter's policy towards the USSR was principally shaped by the perceived need to reach some kind of meaningful arms control deal, thereby responding to innovations in the Soviet nuclear programme. Until 1979, the relationship with Moscow was conducted broadly within the framework of *détente*, despite Carter's earlier criticisms that the Ford–Kissinger understanding of *détente* had yielded too much to Moscow, not least in the area of internal freedoms. Following the Soviet invasion of Afghanistan, SALT II (the strategic arms treaty signed in June 1979) was withdrawn from consideration by the Senate. The regime of international détente – the centrepiece of the Nixon–Kissinger–Ford foreign policy – was now at an end. In Presidential Directive 59, issued in July 1980, the administration moved in effect to a 'nuclear war-fighting' doctrine in the event of deterrence failing. Carter recommended massive defence spending increases, ending the squeeze on military outlays that had prevailed since the defeat in Vietnam. He committed himself additionally to the new accurate and mobile MX missile system, essentially opening the way for the policies of the Reagan administration.[41]

In this story of collapsing *détente* and the failure of arms control, where exactly did the administration's commitment to promoting democratic freedoms in the USSR sit? How did it relate to the inheritance from Nixon and Ford? Carter welcomed, and sought to extend the Helsinki process – especially the so-called 'basket three' provisions on human rights. He regarded Washington's support for rights within the USSR under the Helsinki Final Act as having been forced on Ford and Kissinger by Congress, and undertook to take up the cause of internal freedoms within the USSR in a way that broke with the approach of the Republican years. Central here was Carter's early explicit rejection of the Kissingerian concept of 'linkage'. At a press conference in February 1977, Carter declared: 'I think we come out better in dealing with the Soviet Union if I am consistently and completely dedicated to the enhancement of human rights.' Human rights concerns

> can legitimately be severed from our inclination to work with the Soviet Union, for instance, in reducing dependence upon atomic weapons ... I don't want the two to be tied together. I think the previous administration, under Secretary Kissinger, thought there ought to be this linkage.[42]

Carter sought, in effect, to manage competitive and cooperative aspects of the American–Soviet relationship separately. This put him at odds, not only with the Kissinger legacy, but also with efforts to tie internal freedoms (notably in relation to Jewish emigration) to progress in other areas. Carter thus opened himself to attack from *Realpolitik* conservatives, from pro-*détente* liberals *and* from moralistic anti-Soviet neoconservatives.[43]

Carter pressed ahead with verbal attacks on Soviet treatment of dissidents. To some extent, the president was running against the grain of bureaucratic commitments to arms control, though the official line remained that 'linkage' was a doctrine of the past. Both Marshall Shulman (chief adviser to Vance on Soviet affairs) and Malcolm Toon (retained as the American Ambassador in Moscow from the Ford years) were more or less openly dismissive of the wisdom and practical purpose of advancing the cause of personal freedoms in the USSR. In fact, Moscow's persecution of dissident intellectuals in particular had intensified in the wake of the Helsinki agreement. The Helsinki Final Act had been accepted by Moscow as recognizing the Soviet sway in Eastern Europe and as making only symbolic commitments to internal Soviet freedoms. Carter's championing the cause of intellectuals such as physicist Andrei Sakharov and Jewish dissident leader Anatoly (Natan) Sharansky was greeted by the Soviets with a mixture of incomprehension and irritation. Soviet Foreign Minister Andrei Gromyko in 1978 was apparently unaware of who Sharansky was, and subsequently regarded his arrest as an 'absurd' matter. Carter was accused by the Henry Jackson wing of his own party of downplaying human rights issues during the SALT negotiations; though at the Vienna summit (where SALT was finally agreed) Carter made a personal appeal to Soviet leader Leonid Brezhnev for Sharansky's release. (The appeal was ineffectual and he was finally released in 1986.) President Carter was aware of Soviet sensitivities over the dissident intellectuals. He was also aware that some members of his own administration (including Young) tended to see Sakharov and Sharansky as figureheads of an unrepresentative elite in the USSR. Carter emphasized that his calls for democratic freedoms had very wide implications; for example, for those Soviet and Eastern European citizens (like his fellow Baptists) suffering religious persecution. He condemned the 1978–79 dissident trials of Sharansky, Aleksandr Ginzburg, Victoras Pektus and others as an 'attack on every human being in the world who believes in basic human freedoms'.[44]

What did Carter's stance on internal freedoms in the USSR, clearly very personal and deeply felt as it was, actually achieve? According to Anatoly Dobrynin, the veteran Soviet ambassador to Washington, Carter's insistence on raising these issues prevented an arms deal being agreed in late 1977 or early 1978.[45] Such a judgement probably understates the non-human-rights-related obstacles to an arms control deal, notably American normalization with China. However, the general scholarly verdict on Carter's Soviet policy is that it was muddled from the very start (when Vance made his 1977 arms cuts proposals) to the end (when Moscow reacted to Presidential Directive 50 by announcing the start of a new arms race). The efforts to promote internal freedoms in the Soviet Union were, in this line of criticism, worthy but essentially naive and counter-productive. For Burton Kaufman, Carter 'was long on good intentions, but short on know-how'.[46] Strobe Talbott, later chief Russia adviser to President Bill Clinton, regarded the Carter stance as 'little more than a combination of symbolic gestures'.[47] In this analysis, the Helsinki process went nowhere after 1975. Moscow reacted to Carter's 'interference' by ratcheting up repression in the 1978–79 dissident trials while the collapse of *détente* removed any possible restraint on Soviet behaviour.

It cannot be pretended that, any more than in Latin America, Carter's human rights activism in regard to the USSR achieved much measurable progress in the short run, though there is some evidence of emigration restrictions being eased after 1978. Moscow began to exile dissidents rather than to subject them to arrest and formal show-trial.[48] A positive interpretation of Carter's policy, however, is possible. This would recognize the encouragement given to dissent in the Soviet Union. Dissidents *welcomed* Carter's interventions, in spite of the common view that this made it impossible for Moscow to make concessions. In a television interview in March 1977, Sakharov answered 'categorically – no!' to the question of whether Carter's line might stimulate greater abuses of human rights. Ida Milgrom, mother of Sharansky, wrote in an open letter to Carter:

> All the difficult days of the trial, I have been standing in front of the iron barriers, in front of a thick wall of KGB and militiamen … All these days I have heard your sincere, authoritative voice in defence of innocent men.[49]

Such considerations lead us to the final concern of this chapter: Carter's putative role in the ending of the Cold War.

The collapse of the Soviet Union and its empire in the late 1980s represented the major achievement for the cause of democracy promotion since the allied victory in the Second World War. When the Berlin Wall fell, various explanations for the breakthrough were advanced. These ran the gamut from 'Reagan victory' (the view that the American policy of negotiating from strength in the 1980s had delivered the goods) through 'autonomous Soviet collapse' (the argument that the Soviet system, whether or not squeezed by American policies of containment, had simply become unviable by 1989) to the triumph of the 'liberal idea'. While Carter generally receives little direct credit in any of these explanations, it is possible to present his policies as contributing to the plausibility of at least some of them. After all, if Ronald Reagan's tough anti-Soviet policies are seen as having caused the Soviet system to implode, then Carter should be given credit for returning to militarized containment in 1979. The Carter administration's reaction to the Soviet invasion of Afghanistan, rather than Reagan's election in 1980, was the key turning point in America's recommitment to the Cold War. This chapter concludes, however, not by arguing along these lines, but by suggesting that Carter's early, human rights-oriented foreign policy deserves to be taken seriously by students of the Cold War's end.

Part of the argument here relates to the question of 'overstretch'. One plausible narrative of the end of the Cold War involves the dialectical dance between American and Soviet overreaching. The American defeat in Vietnam – itself the product of American overstretching in a country far removed from its core security interest – led to excessive Soviet confidence and emboldening. As the USSR became increasingly active in the revolutionary politics of the developing world in the post-1975 years, it took over the role of global overstretcher from the United States. Under Carter, the United States initially stepped back from the Cold War, focusing on the kind of north–south human rights and post-imperialist democracy promotion policies considered above. Such a stance proved beneficial to the United States, even as Moscow's enervating overstretch led it into the eventually disastrous military occupation of Afghanistan.[50]

Beyond this argument regarding 'overstretch', the case for seeing Carter's version of democracy promotion as part of the story of the Cold War's end rests upon the degree to which the fall of Soviet communism was linked to a triumph of values. By 1989, the mass emotional and intellectual appeal of Soviet communism was at a very low ebb. To some degree this was simply due to the failure of the Soviet system to deliver the economic goods. The values and glamour of Western consumerism had been communicated eastwards. To quote Fred Halliday, 'It was the T-shirt and the supermarket, not the gunboat or the cheaper manufacturers that destroyed the legitimacy and stability of the Soviet system.'[51] Beyond the values of consumerism, however, the 'liberal idea' in its political guise had also grown globally. The values of free expression espoused by the Soviet dissidents, and encouraged by Carter, played an important role here. Carter's human rights policy had many inconsistencies. The State Department condemned the persecution of pro-democracy Charter 77 intellectuals in Czechoslovakia, yet the United States had little alternative but to recognize Moscow's domination of Eastern Europe. Polish democracy activist and later Prime Minister Tadeusz Mazowiecki later testified to the potency of Carter's support for human rights in encouraging Eastern European democratic opponents of Moscow.[52] However, as we have seen, when Washington sought to encourage this defiance of Moscow, it fell into the awful trap of wooing the rights-abusing Ceausescu regime in Romania. Nevertheless, and despite all the imperfections of the human rights policy, the Carter administration did manage to identify itself with democratic values. It did so, to a significant extent, in a way that distinguished American democracy promotion from the ways of imperialism. Lest such arguments be regarded as special pleading, it is worth pointing out that, in his memoir, *From the Shadows*, Robert Gates (CIA Director under George H. W. Bush and Secretary of Defence under George W. Bush and Barack Obama) made precisely this point: that Carter managed in his human rights policy – not least regarding the Soviet dissidents – to defend and spread the liberal idea.[53] Gates was correct. Jimmy Carter's greatest contribution to democracy promotion consisted in putting the United States (however imperfectly) at least for a time on the side of post-imperial democratic values.

Notes

1 See William I. Robinson, *Promoting Polyarchy: Globalization, US Intervention, and Hegemony* (Cambridge: Cambridge University Press, 1996).

2 For a linking of Carter to the paradoxes of Wilsonian democracy promotion, see Gaddis Smith, *Morality, Reason and Power: American Diplomacy in the Carter Years* (New York: Hill and Wang, 1986) and Betty Glad, *An Outsider in the White House: Jimmy Carter, His Advisors, and the Making of American Foreign Policy* (Ithaca: Cornell University Press, 2009), pp. 279–82. Critiques from the right include: Joshua Muravchik, *The Uncertain Crusade: Jimmy Carter and the Dilemmas of Human Rights* (Lanham MD: Hamilton Press, 1986) and Brian Auten, *Carter's Conversion: The Hardening of American Defense Policy* (Columbia: University of Missouri Press, 2008). For a variety of more positive views, see Jerel A. Rosati, *The Carter Administration's Quest for Global Community: Beliefs and their Impact on Behavior* (Columbia: University of South Carolina Press, 1991); John Dumbrell, *The Carter Presidency: A Reevaluation* (Manchester: Manchester University Press, second edition, 1995); Douglas Brinkley, 'The Rising Stock of Jimmy Carter: The "Hands On" Legacy of our Thirty-ninth President', *Diplomatic History*, 20, 1996, 505–29; Robert A. Strong, *Working the World: Jimmy Carter and the Making of American Foreign Policy* (Baton Rouge: Louisiana State University Press, 2000); and David F. Schmitz and Vanessa Walker, 'Jimmy Carter and the Foreign Policy of Human Rights: The Development of a Post-Cold War Foreign Policy', *Diplomatic History*, 28, 2004, 113–43. For a clear statement of the putatively confused nature of Carter's foreign policy, see Scott Kaufman, *Plans Unraveled: The Foreign Policy of the Carter Administration* (DeKalb: Northern Illinois University Press, 2008), pp. 13–17, 237–41.

3 William L. Miller, *Yankee from Georgia: The Emergence of Jimmy Carter* (New York: Times Books, 1978), p. 220; Jimmy Carter, *Why Not the Best? The First Fifty Years* (New York: Bantam Books).

4 Jimmy Carter, Inaugural Address, available via Carter Presidential Library website; Jimmy Carter, *Why Not the Best? The First Fifty Years* (New York: Bantam Books, 1975).

5 Jimmy Carter, Commencement Address, University of Notre Dame, 22 May 1977, available via Carter Presidential Library website.
6 ibid.
7 Daniel Patrick Moynihan, 'The Politics of Human Rights', *Commentary*, August 1977, p. 22.
8 See Dumbrell, *The Carter Presidency*, pp. 119–20; Jimmy Carter, *Keeping Faith: Memoirs of a President* (London: Collins, 1982), p. 144; Muravchik, *Uncertain Crusade*, p. 96.
9 See, for example, Bruce Ackerman, *Social Justice in the Liberal State* (New Haven: Yale University Press, 1980).
10 Carl Gershman, 'The World According to Andrew Young', *Commentary*, March 1978, p. 20; see also Donald S. Spencer, *The Carter Implosion: Jimmy Carter and the Amateur Style of Diplomacy* (New York: Praeger, 1988), p. 55.
11 Elizabeth Drew, 'A Reporter at Large: Human Rights', *The New Yorker*, 18 July 1977, p. 42; Glad, *An Outsider in the White House*, p. 70.
12 Anthony Lake, *Somoza Falling: A Case Study of Washington at Work* (Boston: Houghton Mifflin, 1989), p. 21.
13 Glad, *Outsider in the White House*, p. 23.
14 See Stephen B. Cohen, 'Conditioning US Security Assistance on Human Rights Practices', *American Journal of International Law*, 76, 1982, pp. 246–72, 259.
15 Memo to Robert Lipshutz from Joyce Starr, 19 June 1978, Box 46, SO: Lipshutz (folder, 'Soviet Jewry') (Carter Presidential Library).
16 D. C. McGaffney, 'Policy and Practice: Human Rights in the Shah's Iran', in David D. Newsom, ed., *The Diplomacy of Human Rights* (Lanham MD: University Press of America, 1986), pp. 69–79, 69; see also Cyrus Vance, *Hard Choices: Critical Years in America's Foreign Policy* (New York: Simon and Schuster, 1983).
17 See Kaufman, *Plans Unraveled*, pp. 30–31.
18 Edwin S. Maynard, 'The Bureaucracy and Implementation of US Human Rights Policy', *Human Rights Quarterly*, 11, 1989, pp. 175–248, 217.
19 William M. Schmidli, 'Institutionalizing Human Rights in US Foreign Policy: US-Argentine Relations, 1976–80', *Diplomatic History*, 35, 2011, 351–77, 373; A. Glenn Mower, *Human Rights and American Foreign Policy* (New York: Greenwood, 1987), p. 75.
20 Glad, *An Outsider in the White House*, p. 25.
21 Zbigniew Brzezinski, *Power and Principle: Memoirs of the National Security Advisor, 1977–81* (New York: Farrar, Straus and Giroux, 1983), pp. 49, 128, 149, 432, 514–15, 520.
22 ibid., pp. 52–54.
23 Glad, *An Outsider in the White House*, p. 249 (also p. 74).
24 Memo from Z. Brzezinski to T. Thornton, 15 June 1979, Box CO-10, White House Central Files, SF: Human Rights (Carter Presidential Library); Christopher C. Shoemaker, *The NSC Staff: Counseling the Council* (Boulder: Westview, 1991), p. 87; Kaufman, *Plans Unraveled*, p. 36.
25 See Muravchik, *The Uncertain Crusade*, p. 170; Steven C. Poe, 'Human Rights and Economic Aid Allocation under Ronald Reagan and Jimmy Carter', *American Journal of Political Science*, 36, 1992, 147–67; John Salzberg, 'The Carter Administration: an Appraisal', in V. P. Nanda, J. Scarritt and G. W. Shepherd, eds., *Global Human Rights* (Boulder: Westview, 1982), pp. 11–22; Steven C. Poe, 'Human Rights and US Foreign Aid', *Human Rights Quarterly*, 12, 1990, 499–512.
26 Jimmy Carter, *White House Diary* (New York: Farrar, Straus and Giroux, 2010), p. 94.
27 For various positions, see Muravchik, *The Uncertain Crusade*; Mark Falcoff, 'Argentina under the Junta', in Daniel Pipes and Adam Garfinkle, eds., *Friendly Tyrants: An American Dilemma* (London: Macmillan, 1991), pp. 153–76; Michael T. Klare and Cynthia Arnson, *Supplying Repression* (Washington, DC: Institute for Policy Studies, 1981); Jenny Pearce, *Under the Eagle* (London: Latin America Bureau, 1982).
28 Quoted in Lars Schoultz, *National Security and United States Policy Toward Latin America* (Princeton: Princeton University Press, 1987), p. 290.
29 Carter, *White House Diary*, p. 91.

30 Schmidli, 'Institutionalizing', pp. 371–72.
31 Cited in David Carleton and David Stohl, 'The Foreign Policy of Human Rights: Rhetoric and Reality from Jimmy Carter to Ronald Reagan', *Human Rights Quarterly*, 7, 1985, 205–29, 226.
32 See Robert Wesson, *The United States and Brazil: Limits of Influence* (New York: Praeger, 1981), p. 151; G. W. Grayson, 'The United States and Latin America: the Challenge of Human Rights', *Current History*, 76, 1979, 38–55; Scmidli, 'Institutionalising', p. 371; Carter, *White House Diary*, pp. 181–82; Glad, *An Outsider in the White House*, p. 242.
33 Schmidli, 'Institutionalising', p. 376.
34 On Carter's policy towards Central America, see Lake, *Somoza Falling*; Robert Pastor, *Condemned to Repetition: The United States and Nicaragua* (Princeton: Princeton University Press, 1987); Dumbrell, *The Carter Presidency*, pp. 150–61; Kaufman, *Plans Unraveled*, pp. 192–93, 229–31.
35 Drew, 'A Reporter at Large', p. 45.
36 Glad, *An Outsider in the White House*, p. 241.
37 See M. G. Schatzberg, 'Zaire under Mobutu', in Pipes and Garfinkle, eds., *Friendly Tyrants*, pp. 420–47.
38 See Muravchik, *The Uncertain Crusade*, p. 122.
39 See Gary Sick, *All Fall Down: America's Tragic Encounter with Iran* (New York: Random House, 1985); David Farber, *Taken Hostage: The Iran Hostage Crisis and America's First Encounter with Radical Islam* (Princeton: Princeton University Press, 2006).
40 Glad, *An Outsider in the White House*, p. 237; Joseph F. Harrington, 'American-Romanian Relations, 1977–81: A Case Study in Carter's Human Rights Policy', in Herbert D. Rosenbaum and Alexej Ugrinsky, eds., *Jimmy Carter: Foreign Policy and the Post-Presidential Years* (Westport: Greenwood, 1994), pp. 89–102; Craig Baxter, 'The United States and Pakistan', in Pipes and Garfinkle, eds., *Friendly Tyrants*, pp. 479–506.
41 See Auten, *Carter's Conversion*; Brzezinski, *Power and Principle*, pp. 455–59; Richard C. Thornton, *The Carter Years: Toward a New Global Order* (New York: Paragon House, 1991).
42 Dumbrell, *The Carter Presidency*, p. 121.
43 See Brzezinski, *Power and Principle*, pp. 150–53.
44 See Spencer, *The Carter Implosion*, p. 45; Carter, *Keeping Faith*, p. 221; Andrei A. Gromyko, *Memoirs* (New York: Doubleday, 1989), p. 293; Anatoly Dobrynin, *In Confidence: Moscow's Ambassador and Six Cold War Presidents* (New York: Crown), p. 399; Dumbrell, *The Carter Presidency*, pp. 124–25.
45 Cited in Kaufman, *Plans Unraveled*, p. 41.
46 Burton I. Kaufman, *The Presidency of James Earl Carter Jr.* (Lawrence: University Press of Kansas, 1993), p. 201 (also p. 193).
47 Strobe Talbott, 'Social Issues', in Joseph S. Nye, ed., *The Making of America's Soviet Policy* (New Haven: Yale University Press, 1984), pp. 183–208, 199.
48 Glad, *An Outsider in the White House*, p. 76.
49 *Prisoners of Conscience in the USSR: Their Treatment and Condition* (London: Amnesty International Report, 1980), p. 2; Andrei D. Sakharov, *Memoirs* (London: Hutchinson, 1990), pp. 462–70.
50 See George C. Herring, 'The Cold War and Vietnam', *Organization of American Historians Magazine of History*, 18, 2004, 18–21; Christopher Andrew and Vasili Mitrokhin, *The World Was Going Our Way: The KGB and the Battle for the Third World* (New York: Basic Books, 2005), pp. 16, 23.
51 Fred Halliday, *Rethinking International Relations* (Basingstoke: Macmillan, 1994), p. 97.
52 Jason Ralph, '"High Stakes" and "Low-Intensity Democracy": Understanding America's Policy of Promoting Democracy', in Michael Cox, G. John Ikenberry and Takashi Imoguchi, eds., *American Democracy Promotion: Impulses, Strategies, and Impacts* (Oxford: Oxford University Press, 2000), pp. 200–217.
53 Robert M. Gates, *From the Shadows: The Ultimate Insider's Story of Five Presidents and How They Won the Cold War* (New York: Simon and Schuster, 1996), p. 177.

8

RONALD REAGAN

Henry R. Nau

Ronald Reagan did much to propel the third great wave of democracy from the late 1970s to the late 1990s. His policies not only vanquished the Soviet Union, the greatest threat to democracy, but they also established the National Endowment for Democracy and inaugurated the era of democracy promotion. Over the next 20 years, 63 of 110 countries that were not free became democratic. Nothing like that ever happened before or is likely to occur again. Since 2006, however, the tide of freedom has crested; more and more countries have become less free. This may be a good moment, therefore, to assess how Reagan thought about the role of democracy in world affairs, what he did to promote it and what his legacy suggests for democracy promotion today.

Ideas, not power or institutions

Why should we care about Reagan's ideas concerning democracy promotion? Isn't democracy a consequence rather than a cause of events? Doesn't it develop mostly from peace and security, economic progress and the habit of international cooperation? Realist and liberal scholars have long argued that ideas are consequences not causes. But constructivists (and earlier idealists) disagree. They contend that ideas have consequences. Ideas interpret or give meaning to material and institutional realities, and in many but not all cases shape those realities more than the reverse.[1]

Reagan's ideas of freedom and democracy clearly influenced the outcome of the Cold War. If power realities had been the primary cause of the end of the Cold War, the Cold War would have ended by the emergence of spheres of influence in Europe. The Soviet Union would have been preserved and the competition between East and West would have reverted to traditional great power relations without ideological overtones, as in the nineteenth century. Similarly, if liberal factors had been the primary forces ending the Cold War, the Cold War would have ended with a revitalized United Nations (UN), as its founders envisioned in 1945. For a first time during the Gulf War of 1991, the UN did appear to function as a collective security operation. But in Bosnia and Kosovo it quickly passed the baton to the North Atlantic Treaty Organization (NATO). The Cold War ended in neither power balancing nor collective security. It ended instead in the disappearance of one set of ideas represented by the Soviet Union and in the spread of another set of ideas represented by democracy and the expansion of the European Union (EU) and NATO. It ended the way it did because ideas proved more powerful than relative power or institutions.[2]

Reagan's rationale for democracy promotion

Reagan's ideas about democracy and world affairs unfolded in four parts: (1) the world works through a competition of ideas more so than a balance of power or international institutions; (2) there is no moral equivalence or 'peaceful coexistence' among ideas – freedom trumps totalitarianism and the United States is an exceptionalist nation; (3) the competition of ideas drives the balance of power that is the only basis for security in a morally contested world; and (4) the goal of the balance of power is to tilt the world towards freedom and the elimination of nuclear weapons, not to preserve the status quo or replace national sovereignty by centralized international institutions.

Relative ideas, not relative power, create distrust

For Reagan, the bedrock force in international affairs was ideas – differing cultural, social, religious, moral and ideological orientations – which defined the identities of nations and motivated the way they used their power and behaved in institutions. As early as June 1952, he said to a graduating class at William Woods College in Fulton, Missouri (where Winston Churchill delivered his famous Iron Curtain speech):

> America is less a place than an idea […] the idea of the dignity of man, the idea that deep within the heart of each one of us is something so God-like and precious that no individual or group has a right to impose his or its will upon the people.[3]

Reagan was self-conscious about his orientation. As he told Peggy Noonan, a former speechwriter, 'there is no question that I am an idealist, which is another way of saying I am an American'.[4] For Reagan, the idea and the nation were the same.

For Reagan, the identities of domestic regimes set the parameters of international affairs, not geopolitical circumstances or diplomatic and personal interrelationships. As national identities crystallized and shifted, they established the degree of convergence or divergence between nations and thereby bracketed the basic conditions under which power and institutional factors operated, limiting what these factors could achieve. When identities converged, trust and communications became easier. When they diverged, misperceptions and misunderstandings multiplied. Reagan saw the world in terms of an ideological struggle that did not displace material and institutional realities but gave meaning to them.[5]

Reagan laid out his worldview at the very beginning of his conversations with Mikhail Gorbachev. At Geneva in November 1985, he told the leader of the Soviet Union:

> Countries do not mistrust each other because of arms, but rather countries build up their arms because of the mistrust between them. I hope that in our meetings both of us can get at the source of the suspicions that exist.[6]

And again at Reykjavik: 'We arm because we don't trust each other. So we must get at the human rights problems and regional disputes that are the sources of distrust.'[7] For Reagan, the root causes of international disagreements were political and ideological, not military or diplomatic.

The nature of the political system or type of regime a nation championed mattered more than personalities or relationships. Queried in June 1985 about the newly appointed Gorbachev, Reagan responded: 'Well, I don't think there's any evidence that he is less dominated by their system and their philosophy than any of the others.'[8] And political systems, such as the Soviet Union, that mistreated their own citizens could not be trusted in international affairs. After the inconclusive summit at Reykjavik, Reagan told the American people: 'For a government that will break faith with its own people cannot be trusted to keep faith with foreign powers [...] When it comes to judging Soviet intentions, we're all from Missouri – you got to show us.'[9] Again in Berlin in June 1987:

> We will closely watch the condition of human rights within the Soviet Union. It is difficult to imagine that a government that continues to repress freedom in its own country, breaking faith with its own people, can be trusted to keep agreements with others.[10]

No moral equivalence

One of Reagan's most controversial steps was to call the Soviet Union an 'evil empire'. He did so deliberately: 'I made the "Evil Empire" speech and others like it with malice aforethought.'[11] At his very first press conference in January 1981, Reagan shocked the press corps: 'the only morality they [the Soviets] recognize is what will further their cause, meaning they reserve unto themselves the right to commit any crime, to lie, to cheat, in order to attain [that cause]'. There was good and evil in the world, and Reagan meant to identify the Soviet government and totalitarian governments in general with evil. On 8 March 1983, before the National Association of Evangelicals, he flatly rejected moral equivalence:

I urge you to beware the temptation of pride – the temptation of blithely declaring yourself above it all and label both sides as equally at fault, to ignore the facts of history and the aggressive impulses of an evil empire, to simply call the arms race a giant misunderstanding and thereby remove yourself from the struggle between right and wrong and good and evil.[12]

Referring to the Soviets, he added pointedly: 'they are the focus of evil in the modern world'. He had changed the wording of earlier drafts from 'surely historians will see there the focus of evil' to '*they are* the focus of evil (italics added)'.[13]

By contrast, the United States represented freedom and what was good in the world. As Lou Cannon points out, 'Reagan held an innocent and unshakable belief in the myth of American exceptionalism'.[14] Cannon calls it a 'myth', but for Reagan it was truth:

I've always believed that individuals should take priority over the state. History has taught me that that is what sets America apart – not to remake the world in our own image, but to inspire people everywhere with a sense of their boundless possibilities.[15]

'If we lose freedom here [in America],' Reagan told the 1964 Republican convention, 'there is no place to escape to.'[16]

Some historians dismiss these flourishes as mere rhetoric.[17] And, to be sure, Reagan was a commander, not a captive, of his language. Tony Dolan, the aide who worked with him on the evil empire speech, wrote in an early draft: 'Now and forever, the Soviet Union is an evil empire.' Reagan crossed out the words 'now and forever'.[18] Already by the end of 1983, he told *Time* magazine: 'No, I would not say things like that again, even after some of the things that have been done recently', referring to the Soviets shooting down the Korean airliner in September 1983 and storming out of arms control talks after the deployment of NATO missiles in November 1983.[19] And five years later in Red Square, he consigned the evil empire phrase to the ash heap of history: 'No, I was talking about another time in another era.'[20] Nevertheless, in April 1988, just a few weeks before going to Moscow, Reagan said to an audience in Springfield, Massachusetts:

We spoke plainly and bluntly [...] We said freedom was better than totalitarianism. We said communism was bad [...] experts said this kind of candor was dangerous [...] But far to the contrary, this candor made clear to the Soviets [...] that the differences that separated us and the Soviets were deeper and wider than just missile counts and number of warheads.[21]

Even at this late date, the message stung in Moscow. Gorbachev threw a 'tantrum' over the speech when he met the next day with Shultz.[22] Natan Sharansky, the Soviet dissident who spent years in the Gulag before his release in 1986, testified most credibly to the power of Reagan's rhetoric: 'I think the most important step in the Cold War and the defeat of the Soviet empire was his words and actions at the beginning of his Presidency.'[23]

Arms are necessary in a world of diverging ideologies

The moral struggle informed the military struggle. Right made might, not might makes right, as the old realist dictum would have it. '[T]he ultimate determinant in the struggle that's now going on in the world,' Reagan told the British parliament in June 1982, 'will not be bombs and rockets, but a test of wills and ideas, a trial of spiritual resolve, the values we hold, the beliefs we cherish, the ideals to which we are dedicated.'[24] The 'test of wills and ideas' drove the balance of power, but the balance of power was not a perversion. It was needed to provide safety in a world in which ideological divisions created distrust. And the balance of power was also needed to win, not in a conventional military sense but in a contest of political resolve and commitment. Already in 1963, Reagan laid out his prescription for how arms would tilt the balance of power towards freedom:

> The only sure way to avoid war is to surrender without fighting […] the other way is based on the belief that in an all out race our system is stronger, and eventually the enemy gives up the race as a hopeless cause. Then a noble nation believing in peace extends the hand of friendship and says there is room in the world for both of us.[25]

Again, in early January 1977, Reagan told Richard Allen, who became his first national security adviser: 'Some people think I'm simplistic but there's a difference between being simplistic and being simple. My theory about the Cold War is that we win and they lose? What do you think about that?' When Allen asked if he meant that, Reagan responded: 'Of course, I mean it. I just said it.'[26]

Here was vintage Reagan, persistently pointing out that ideas drive arms races, not the reverse, and that in the competition of ideas all ideas are not morally equivalent. History involves moral struggle, and some ideas win while others lose. Certainly, an arms race bore risks. But it was necessary to make diplomacy effective. Reagan believed that arms leveraged diplomacy rather than impeded it. By closing off options *outside* the negotiating process, an arms contest made serious bargaining possible *inside* negotiations. On the campaign trail in 1980, he told *Washington Post* editors that a rapid arms build-up would be good because it would bring the Soviet Union to the bargaining table.[27] And, once negotiations were under way, an arms race ensured a negotiating posture from strength and provided bargaining chips to expedite the negotiations themselves.

Freedom is universal

Finally, the purpose of negotiations was not just to preserve the status quo but also to win the moral contest *and* to win it peacefully. At Westminster, Reagan called for 'a crusade for freedom [...] toward a world in which all people are at last free to determine their own destiny'.[28] He said: 'what we have to consider here today while time remains is the permanent prevention of war and the establishment of the conditions of freedom and democracy as rapidly as possible in all countries'.[29] This was a tall order. Reagan's vision was anything but simplistic. He wanted to end communism, and he wanted to rid the world of nuclear weapons. How could he do both, if aggressively challenging communism increased the risks of nuclear war, and the desire to eliminate nuclear weapons removed a bulwark of deterrence while communism still existed? This is a puzzle that still baffles Reagan's supporters and opponents.

Reagan's desire to end communism was well known. And he stated it often. At the University of Notre Dame in May 1981, he declared: 'The West won't contain communism; it will transcend communism [...] it will dismiss it as some bizarre chapter in human history whose last pages are even now being written.'[30] In a press conference in June 1981, he said in reference to the crisis developing in Poland: 'communism is an aberration. It's not a normal way of living for human beings, and I think we are seeing the first, the beginning cracks, the beginning of the end'.[31] And at Westminster in 1982, he drove a stake into the heart of communism:

> What I am describing now is a plan and a hope for the long term – the march of freedom and democracy that will leave Marxist-Leninism on the ash heap of history as it has left other tyrannies, which stifle the freedom and muzzle the self-expression of the people.[32]

There is no doubt here that Reagan aimed to spread democracy 'as rapidly as possible to all countries' and 'all people'. Reagan went on:

> The objective I propose is quite simple to state: to foster the infrastructure of democracy, the system of a free press, unions, political parties, universities, which allows a people to choose their own way to develop their own culture, to reconcile their own differences through peaceful means.[33]

In the same year, Reagan presented legislation to Congress to create the National Endowment for Democracy (NED) and its affiliated institutes – the International Republican Institute, the National Democratic Institute for International Affairs, the Center for International Private Enterprise and the Free Trade Union Institute. Modelled after similar German institutes, the creation of the NED launched the era of democracy promotion that dominated world affairs over the next three decades (see below).

Reagan was talking about regime change, first and foremost in the Soviet Union. In May 1982, before going to Europe, he approved NSDD-32, the first comprehensive study by the administration of US policy towards the Soviet Union. As Paul Lettow describes, 'that document introduced and formalized the notion that the

United States should seek not simply to contain the spread of Soviet influence but to reverse it as well, and to pressure the internal Soviet system so as to encourage change'.[34] This guidance was reissued in January 1983 as NSDD-75, which spelled out the goal

> to contain and over time reverse Soviet expansionism by competing effectively on a sustained basis with the Soviet Union in all international arenas – particularly in the overall military balance and in geopolitical regions of priority concern to the United States [...] [and] to promote, within the narrow limits available to us, the process of change in the Soviet Union toward a more pluralistic political and economic system.[35]

This was prudent (notice, 'within the narrow limits available to us') rollback language, not the procrustean language of containment and peaceful coexistence that had dominated American Soviet policy since the 1950s.

Reagan never accepted a divided Europe as legitimate. As early as 1967, he advocated knocking down the Berlin Wall. In a debate with Robert F. Kennedy, he explained:

> We don't want the Berlin Wall knocked down so that it's easier to get at the throats of the East Germans. We just think that a wall that is put up to confine people and keep them within their own country instead of allowing them the freedom of world travel, has to be somehow wrong.[36]

Reagan seized on the Polish crisis in 1981 to take the first step. He constructed it not as another challenge to preserve stability in Europe but as 'the last chance in our lifetime to see a change in the Soviet empire's colonial policy'.[37] And he told the reporter Laurence Barrett on 29 December 1981:

> there is reason for optimism because I think there must be an awful lot of people in the Iron Curtain countries that feel the same way [as the Poles ...]. Our job now is to do everything we can to see that [the reform movement] doesn't die aborning. We may never get another chance like this in our lifetime.[38]

When Reagan visited the wall in June 1982, he called it 'as ugly as the idea behind it'. Asked at the time if Berlin would ever reunite, he replied simply, 'Yes'.[39] On the fortieth anniversary of Yalta in 1985, he reiterated:

> there is one boundary that can never be made legitimate, and that is the dividing line between freedom and repression. I do not hesitate to say we wish to undo this boundary [...] Our forty-year pledge is to the goal of a restored community of free European nations.[40]

And in 1987 he challenged Gorbachev brashly to 'tear down this wall'. Reagan had a fixed moral compass, and it excluded communism.

Eliminate nuclear weapons

Reagan's desire to eliminate nuclear weapons was less well known, even though it too was often repeated. He was preoccupied with the spectre of nuclear war at the Republican convention in 1976 when he made an impromptu speech about a time capsule that would tell the world whether nuclear weapons had been used or not.[41] In meetings with papal emissaries in December 1981 he called nuclear conflict, 'the last epidemic of mankind'. And he mentioned the elimination of nuclear weapons publicly for the first time in an interview with *New York Post* reporters on 23 March 1982.[42] Over the next seven years, he 'referred again and again – over 150 times – to the necessity of wiping out nuclear weapons'.[43] But no one took him seriously. Apparently the press not Reagan was 'sleepwalking through history'.[44] When Reagan announced the Strategic Defense Initiative (SDI) in March 1983, critics argued it would only add to the proliferation of nuclear weapons. Reagan predicted confidently it would 'pave the way for arms control measures to eliminate the weapons themselves'.[45] From the very beginning, he saw a non-nuclear SDI system as a means to eliminate offensive nuclear weapons and provide deterrence through enhanced defensive systems rather than retaliatory offensive systems.

How do we square Reagan's desire to defeat communism with his desire to eliminate nuclear weapons? The answer lies in the tight connection Reagan made between arms and diplomacy. He was just as firm in setting diplomatic goals as he was prudent and flexible in negotiations. In a National Security Council (NSC) meeting on 16 April 1982, in which he called for 'a vigorous defense build-up', Reagan also cautioned that the Soviets 'will not engage us if they feel threatened. What we need is presence so that if they come in, they will have to confront the United States. Can we use our presence in Europe to obtain that effect?'[46] Presence is an interesting term for deterrence. It is an actor's concept. It implies an impenetrable profile but not pugnacity. At Westminster he said: 'we must be cautious about forcing the pace of change, [but] we must not hesitate to declare our ultimate objectives and to take concrete actions to move toward them'.[47] Arms acted as leverage to close off avenues of advance by which the Soviets might achieve their goals outside negotiations and to prod them towards compromise inside negotiations. Once at the table, the United States offered them an attractive alternative they could not resist – relief from an arms race that they could not win and access to a global economy that they desperately needed if they were to modernize.

Reagan's view of the way the world worked was so visionary few shared it at the time. One was Daniel Patrick Moynihan. In a commencement address at New York University in 1984, he said: 'The truth is that the Soviet idea is spent [...] it is as if the whole Marxist-Leninist ethos is hurtling off into a black hole in the universe.'[48] But Seweryn Bialer, a Russian expert at Columbia University, wrote in *Foreign Affairs*: 'The Soviet Union is not now nor will it be during the next decade in the throes of a true economic crisis.'[49] The vast majority of experts agreed with Bialer. As biographer Lou Cannon notes, 'hardly anyone in the West believed at the time of the Westminster speech that the Soviet Union was on its last legs'.[50]

Even Reagan's own staff did not share his complete vision. In the instant history of the time, Reagan was often viewed as a puppet of his staff.[51] But, in truth, Reagan went through staff like water – six national security advisers, four chiefs of staff and 14 speechwriters. While he needed them all, he did not need any one of them in particular. He took his most significant initiatives against the advice of staff – SDI, the evil empire speech, zero nukes and the tear down this wall speech. The soft liners opposed the harsh rhetoric and the arms build-up, especially SDI.[52] The hardliners opposed negotiations with the Soviet Union and were aghast at Reagan's desire to eliminate nuclear weapons. Only Reagan brought the arrows (arms) and olive branch (diplomacy) of the American eagle on the presidential seal together. As early as May 1983, he described the synthesis:

> some of the N.S.C. staff are too hard line and don't think any approach should be made to the Soviets. I think I'm hard-line and will never appease but I do want to try and let them see there is a better world if they show by deed they want to get along with the free world.[53]

He combined, in an uncanny brew: the clarion statement of principles, the use of force as leverage both inside and outside negotiations, and the articulation of alternatives that offered opponents a way out of confrontation rather than running over them.

Democracy: definition, evolution and promotion

Any approach to democracy promotion involves understanding what a democracy is, how it develops and which mechanisms promote it.

What do we mean by democracy, and what are the different causal paths by which it may be created? Democracy can be distinguished in terms of 'thin' or 'thick', 'weak' or 'strong' democracies.[54] Essentially, three broad dimensions are involved: (1) free and fair elections in which all adult citizens participate and multiple parties compete; (2) divided and independent institutions (checks and balances, federalism etc.) that provide for the rule of law (independent judiciary), control the military and are accountable to elected officials; and (3) civil liberties to include basic freedoms of assembly, organization, ethnicity, religion, speech, press, and so on that underpin free elections and democratic norms of pluralism and tolerance.[55] If a country scores high on all three dimensions, it counts as a strong or liberal democracy. If it is missing the third dimension, it qualifies as a weak or illiberal democracy.[56] And if it has reasonably free and fair elections but a military or other institutions that are less accountable to elected officials, it is sometimes called a pseudo-democracy or electoral authoritarian regime.

As Larry Diamond elaborates, there are two broad causal pathways by which democracies emerge.[57] The first is through a competition among elites that eventually widens and draws in a larger and larger number of citizens. This competition is driven by the success or failure of elites in providing and sustaining legitimacy. This type of evolution from authoritarian to democratic rule characterized the experiences of Greece, the Philippines, South Korea and Taiwan, among others, in the post-war period. A second pathway is through structural change, the evolution of a middle class and civil society that demand participation in the political process. Economic growth is a key driver of this pathway to democracy. Early Western states, such as the Netherlands, Great Britain and the United States, followed this type of route to democracy.

There are five principal mechanisms for implementing democracy promotion: (1) setting a domestic example of democracy for others to emulate (for example, 'shining city on a hill'); (2) creating general international conditions of security and political and economic openness that foster freedom (for example, support for human rights, NATO and international economic institutions); (3) providing specific assistance to promote democracy in individual countries or regions (for example, National Endowment for Democracy and conditional assistance under the Millennium Challenge Corporation); (4) applying diplomatic and economic pressure to weaken non-democratic states (such as diplomatic isolation and economic sanctions); and (5) direct military intervention, either covert or overt, to overthrow non-democratic regimes and establish more democratic ones.[58]

Reagan's practices of democracy promotion

A devout advocate of limited government and strong civil society, Reagan defined democracy largely in liberal rather than electoral terms. The bedrock of democracy was individual self-government and responsibility, not the care and feeding of individuals by state elites and institutions. He was unusually fond of Jefferson's famous inaugural lines: 'Sometimes it is said that man cannot be trusted to govern himself. Can he then be trusted with the government of others?'[59] He paraphrased Jefferson's comment in his own Inaugural Address and included it in a letter he sent to the Soviet Leader Leonid Brezhnev in April 1981: 'If they [the people of the world] are incapable of self-government, as some would have us believe, then where in the world do we find people who are capable of governing others.'[60] Like Jefferson, Reagan believed the people could make better decisions than elites or experts. 'My attitude is', he said, 'let the people flourish.'[61] People *could* 'make the world over again', as Thomas Paine proclaimed, even if at the outset many of those people were uneducated and excluded. The people, not institutions, were supreme.[62]

Reagan, therefore, was sympathetic to the civil society rather than elite pathway to democracy. Government was constructed from the bottom up, not the top down. And it was internally moulded, not externally imposed. During his China trip in 1984 Reagan told his audience: 'We believe in the dignity of each man, woman and child [...] the special genius of each individual, and of his special right to make his own decisions and lead his own life.'[63] In Beijing, he quoted Abraham Lincoln: 'No man is good enough to govern another without that other's consent.' And when the Chinese government censored this quote, Reagan made sure to repeat it in Shanghai where it was reported.[64] In Moscow in 1988, Reagan explained how freedom would sprout from the bottom up in the Soviet Union:

> political leadership in a democracy requires [...] embracing the vast diversity of humanity and doing it with humility, listening as best you can not just to those with high positions but to the cacophonous voices of ordinary people and trusting those millions of people, keeping out of their way [...] We hope that one freedom will lead to another; that the Soviet government will understand that it is the individual who is always the source of economic creativity, the inquiring mind that produces a technical breakthrough, the imagination that conceives of new products and markets; and that in order for the individual to create, he must have a sense of just that – his own individuality, his own self-worth. He must sense that others respect him and, yes, that his nation respects him – respects him enough to grant him all his human rights.[65]

Reagan's strategy to promote democracy was comprehensive and priority-driven. Scholarly studies seldom adopt this strategic view to assess democracy promotion. They usually evaluate the mechanisms and outcomes of democracy promotion, country-by-country or mechanism-by-mechanism. For example, evaluations focus on countries in particular regions or at particular stages of development.[66] Or they evaluate specific instruments of democracy promotion such as economic sanctions or military intervention.[67] This is a mistake. Democracy is deeply embedded in its circumstances, and any effort to judge its progress and promotion must take into account the comprehensive factors affecting its evolution.

Reagan was above all a strategist.[68] He approached foreign policy comprehensively and incorporated all five mechanisms of democracy promotion in his strategy to end communism and spread freedom.

With respect to the United States as an example of democracy, Reagan addressed its political, economic and military revitalization, most importantly the revival of its moral self-confidence after the Vietnam experience. He spoke eloquently and often about 'the shining city on the hill'. There was no hope for a crusade for freedom in the world if the United States flagged. In his first year of office, and indeed throughout his first term, Reagan was often criticized for not having a clear foreign policy. But in those early days, his foreign policy was domestic policy, and to say that he had no foreign policy ignores the fact that in the first eight weeks of his administration between February and the end of March, he chaired ten national security meetings and in his first three years supervised and signed more than 100 national security decision studies and directives.[69] As noted above, he thought about his foreign policy strategy from the early 1950s on; and, although he was in no rush to negotiate until he had revitalized America and its alliances, he initiated a personal correspondence with his Soviet counterparts as early as April 1981. By the end of 1983 his strategy and leverage to deal with the Soviet Union were in place, and the negotiations unfolded from 1984 almost in lockstep, as Reagan foresaw.[70]

On the second mechanism – to create favourable international conditions for the spread of democracy – Reagan was determined to restore American leadership in the transatlantic alliance and the global economy. He rallied NATO to deploy INF missiles in Europe and led the global economy into the information age by restoring American growth, encouraging worldwide reductions in inflation, state controls and protectionism (especially in services, such as telecommunications and financial services), and defended the free-market-oriented international economic institutions, the World Bank and International Monetary Fund (IMF), from statist solutions such as the 'New International Economic Order'. Democracy could not advance until it was solidly shored up where it already existed.

The INF deployments and Reagan's related military build-up, including SDI, are seldom seen as elements of his democracy promotion strategy, but they were. Like the United States' domestic example, the free world is democracy's 'shining city on the hill' for the rest of the globe. In the late 1970s that free world was demoralized by the threat of Soviet SS-20s in eastern Europe and aggressive Soviet interventions in Africa and Afghanistan. Europe's leaders sounded the first alarms. Chancellor Helmut Schmidt of Germany asked NATO in 1977 to deploy counterbalancing INF missiles, and Reagan with British Prime Minister Margaret Thatcher, Helmut Kohl (Schmidt's successor) and French President Francois Mitterrand faced down massive street protests in Europe and media-driven war scares in the United States (for example, ABC's *The Day After*) to deploy INF weapons at the end of 1983. In pique, the Soviets withdrew from arms control talks in Geneva, but then quickly returned once Reagan was re-elected and they knew they had to deal with him for another four years.

In the strategic negotiations that followed, nothing was more significant for what followed than SDI.[71] For Reagan, it was a technological insurance policy to enable him to rid the world of nuclear weapons.[72] For Soviet leaders, SDI represented the prospect of a new arms race in space at the dawn of the information age, a race they knew they could not win. Reagan used SDI deftly to force Soviet leaders to take arms reductions seriously.

Reagan's programme to revitalize the world economy and free market institutions such as the World Bank and the IMF was the other big element of his broad international strategy to defend and promote democracy.[73] If the United States and its allies had not rebounded from the capitalist crisis of the 1970s, Soviet economic difficulties might have had far less significance and almost certainly would not have spelled the end of the Soviet Union. It is easy to forget that the world economy of the 1970s, with its high prices for oil and other commodities, favoured resource-rich countries such as the Soviet Union. While it is fashionable now to point out that the Soviet economy peaked in the early 1970s and declined thereafter, that was evident to practically no one at the time. In fact it was Reagan in the early 1980s who was one of the first to spot the vulnerabilities of the Soviet Union and to seek to exploit them.[74]

In the end this larger campaign by Reagan to strengthen the West militarily and economically and shape the choices for the Soviet Union was perhaps the biggest factor propelling the third great wave of the spread of democracy. Reagan's strategy contributed to the end of the Cold War, and in its wake democracy surged across Europe and much of the rest of the world. From 1980 to 1990, 14 countries became free; from 1990 to 2000, another 63 countries joined the free world.

One might have expected Reagan, focusing on the big picture, to ignore the nuts and bolts of democracy promotion. But in fact he became the author of the third mechanism to promote democracy-specific programmes to assist the development of democracy. Reagan founded the NGOs that became the flagship of democracy promotion over the next three decades.[75] As noted earlier, his pledge at Westminster 'to foster the infrastructure of democracy' led to the establishment of NED and its four affiliated institutes. The NED introduced the idea of giving direct grants to NGOs to foster democracy, 'a radical innovation at the time', as Michael McFaul notes.[76] It reflected Reagan's commitment to building democracy from the bottom up, from civil society organizations that are closest to the people and connect with indigenous sources of personal and local responsibility.

The NED flourished and spawned 'look-alikes' over the next 30 years. From modest beginnings, American spending for democracy assistance increased from $100 million in the late 1980s to over $2.5 billion in fiscal year 2011.[77] More importantly, subsequent presidents added to the machinery of democracy promotion. Bill Clinton expanded funding for the NED and created a new bureau in the State Department for Democracy, Human Rights and Labor (DRL). George W. Bush created the Millennium Challenge Account (MCA) and Corporation (MCC) to link development aid with democratic governance – based on rooting out corruption, enhancing respect for human rights and upholding the rule of law.[78] And Bush launched the Middle East Partnership Initiative (MEPI) to foster freedom in Arab societies by providing small grants to civil society actors.

Democracy promotion also became a new focus in international organizations. Spending for democracy promotion among advanced countries in the Organization for Economic Cooperation and Development totalled $12 billion in 2008. The UN, where despotic governments often chaired key committees and groups such as the G-77, founded a Democratic Caucus, and democratic nations met in Warsaw, Poland in 2000 to launch the Council of Democracies.[79] The democracy movement spawned election-monitoring programmes and institutes, and trained thousands of personnel worldwide to verify election results. The International Foundation for Election Systems and the International Institute for Democracy and Electoral Assistance are but two examples.

At the same time that Reagan was giving novel attention to NGOs, he actively deployed the fourth mechanism to promote democracy – government-to-government policies. He applied persistent diplomatic pressure to support domestic dissidents and economic sanctions to weaken non-democratic governments, most notably in the Soviet Union. He did not do this across the board, especially at the outset – for example, with Cuba, South Africa or the Philippines. Strategy and limited resources required setting priorities. And Reagan always gave Europe priority in the struggle against autocratic governments. Following the imposition of martial law in Poland in December 1981, he held four NSC meetings in one week and in a lengthy disquisition at one of them called for 'a total quarantine of the Soviet Union'. He laid down the gauntlet for the allies: 'those who do not go along with us will be boycotted, too, and will be considered against us'.[80] Reagan subsequently imposed sanctions against the Soviet pipeline carrying gas to Europe and applied them extraterritorially to affect American firms based in Europe. The allies strenuously objected in public, but behind the scenes they closed ranks and eventually deployed INF weapons, turning the tide in the arms race with the Soviet Union. When his priorities were on the line, Reagan held nothing back.

While he was liberating Europe, however, Reagan was reluctant to promote democracy in all countries at all times. He told an NSC meeting on 6 February 1981: 'We don't throw out our friends just because they can't pass the "saliva test" on human rights.' He called for aid to Jonas Savimbi in Angola, better relations with Chile and support for non-communist forces in El Salvador where 'a victory […] could set an example'. However bad these governments were, Reagan believed 'none of them is as guilty of human rights violations as are Cuba and the Soviet Union'.[81] He was following John F. Kennedy's dictum: before you over-turn an autocratic government to install a democratic one, make sure you don't get a communist one.[82]

But once the struggle in Europe turned the corner, Reagan pressed human rights and democracy in these countries as well. Under his watch, Chile, the Philippines, South Korea and Taiwan – all went from military or autocratic regimes to democracy. Reagan's record is hardly perfect. If he believed Jeane Kirkpatrick's argument that autocratic governments were always better than com-munist ones because they could become democratic and communist governments could not, he was wrong.[83] Communist governments too became democratic. But he was right to husband as allies autocratic governments on the periphery of the Cold War conflict to win the battle against communism on the Cold War's central front in Europe. Once the Berlin Wall fell, communism fell worldwide and lingers today in barely recognizable form only in China, Cuba, Vietnam and North Korea.

Finally, Reagan did not shy away from the fifth mechanism to promote democracy, namely military interventions to subvert non-democratic governments, particularly by covert actions. He supported 'freedom fighters' in Central America, southern Africa and Afghanistan, and intervened directly with military forces in Lebanon and Grenada.[84] However, compared to George H. W. Bush, who led the first Gulf War, and his son, George W. Bush, who invaded both Afghanistan and Iraq, Reagan did not appear to use force very much. In retrospect, some analysts portray Reagan as a dove. Lou Cannon writes, for example: 'Reagan was reluctant to take major military risks.'[85] If so, it depends on how Cannon defines 'major';

and few people, including Cannon, believed at the time that Reagan was reluctant to use force. Just the opposite, he was accused of fomenting a new Cold War and nearly starting a hot one.[86]

Reagan's reluctance to intervene with ground forces in Third World situations was a function of two factors: the structure of deterrence in the Cold War and limited resources. Deterrence meant that direct military intervention risked Soviet reaction and a potential nuclear confrontation. Neither Bush faced that same risk. If using force meant confrontation with the Soviets, Reagan's priority was to challenge Soviet forces in Europe, not in Lebanon or Grenada.

Moreover, both Bushes benefited from Reagan's military build-up. In Reagan's time, resources were limited. He gives us a hint of what he might have done in Europe during the Polish crisis of 1981 if he had had the resources. On 14 July 1981 he wrote in his diary: 'Can we afford to let Poland collapse? But in the state of our present economy can we afford to help in any meaningful way?'[87] Secretary of Defence Caspar Weinberger told Reagan that 'we don't have the ability to project our power that far and we could not, without very substantial help, successfully come to the aid of the Poles if they were invaded'. The president responded: 'Yes, I know that Cap. But we must never again be in this position.'[88] Had he had the military he bequeathed to the Bushes and Clinton, he might have manoeuvred tanks and troops on the western side of the central frontier in Europe in 1981 the way the Soviets mobilized 25 divisions on the eastern side to impose military government and then martial law on Poland. After all, that is precisely what Reagan did with military forces at the nuclear level. At considerable risk, he deployed INF missiles in western Europe to push back against the SS-20 missiles the Soviet Union had already deployed in eastern Europe.

Reagan's legacy in democracy promotion

Reagan's approach to democracy promotion has been followed by that of other presidents. George H. W. Bush saw world affairs and democracy less in terms of ideas and regime change than in terms of stability and the status quo. He had problems, as he said, with the 'vision thing'. He was more realist than idealist towards the Soviet Union and the Middle East. He was reluctant to break up the Soviet Union and warned the Ukraine in his famous 'chicken Kiev' speech not to move hastily to independence and threaten stability. In the Gulf War, he deployed forces to restore Kuwaiti sovereignty and the status quo ante, hallmark features of a realist world. He explicitly rejected the option to go on to Baghdad and overthrow the regime of Saddam Hussein.[89]

Bill Clinton adopted a policy of 'democratic enlargement' and expanded NATO to include newly liberated communist countries.[90] He faced a world with no Soviet Union and downplayed the use of force while upgrading the role of 'assertive multilateralism' and international organizations. A new threat of ethnic division, however, prompted him to revive a more muscular approach to defend and promote democracy. Clinton deployed NATO in its first 'out-of-area' missions to quell ethnic violence in Bosnia and Kosovo, earning in response the ire of Russia, which clamped down on democratic reforms under Vladimir Putin.

George W. Bush encountered 9/11 and the emergence of another globalized threat against freedom. He responded initially to punish the perpetrators in Afghanistan and then to pre-empt what he believed to be an 'evil nexus' of terrorism and nuclear proliferation in Iraq (alongside Iran and North Korea). He invaded Iraq mostly on realist grounds of pre-emption but when no weapons of mass destruction were found, he stressed the idealist rationale of spreading democracy to Iraq. Bush did not stop with Iraq, announcing in his second Inaugural Address that 'it is the policy of the United States to seek and support the growth of democratic movements and institutions in every nation and culture, with the ultimate goal of ending tyranny in our world'.[91] He went on to promote democracy throughout the Middle East, giving a militant cast to the policy of spreading democracy that rivalled Woodrow Wilson's imperialist policies in Mexico and Latin America.

Barack Obama deliberately pulled back from the Bush approach. He soft-pedalled human rights and democracy promotion. In Prague in April 2009, he said: 'when nations and peoples allow themselves to be defined by their differences, the gulf between them widens'.[92] He preferred to see the world in terms of multilateralism rather than political ideas. He embraced engagement with governments to solve common problems of proliferation, climate change and energy resources and withheld support for dissident movements trying to overthrow despotic regimes.[93] He sustained funding for democracy promotion programmes but implemented an overall foreign policy premised on an expected decline in American influence, a reduction of American military forces and recantation of American exceptionalism around the world.[94]

What does Reagan's legacy offer for evaluating subsequent presidents and designing democracy promotion policies for the future? Four observations seem warranted.

First, circumstances change and there is no one-setting-fits-all approach to democracy promotion. Reagan dealt with the Cold War, a greater threat to democracy than any threat since. When the Cold War was won, democracy sprouted in its wake, in a manner unlikely to be repeated. Whatever the circumstances, however, Reagan's approach suggests the need to develop an overall strategy and set priorities. Do not just react to events – as a pragmatist does – shape them – as a statesman does. Reagan knew where he wanted to go, and he was patient in getting there. Subsequent presidents have been less visionary.

Second, whether presidents think about the world *primarily* in terms of ideas, power or institutions (multilateralism) matters. Strategy involves making assumptions about what factors drive the world. Without doubt causality is complex, but, the complexity lies in the way causal variables interact, not in their multiplication. Ideas, institutions and power exist in all situations. But, in any given situation, one factor is the key to the others. Leaders have to choose. If they repeatedly choose different factors in different situations, they are more likely to manage events than to shape them. Their worldview is less coherent, and they will have less cognitive impact on expectations. Reagan saw the world as a moral struggle. Power and negotiations were simply ways to influence that moral struggle. He never wavered from that view, and he moved the world decisively in his direction. Presidents since have been more realist – and less consistent.[95]

Third, strategy involves using all mechanisms to promote democracy simultaneously. Reagan integrated defence, economic and democracy promotion policies. A strong America and Western alliance were the *sine qua non* of first defending and then spreading democracy. The NED would have had much less effect without the larger web of policies in which it was embedded. Compare the NED's influence today with that of China's Confucius Institutes abroad. The latter are numerous but they do not resonate, as the NED does, with larger structures of free world trade and diplomacy. This point is particularly relevant for President Obama. It is hard for America to have an effective policy to promote democracy around the world, if its contribution to the security and prosperity of the world community declines.

Fourth, democracy is *self*-government, so there will always be limits to how much it can be aided and abetted from abroad. In the end, democracy promotion depends on culture, religion and other aspects of *indigenous,* not foreign, societies. Reagan's insight through the NED was to link the indigenous societies of different countries through NGOs. But such organizations do not thrive in all cultures. Russia keeps a tight rein on foreign NGOs, China does not permit them, and Egypt imprisons their leaders. At times, for larger (for example, security) and hopefully coherent reasons (why strategy is important), the United States needs these countries and balances support for local opposition groups with close government ties. As Michael McFaul suggests, the best approach is a dual-track one, i.e. one that engages governments and NGOs simultaneously.[96] Reagan aided dissidents and pounded away at human rights in the Soviet Union, as late as his trip to Moscow in May 1988, even as he negotiated with the Soviet Union to end the arms race and bring the Soviet Union into the world economy.

Ronald Reagan's approach to democracy promotion is instructive and to date has been understudied. The newly declassified record is voluminous and deserves greater attention from scholars and practitioners alike.

Notes

1 See my essay, 'America's Identity, Democracy Promotion, and National Interests: Beyond Realism, Beyond Idealism', in Michael Cox, G. John Ikenberry and Takashi Inoguchi, eds., *American Democracy Promotion: Impulses, Strategies, and Impact* (Oxford University Press, 2000) and my textbook, *Perspectives on International Relations: Power, Institutions, and Ideas* (Washington, DC: CQ Press, 2011, 3rd edition), chapter 1.
2 See my essay, 'Ideas have Consequences: The Cold War and Today', *International Politics*, Vol. 48 (July/September 2011). For other empirical demonstrations of the causal power of ideas, see Peter Katzenstein, ed., *The Culture of National Security: Norms and Identity in World Politics* (New York: Columbia University Press, 1996); John M. Owen IV, *The Clash of Ideas in World Politics: Transnational Networks, States, and Regime Change 1510–2010* (Princeton University Press, 2010); Mark L. Haas, *The Ideological Origins of Great Power Politics, 1789–1989* (Ithaca: Cornell University Press, 2005); Mark L. Haas, *The Clash of Ideologies: Middle Eastern Politics and American Security* (New York: Oxford

University Press, 2012); and Martha Finnemore, *The Purpose of Intervention: Changing Beliefs about the Use of Force* (Ithaca: Cornell University Press, 2004).

3 Martin Anderson and Annelise Anderson, *Reagan's Secret War: The Untold Story of His Fight to Save the World from Nuclear Disaster* (New York: Crown Publishers, 2009), pp. 248–49. Nationalists and realists, by contrast, see the United States more as a geographic and cultural entity rather than an idea. For example, Walter McDougall, sceptical of American internationalism, refers to the United States as 'a delightful spot'. See *Promised Land: Crusader State* (Boston: Houghton Mifflin, 1997).

4 Peggy Noonan, *When Character was King: A Story of Ronald Reagan* (New York: Viking, 2001), p. 317.

5 In this sense, Reagan was a 'classical liberal' constructivist who saw individuals as the source of independent ideas, not a social constructivist who sees societal dialogue as the source of collectivist ideas.

6 Anderson and Anderson, *Reagan's Secret War*, p. 233.

7 Quoted in George P. Shultz, *Turmoil and Triumph: My Years as Secretary of State* (New York: Charles Scribner's Sons, 1993), p. 762.

8 Then Reagan quipped: 'But it isn't true that I don't trust anyone under 70.' Quoted in Anderson and Anderson, *Reagan's Secret War*, p. 207.

9 ibid., p. 313.

10 ibid., pp. 357–58.

11 Quoted in Stephen F. Hayward, *The Age of Reagan: The Conservative Counterrevolution 1980–1989* (New York: Crown Forum, 2009), p. 289.

12 Quoted in Lou Cannon, *President Reagan: The Role of a Lifetime* (New York: Public Affairs, 2000), p. 273.

13 See Anderson and Anderson, *Reagan's Secret War*, pp. 122–23.

14 Cannon, *President Reagan*, p. 711.

15 Noonan, *When Character Was King*, p. 317.

16 Quoted in Peter Robinson, *How Ronald Reagan Changed My Life* (New York: ReganBooks, 2003), pp. 88–89.

17 As John Patrick Diggins writes: 'Religious conservatives regarded evil as real; for Reagan, it was rhetorical', *Ronald Reagan: Fate, Freedom, and the Making of History* (New York: W. W. Norton & Company, 2007), p. 2.

18 ibid., pp. 373–74.

19 Quoted in Hayward, *The Age of Reagan*, p. 337.

20 ibid., p. 606.

21 ibid., p. 605.

22 ibid.

23 Quoted in Noonan, *When Character Was King*, p. 213.

24 ibid., p. 207.

25 Quoted in Anderson and Anderson, *Reagan's Secret War*, p. 42.

26 Robinson, *How Ronald Reagan Changed My Life*, pp. 71–72.

27 Lou Cannon, 'Arms Boost Seen as Strain on Soviets', *Washington Post*, 18 June 1980, A3.

28 Quoted in Cannon, *President Reagan*, p. 272.

29 Quoted in Hayward, *The Age of Reagan*, p. 255.

30 ibid., p. 114.

31 ibid., p. 123.

32 Quoted in Noonan, *Character*, p. 207.

33 Quoted in Hayward, *The Age of Reagan*, pp. 255–56.

34 Paul Lettow, *Ronald Reagan and His Quest to Abolish Nuclear Weapons* (New York: Random House, 2006), p. 70.

35 Summary from Jack F. Matlock, Jr., *Reagan and Gorbachev: How the Cold War Ended* (New York: Random House, 2005), pp. 53–54.

36 Quoted in Anderson and Anderson, *Reagan's Secret War*, p. 249. Richard Reeves, a liberal reporter for the *New York Times*, commented that 'Reagan just cleaned his [Kennedy's]

clock' in the debate. Kennedy apparently agreed, telling his staff: 'Don't get me alone with this guy again', p. 249.

37 Ronald Reagan, *The Reagan Diaries*, Douglas Brinkley, ed. (New York: HarperCollins, 2007), p. 57.

38 Laurence J. Barrett, *Gambling with History: Ronald Reagan in the White House* (New York: Doubleday, 1983), p. 298.

39 Cannon, *President Reagan*, p. 414.

40 Quoted in Paul Kengor, *The Crusader: Ronald Reagan and the Fall of Communism* (New York: Regan, HarperCollins, 2006), p. 220. The Yalta message was carefully targeted. Over the previous year, Gromyko complained to Shultz (and no doubt the president as well) that Reagan's 'rollback' rhetoric was dangerous. 'No one – no one – can change the reality of the situation in Europe', Gromyko warned, and he called 'shocking' the administration's talk about the 'artificial division' of Europe. See Shultz, *Turmoil and Triumph*, pp. 467–68, 484–85.

41 Martin Anderson, *Revolution* (San Diego: Harcourt Brace Jovanovich, 1988), p. 71.

42 Anderson and Anderson, *Reagan's Secret War*, p. 94. This is one year before Shultz hears it for the first time in February 1983.

43 ibid.

44 Haynes Johnson, *Sleepwalking Through History: America in the Reagan Years* (New York: W. W. Norton & Company, 2003). Johnson had the good grace to admit later that he was wrong. Hayward, *The Age of Reagan*, p. 16.

45 Quoted in Anderson and Anderson, *Reagan's Secret War*, p. 129.

46 ibid., p. 102.

47 Hayward, *The Age of Reagan*, p. 255.

48 Quoted in Anderson, *Revolution*, p. 36.

49 Quoted in Hayward, *The Age of Reagan*, p. 115.

50 Cannon, *President Reagan*, p. 760. The CIA concluded in November 1984 that 'Soviet economic problems were unlikely ... to cause them to limit their strategic programs', Anderson and Anderson, *Reagan's Secret War*, p. 182. In fact the Soviets increased their military budget right through 1988. At Westminster Reagan noted the decline in the rate of growth of the Soviet economy since the 1950s (not the same as a decline of the economy), which was then half what it was earlier. See Hayward, *The Age of Reagan*, p. 255. Oil price increases propped up the Soviet Union in the 1970s, and oil price drops probably had a lot to do with its precipitous decline after the mid-1980s.

51 Cannon makes this point repeatedly in *President Reagan*.

52 According to some accounts, Shultz thought SDI was 'lunacy'. See Strobe Talbott, *The Master of the Game: Paul Nitze and the Nuclear Peace* (New York: Knopf, 1988), p. 193. He was sceptical, as he reveals in his own account. See Shultz, *Turmoil and Triumph*, pp. 246–65.

53 Reagan, *Diaries*, p. 142; and Paul Kengor and Patricia Clark Dorner, *The Judge William P. Clark: Reagan's Top Hand* (San Francisco: Ignatius Press, 2007), p. 199.

54 Larry Diamond, *The Spirit of Democracy: The Struggle to Build Free Societies Throughout the World* (New York: A Holt Paperback, 2008), pp. 20–26.

55 See my book, *At Home Abroad: Identity and Power in American Foreign Policy* (Ithaca: Cornell University Press, 2002), pp. 22–23. These three categories cover the ten attributes identified by Diamond for 'thick' democracies, as well as the three targets of democracy assistance identified by Thomas Carothers: elections, institutions and civil society. See Carothers, *Aiding Democracy Abroad: The Learning Curve* (Washington, DC: Carnegie Endowment for International Peace, 1999).

56 Fareed Zakaria, *The Future of Freedom: Illiberal Democracy at Home and Abroad* (New York: W. W. Norton & Company, 2003).

57 Diamond, *Spirit of Democracy*, pp. 70–106.

58 A sixth mechanism may be disaster relief or humanitarian intervention, but that is generally considered a part of development rather than democracy assistance.

59 Quoted in Henry Adams, *History of the United States During the Administrations of Thomas Jefferson* (Library of America, 1986; originally published 1889–91), p. 137.

60 Anderson and Anderson, *Reagan's Secret War*, p. 51.

61 Cannon, *President Reagan*, p. 197.

62 Some more traditional conservatives had trouble understanding Reagan's 'classical liberal' commitment to the people as opposed to institutions. At the end of his presidency, Reagan startled George Will and William Buckley at a White House dinner with the following remark: 'Well, you know, is it possible that we conservatives are the real liberals and the liberals are the real conservatives?' Buckley absorbed the comment affably, but Will took offence, calling the remark 'banal' and retorting to the president: 'I knew you were a liberal all along.' Quoted in Cannon, *President Reagan*, p. 106.

63 ibid., p. 404.

64 ibid., p. 422.

65 Cannon, *President Reagan*, pp. 705–6. By contrast, Gromyko once called human rights issues a 'tenth rate question'. See Shultz, *Turmoil and Triumph*, p. 122.

66 See discussion in Michael McFaul, *Advancing Democracy Abroad: Why We Should and How We Can* (Stanford, CA: Hoover Institution, 2010), p. 163.

67 For example, see Jeffrey Pickering and Mark Peceny, 'Forcing Democracy at Gunpoint', *International Studies Quarterly*, Vol. 50, No. 3 (2006); and Nikolay Marinov, 'Do Economic Sanctions Destabilize Country Leaders?', *American Journal of Political Science*, Vol. 49, No. 3 (2005).

68 See John Lewis Gaddis, *Strategies of Containment: A Critical Appraisal of American National Security Policy During the Cold War* (Oxford University Press, revised and expanded edition, 2005), especially his conclusions, p. 375; Kengor and Doerner, *The Judge*, pp. 237–41; and Steven R. Weisman, 'The influence of William Clark', *New York Times Magazine*, 14 August 1983.

69 Anderson and Anderson, *Reagan's Secret War*, p. 34.

70 In one instance, Reagan foresaw in his diary in December 1984 that the Soviet Union were coming into the negotiations to get SDI and that they would walk out of the arms control talks when they did not succeed. This was an uncanny prediction of the outcome of the Reykjavik summit two years later. See *Reagan Diaries*, p. 288, *and* Anderson and Anderson, *Reagan's Secret War*, p. 189.

71 Soviet leaders themselves attest to this conclusion. Gorbachev's foreign minister Alexander Bessmertnykh said later: 'The atmosphere in Moscow was very tense for the first few years of the Reagan administration especially because of the SDI program, it frightened us very much.' See William C. Wohlforth, ed., *Witnesses to the End of the Cold War* (Baltimore: Johns Hopkins University Press, 1996), p. 14.

72 This is the story of Martin and Annelise Anderson's *Reagan's Secret War*, based entirely on declassified national security documents and other records.

73 This is the story that I tell in considerable detail in *The Myth of America's Decline: Leading the World Economy into the 1990s* (Oxford University Press, 1990).

74 As Gaddis points out, 'Reagan saw Soviet weaknesses sooner than most of his contemporaries did.' *Strategies of Containment*, p. 375.

75 Diamond calls it 'a turning point', *Spirit of Democracy*, p. 121.

76 McFaul, *Advancing Democracy Abroad*, p. 19.

77 Thomas Carothers, *Democracy Policy Under Obama* (Washington, DC: Carnegie Endowment for International Peace, 2012), p. 20.

78 McFaul, *Advancing Democracy Abroad*, pp. 17–23.

79 This work is closely followed and supported by NGOs, such as the Council for the Community of Democracies, on whose board I sit.

80 Quoted in Anderson and Anderson, *Reagan's Secret War*, p. 85.

81 ibid., p. 35.

82 See Tony Smith, *America's Mission: The United States and the Worldwide Struggle for Democracy in the Twentieth Century* (Princeton: Princeton University Press, 1994), p. 226.

83 For Kirkpatrick's argument, see 'Dictatorships and Double Standards', *Commentary*, November 1979.

84 Grenada is one of the few cases in which democracy has been sustained after military interventions. See McFaul, *Advancing Democracy Abroad*, p. 156.

85 Cannon, *President Reagan*, p. 293.

86 Indeed, according to some accounts, his eagerness to use force eventually scared even him and prompted him to reverse course after war scares in late 1983. See Beth A. Fischer, *The Reagan Reversal: Foreign Policy and the End of the Cold War* (Columbia, MO: University of Missouri Press, 1997).

87 Reagan, *Diaries*, p. 30.

88 Caspar W. Weinberger, with Gretchen Roberts, *In the Arena: A Memoir of the 20th Century* (Washington, DC: Regnery, 2001), p. 280.

89 Philip Zellikow and Condoleezza Rice, *Germany United and Europe Transformed: A Study in Statecraft* (Cambridge: Harvard University Press, 1997).

90 Derek Chollet and James Goldgeier, *America Between the Wars: From 9/11 to 11/9* (New York: Public Affairs, 2008).

91 'There is No Justice without Freedom', *Washington Post*, 21 January 2005, A24.

92 See my essay, 'Obama's Foreign Policy: The Swing Away from Bush', *Policy Review*, No. 160, April/May 2010.

93 See my essay, 'The Jigsaw Puzzle and the Chess Board: The Making and Unmaking of Foreign Policy in the Age of Obama', *Commentary*, Vol. 133, No. 5, May 2012.

94 For a sympathetic interpretation of Obama's 'reset' of democracy promotion, see Carothers, *Democracy Policy Under Obama*.

95 Both Clinton and George W. Bush did reversals in their presidency – Clinton from multilateralism to NATO military missions in Bosnia and Kosovo, and Bush from a robust military policy to spreading democracy everywhere at once.

96 McFaul, *Advancing Democracy Abroad*, p. 171ff. McFaul, currently the American ambassador to Moscow, is practising what he preaches, meeting with opposition leaders as soon as he arrived in Moscow, not just presenting his credentials to the government. See Ellen Barry, 'New U.S. Envoy Ruffles Feathers in Moscow', *New York Times*, 23 January 2012.

9

BILL CLINTON

Nicolas Bouchet

Introduction

Containment having become irrelevant with the collapse of the Soviet Union, Bill Clinton was the first president in half a century that did not inherit a ready-made grand strategic concept. He was subsequently criticized for failing to devise a post-Cold War strategy, but his foreign policy was in fact underpinned by a consistent worldview articulated through the concept of 'democratic enlargement'. In developing this, Clinton and his advisers tapped into the liberal internationalist tradition that conceives the United States' national interest partly in terms of promoting its political values abroad. Their ambition to expand the sphere of free markets and liberal democracy in support of American security and prosperity reflected enduring beliefs in the 'unity of goodness'[1] and the 'utilitarian value of democracy'.[2] These assume that all desirable outcomes for the United States can be pursued simultaneously and that the spread of democracy is central to this. Where and when the Clinton administration attempted to implement democratic enlargement, however, it became clear that how to do so through standard tools of international influence was not self-evident. The relatively new policy field of democracy promotion was one obvious avenue for pursuing enlargement and therefore the administration attempted to integrate it more in foreign policy, while framing it explicitly in terms of helping to achieve national security and economic goals. This chapter considers Clinton's democracy promotion with regard both to democratization and to its role in the service of these broader goals. It first looks at the origins of democratic enlargement. It then addresses how enlargement was implemented through the institutionalization and application of democracy promotion. Having considered the impact of the administration's policies on democratization, the chapter sets out some legacies and lessons from its experience with enlargement in relation to the instrumental value of democracy promotion for American foreign policy.

The origins of democratic enlargement

When Clinton left office, judgements on his foreign policy were mixed. Though they have grown more favourable since, the accusation of failing to set the United States on a new post-Cold War course has endured.[3] Clinton is blamed for not developing a strategy for a world in the throes of a historic realignment.[4] Richard Haass, for example, accuses him of having 'inherited a world of unprecedented American advantage and opportunity and [doing] little with it', overseeing an era of 'underachievement and squandered potential'.[5] But the failure to encapsulate Clinton's strategic thinking in a lastingly popular concept should not be confused with the absence of any.[6] Clinton's own defence was that containment was not born fully formed in the immediate aftermath of the Second World War either, and that its architects had improvised on their instincts.[7] With democratic enlargement, his administration did in fact develop a strategic vision based on a mainstream American worldview. As John Dumbrell puts it, Clinton's foreign policy had 'an integrating purpose in its commitment to the expansion of market democracy under conditions of accelerating globalisation'.[8] Walter Russell Mead describes a 'uniquely far-reaching and systematic' Wilsonian agenda.[9] How much this constituted a grand strategy proper is a valid question. As Stephen Krasner argues, though, 'Most foreign policies most of the time have not been guided by a grand strategy', and American foreign policy in the 1990s was informed instead by 'orienting principles'.[10] This is echoed by Clinton's second National Security Adviser Sandy Berger:

> The challenge, which [the president] impressed upon me and his other advisers, is to provide a strategic framework that clarifies our stance to the rest of the world and informs administration decision-makers up and down the line. It's not a blueprint for action but a means to convey the president's principles and priorities.[11]

The 'launch' of democratic enlargement in 1993 can be seen as an attempt to counter criticism in a first presidential year marked by crises in Bosnia, Haiti and Somalia. These had created the impression of an erratic, inexperienced president and an administration out of its depth, and led to Clinton's early reputation for naive idealism and mishandling international affairs, memorably summed up by Michael Mandelbaum as 'foreign policy as social work'.[12] However, democratic enlargement also rose out of wider post-Cold War debates in Washington and from the democracy tradition in American foreign policy. It was also related to Clinton's project of modernization for the Democratic Party, which entailed winning back centrists and neoconservatives disaffected with the party's foreign-policy positions since the Vietnam War by reconnecting to a tradition of liberal anti-communist internationalism.[13] In the 1992 election, needing to defend himself from accusations of inexperience, Clinton tried to project the image of a candidate with a broad strategic ambition, which he couched in the rhetoric of democracy and geo-economics. Speaking at Georgetown University, Clinton criticized President George H. W. Bush for favouring 'political stability and his personal relations with foreign leaders over a coherent policy of promoting freedom, democracy and economic growth' and pointed out 'the dangers of forging strategic relationships with despotic regimes'.[14] He set himself three national security objectives: restructuring the military, working with allies to encourage the spread of democracy abroad, and re-establishing economic leadership at home and in the world. Clinton stressed the need to support democratic transitions, especially in Russia:

> [America] should regard increased funding for democratic assistance as a legitimate part of our national security budget. We should support groups like the National Endowment for Democracy, which work openly rather than covertly to promote democratic pluralism and free markets abroad. I would encourage both the Agency for International Development and the US Information Agency to channel more of their resources to promoting democracy.

On the campaign trail Clinton called for an American-led 'global alliance for democracy as united and steadfast as the global alliance that defeated Communism'.[15] He argued that 'it is more possible for us than ever before to be more consistent in the advocacy of freedom and democracy and human rights, and global economic growth based on market principles, than ever before'.[16] In a speech devoted to the subject in Milwaukee in October 1992, he said that Bush

> simply does not seem at home in the mainstream pro-democracy tradition of American foreign policy. [...] in the long run I believe that Mr Bush's neglect of our democratic ideals abroad could do as much harm as our neglect of our economic needs at home.[17]

That speech has been described as Clinton's 'culminating effort to make democracy the centrepiece of the Democratic Party's foreign policy'.[18]

Clearly a believer in the standard liberal assumption that democracy makes for peace, stability and prosperity, Clinton saw democracy as a goal in itself and as a means to secure the United States' interests. His perspective on the international challenges before the country reflected John Lewis Gaddis' argument that the end of the Cold War would mean a geopolitical paradigm shift from totalitarianism or democracy to integration or fragmentation.[19] Thus, according to Berger, the president wanted 'to encourage to the extent possible the positive forces of integration – while preventing the forces of disintegration from dominating the future'.[20] The articulation of Clinton's foreign policy was in part a search for orienting principles (to take Krasner's term) in this new context. It was within a post-Cold War consensus shaped by the traditional tenets of liberal internationalism that had begun to emerge before he took office.[21] As Colin Dueck sums up, Clinton's national security policy was justified by two central claims: that the

United States was (and ought to be) the pre-eminent world power and that it had a special responsibility to promote a liberal order based on free markets and democracy.[22] Democracy promotion should therefore be a central element of foreign policy since democracy breeds the international stability and peace that preserve American hegemony.[23] Neoconservatives spurred this on with claims about American exceptionalism and the inseparability of American values, national security and international order.[24] Clinton also emphasized a peaceful world of free-trading capitalist democracies. As governor, he had developed an interest in global economics as he sought trade and investment opportunities for his state. In his 1991 Georgetown speech, he argued that 'Global democracy means nations at peace with one another, open to one another's ideas and one another's commerce.'[25] As president, he devoted his first major foreign policy speech to the importance of international economics and globalization for American interests and security (and for new democracies). 'If we believe in the bonds of democracy, we must resolve to strengthen the bonds of commerce', he declared.[26]

In 1993, the Clinton administration set out to define and communicate a strategy based on this mix of beliefs. Having been charged with leading this task, National Security Adviser Tony Lake unveiled the concept of democratic enlargement in a speech at Johns Hopkins University on 21 September.[27] He stated that 'To the extent democracy and market economics hold sway in other nations, our own nation will be more secure, prosperous, and influential, while the broader world will be more humane and peaceful.' Therefore, he concluded, 'The successor to a doctrine of containment must be a strategy of enlargement of the world's free community of market democracies.' A few days later, before the United Nations General Assembly, Clinton declared that

> our overriding purpose must be to expand and strengthen the world's community of market-based democracies. During the Cold War, we sought to contain a threat to survival of free institutions. Now we seek to enlarge the circle of nations that live under those free institutions.

He continued:

> [B]roadly based prosperity is clearly the strongest form of preventive diplomacy, and the habits of democracy are the habits of peace. Democracies rarely wage war on one another. They make more reliable partners in trade, in diplomacy, and in the stewardship of our global environment. And democracies, with the rule of law and respect for political, religious, and cultural minorities, are more responsive to their own people and to the protection of human rights.[28]

The United States, Clinton reassured his audience, was not embarking on 'some crusade to force our way of life and doing things on others or to replicate our institutions', stressing instead that American policy would be selective, patient and aligned with the yearnings of foreign populations. The United States would also seek to 'reduce the threat from regimes that are hostile to democracies and to support liberalization of non-democratic states when they are willing to live in peace with the rest of us'.

Democratic enlargement provided an underlying rhetoric and rationale for American foreign policy during the Clinton years. Lake's speech closely matched the administration's National Security Strategy (NSS) that soon followed. The core objectives of *A National Security Strategy of Engagement and Enlargement* were listed as enhancing the United States' security, promoting prosperity at home and promoting democracy. It pronounced that 'All of America's strategic interests – from promoting prosperity at home to checking global threats abroad before they threaten our territory – are served by enlarging the community of democratic and free market nations.'[29] The 1993 'Bottom Up Review' of military goals and programmes also identified internal threats to democracy in the former Soviet Union and the developing world as one of four fundamental strategic dangers for the United States. The content of the NSS varied little in its iterations throughout Clinton's presidency. Listing the challenges for the second term, Lake gave less prominence to democracy relative to security and economics, and focused more on Europe and away from the earlier global rhetoric. Still he insisted:

> Enlargement of democracy is central to all of the challenges I have mentioned today. A democratic Europe is more likely to remain at peace and to be a strong partner in diplomacy, security, and trade. Democratic nations are less likely to go to war against one another – and more likely to join us in promoting arms control, fighting proliferation, and combating the forces of destruction. And democracy under-girds the open markets that promote prosperity, because the rule of law helps guarantee that contracts are respected just as the searchlight of free media helps expose corruption.[30]

Clinton's rhetoric was consistent, repeatedly referring to human rights, democracy and freedom as core elements of American internationalism. At his second inaugural, he proclaimed that 'the world's greatest democracy will lead a whole world of democracies'.[31] In his 1997 State of the Union address, he told Congress that

> By expanding trade, we can advance the cause of freedom and democracy around the world. [...] Every dollar we devote to preventing conflicts, to promoting democracy, to stopping the spread of disease and starvation, brings a sure return in security and savings.[32]

In 1999, the president was still preaching the same message:

> We have to keep standing by those who risk their own freedom to win it for others. [...] We need to deepen democracy where it's already taking root by helping our partners narrow their income gaps, strengthen their legal institutions, and build well-educated, healthy societies.[33]

In his final State of the Union address, Clinton reiterated that 'globalization is about more than economics. Our purpose must be to bring together the world around freedom and democracy and peace and to oppose those who would tear it apart'.[34]

At home, the immediate reaction to democratic enlargement was unenthusiastic. It was criticized both for not offering a compelling overarching theme and for being overambitious.[35] Some saw it as a 'democratist crusade' pursued by 'new moralists'.[36] Many doubted its usefulness. Lake's speech was 'a rhetorical cul-de-sac [that] contained almost no specific policy prescriptions'.[37] Enlargement may have appealed to American ideals but it suffered from not being based on a threat comparable to that of Soviet power.[38] The prospects for its implementation were undermined by the Republican victory in the 1994 mid-term elections, which produced more legislators exhibiting unilateralist or isolationist tendencies and determined to cut the foreign affairs budget. But, although enlargement did not stick as a label, its rationale was one constant throughout Clinton's presidency. After 1994 the administration adopted a more diffuse rhetoric, shifted the emphasis to 'market' democracy and practised democracy promotion with a lower profile.[39] Most foreign policy principals, while not necessarily champions of democracy promotion, shared the assumptions behind it. Lake's influence on the strategy was considerable but enlargement clearly matched Clinton's views about the relevance of democracy to 'the inexorable logic of globalization'.[40] Vice-president Al Gore and Berger shared Clinton's vision of the importance of geo-economics and were committed to enlargement's free-market dimension. When Berger succeeded Lake as National Security Adviser, there was no radical shift in strategic vision. In policy towards Russia, which he oversaw, Deputy Secretary of State Strobe Talbott conceded democracy's relevance to the United States' national interest.[41] A traditionalist diplomat generally seen as uninterested in democracy promotion, Secretary of State Warren Christopher had headed, however, the Interagency Group on Human Rights and Foreign Assistance that had formulated the Carter administration's human rights policy.[42] He made no notable contribution to the administration's rhetoric, but he did argue that 'promoting democracy is perhaps the best preventive diplomacy there is'.[43] And above all, Madeleine Albright, a former Vice-chair of the National Democratic Institute in the 1980s, pushed for greater attention to democracy, first as Ambassador to the United Nations (UN) and then crucially as Secretary of State.

Democratic enlargement through democracy promotion

The goals of democratic enlargement as laid out in Lake's speech and in the NSS were: strengthening the community of major market democracies, fostering and consolidating new democracies and market economies, countering backlash states and helping market democracy take root in regions of humanitarian concern. Lake said little about the means to pursue these goals, though this was elaborated somewhat in the NSS. The United States would mobilize international resources, integrate new democracies in the international security architecture and global markets, take position on democratic reversals, assist reforms, support human rights, work with non-state agents and use humanitarian aid. In the emerging field of democracy promotion, the administration found tools that seemed designed precisely for enlargement, especially for fostering new democracies. They covered using diplomatic channels, political conditionality, assistance programmes and direct support for pro-democracy forces. Democracy and governance capacity-building assistance could also be included in development, humanitarian and nation-building aid.

Initial democracy assistance programmes developed since the 1980s were scattered. The Clinton administration tried to overhaul and integrate the institutional capacity to deliver them, even if an early attempt to reorganize the international affairs budget was blocked in Congress.[44] A National Security Council (NSC) director for democracy affairs was created, as was an under-secretary of state for global affairs whose remit would include democracy and human rights. The State Department's Bureau of Human Rights and Humanitarian Affairs was redesignated as Democracy, Human Rights and Labor, expanded and given additional responsibilities. Since most democracy funds came under the aid budget, the Agency for International Development (AID) became the main channel for democracy assistance. Under Clinton, the agency extended its nascent work in democracy, which in 1995 was approved as one of four pillars of its mission. Accordingly, AID's Centre for Democracy and Governance and Office of Transition Initiatives were created. Elsewhere in the government, however, there were no comparable efforts to institutionalize democracy promotion. Clinton's appointment of Lake and Albright were key decisions in the process, and both in turn recruited similarly-minded staff to the NSC and State Department. Another important nomination was that of Brian Atwood as AID administrator. Formerly the National Democratic Institute president, he strove to make democracy a central part of AID's work, appointing democracy specialists in an agency that sometimes viewed them as interlopers. Such staffing decisions created an embryonic democracy promotion cadre within the policy-making apparatus that gave a fuller operational dimension to the democracy agenda in Clinton's second term.

The Clinton administration frequently claimed its international economic policy could support the spread of market democracies, leading Douglas Brinkley to argue that 'enlargement was about spreading democracy through promoting the gospel of geoeconomics'.[45] Clinton saw the North American Free Trade Agreement partly as a way to help Mexico's transition to a market economy and multiparty democracy, which would set an example for Latin America.[46] Engaging 'big emerging markets' was partly couched in enlargement rhetoric as they might be regional drivers in democratization.[47] Washington also tried to support the adoption of democracy standards by UN bodies, the Organization for Security and Co-operation in Europe, the Organization of American States and the Organization for Economic Co-operation and Development. The administration was also instrumental in launching in 2000 the Community of Democracies, a multilateral group of new and old democracies devoted specifically to promoting democratization.

Funding for democracy promotion was increased. Summing up this commitment is notoriously difficult given the different budget accounts, the potential for double-accounting and the issue of defining what exactly qualifies as democracy promotion. Thomas Carothers calculates that this aid rose from around $100 million annually at the start of the 1990s to more than $700 million when Clinton left office.[48] While AID's budget declined from $14.1 billion in 1993 to $12.6 billion in 2000,[49] its 'Democracy & Governance' obligations increased from $317 million to $494 million.[50] Clinton also sought a large funding increase for the National Endowment for Democracy (NED) but this was defeated in Congress.[51] However, he did help entrench NED funding, which was still not entirely secure when he took office, and its grant revenues increased from $32 million in 1993 to $42 million in 2001.[52] The role of the NED 'family' grew, especially in countries where there was less scope for action by government agencies.[53]

Listing democracy after national security and economic prosperity in the NSS goals showed that the pursuit of democratic enlargement would be determined by these considerations. In practice, the Clinton administration's democracy promotion was selective, frequently undercut by other interests.[54] The administration lacked a long-term strategy across agencies. Optimism about rapid, easily guided transitions led to overconfidence and generic programmes that tended to be developed reactively. Democracy promotion paid insufficient attention to the socio-economic impediments to democratization in many countries, while simultaneous Washington-driven market liberalization had socio-economic consequences that undermined transitions. Furthermore, democracy funding would have had to be increased much more to match enlargement's ambitious goals. Democracy promotion was tentative during Clinton's first term and more assertive in his second. Despite the global rhetoric of enlargement, the focus was principally on Russia and eastern Europe, while in relations with most countries democracy promotion was only peripheral. There were no serious attempts to target potential regional 'beachheads' until 1999–2000 with the identification of Colombia, Indonesia, Nigeria and Ukraine. Meanwhile Asia and the Middle East were effectively no-go areas. As Carothers summarizes, the administration ranged 'from serious engagement to almost complete disinterest'.[55]

Russia was the cornerstone of democratic enlargement and the highest-profile instance of Clinton's democracy promotion.[56] He committed himself to supporting the country's transition in the belief that American interests were best served by the survival in office of Boris Yeltsin and those identified as reformers. Yet Russia also epitomizes the strategy's contradictions and shortcomings. American policy became a triangulation between the goals of democratization, bolstering Yeltsin, and negotiating clashing American and Russian interests, with democracy usually losing out against security and economics. The decision to support Yeltsin, come what may, ruled out democracy promotion actions that might penalize him, leaving only direct support to pro-democracy actors (taken to be Yeltsin and his allies) and AID-led programmes. Funds for the latter were a small portion of American assistance, however. Many in the administration argued the priority should be a Russian market economy, which would enable democratization. Until the 1998

Russian financial crisis, assistance policy was dominated by the Treasury and the economic agenda took precedence. Between 1992 and 2000, $631 million of Freedom Support Act funds for Russia were allocated to democracy and $1.4 billion to market reforms.[57] Only in 1999 did AID's spending on democracy overtake that on economic liberalization.[58] Equating Yeltsin with Russian democracy led Clinton to acquiesce to his many violations of it. Official and unofficial channels were used to help Yeltsin in deeply flawed polls, especially the 1996 presidential election. For Clinton, what mattered most was keeping the Russian president in power. Thus the administration undermined its democracy agenda in Russia by overpraising small instances of progress while overlooking serious failings, creating the impression that it was content with the appearance of democracy.[59] Unconditional support for Yeltsin brought short-term benefits but left the United States hostage to his fortunes and his caprices. It also discredited the notions of reform and democracy for many Russians, and along with perceived humiliation of Russia on the international stage, led to rising anti-Americanism in the country.

Democracy promotion by the Clinton administration clearly did not speed up Russia's democratization, which after an initial rise went into reverse as the 1990s progressed. For some it even contributed to its retreat.[60] American-backed market reforms are also criticized for causing socio-economic decay, creating a corrupt oligarchy and derailing the transition.[61] Criticism of the Clinton administration's democracy promotion efforts resonates and their impact for good is certainly debatable. At best they had marginal influence in spreading the norm of democracy, in electoral assistance and party-building, and in strengthening governance institutions. Given the alternatives at the time, though, within the United States' broader engagement with Russia they may have helped to avoid a worse trajectory. The size of the challenge of reforming post-Soviet Russia cannot be underestimated either, and nor should the United States' influence for good or bad be overestimated. Russian democratization in the 1990s was ultimately shaped by Russian actors and forces, and Russian decisions that had lasting consequences for democracy were taken before Clinton took office.[62]

Unlike Russia, post-communist eastern Europe continued to make democratization progress throughout the 1990s. In this it was helped by more consistent, less conflicted American democracy promotion. Building on inherited initiatives, the Clinton administration used diplomatic channels to emphasize democracy issues and assistance programmes to consolidate transitions. AID democracy funding for eastern Europe rose from $21.6 million in 1992 to $93.9 million in 2000, with the Balkan countries accounting for more than half, and Poland, Bulgaria and Romania as the other major recipients. American assistance for building civil society, strengthening institutions and improving electoral processes contributed to democratic consolidation. Where backsliding threatened, assistance played a role in 'electoral revolutions' in Bulgaria, Romania, Slovakia, Croatia and Serbia.[63] Serbia's case is the most striking. The Clinton administration first downplayed democracy there, considering Slobodan Milosevic a necessary evil for implementing the Dayton peace accord, but this gradually changed, especially with the advent of the Kosovo conflict. American policy grew into a successful engagement in 1998–2000, alongside European partners, in supporting opposition efforts to unseat Milosevic, with the State Department, AID, the NED institutions and other American states and non-state actors spending around $40 million.[64] Across eastern Europe, the North Atlantic Treaty Organization (NATO) expansion helped to 'lock in' democratic progress for the countries that joined in 1999 and those that would in 2004.[65] Secretary of Defence William Perry's principles for expansion included using the prospect of membership as an incentive for aspirants to ensure civilian command of the military, economic liberalization and minority rights. This was put into practice through the Partnership for Peace process while democracy was declared one of NATO's concerns at its 1997 Summit. Democratic enlargement should not be taken as synonymous with NATO expansion. Enlargement was a lasting influence on Clinton's foreign policy and dealing with security issues in eastern Europe was a strategic priority, so it was logical for them to combine in NATO expansion.

It was not until later in Clinton's second term that more democracy attention was paid to the post-Soviet Newly Independent States (NIS).[66] Partly this was because Russia took up most American time and resources, but also because of a belief that their democratization would be served by focusing efforts on the region's dominant country, whose progress would then influence its neighbours. The shift towards the NIS in 1999–2000 was part of a reorientation of American policy, especially after the 1998 financial crisis had deepened disillusion with Russia. After initial progress at the collapse of the Soviet Union, democratization in almost all the NIS was either static or in retreat in the 1990s. Autocratic regimes quickly entrenched themselves from Belarus to Central Asia. For strategic reasons, only the Ukraine was the recipient of sustained democracy assistance, yet for the same reasons Washington refrained from criticizing President Leonid Kuchma as accusations of corruption and authoritarianism grew. Otherwise, democracy promotion was limited, late and ineffective in most countries, with only Armenia, Georgia and Kazakhstan receiving any notable assistance. Engagement with the NIS was security-oriented and led by the Defence Department. Along with accessing energy resources, countering Russian influence and preventing the spread of Islamism, this meant an acceptance of regimes even less democratic than Moscow's. Lack of knowledge about the NIS, the low geopolitical importance of several of them, and pessimism about their prospects were also limiting factors. Whatever democracy promotion efforts there were, they fared marginally better in resource-poor countries (Georgia, Armenia and Kyrgyzstan) than in resource-rich ones that could ignore them (Azerbaijan, Kazakhstan, Turkmenistan, Uzbekistan).[67] The belief that the NIS should be given time receded as it became clear democratization was failing, but by then the United States' 'moment for leverage' during the initial state-building phase was over.[68] As with Russia, economic liberalization was seen as enabling democracy and prioritized, with similar consequences. There was also an assumption that the NIS were mostly identical, meaning that the few democracy programmes were insufficiently country-specific and replicated those in

Russia. Furthermore, when the United States did not condemn the deterioration of Russia's democracy or alter its stance towards Yeltsin, this sent the message to NIS leaders that they could ignore the democracy rhetoric as long as they cooperated with the United States on other interests.

In Latin America, the Clinton administration's democracy promotion was intermittent.[69] AID democracy funding fluctuated, with Haiti the largest recipient, followed by El Salvador, Nicaragua and Guatemala. Attention was only occasionally paid to Peru and Colombia since their rulers' cooperation was needed against the narcotics trade and transnational crime. When Albright identified Colombia as a priority country in 1999, democracy assistance was included as a minor component of the Plan Colombia initiative. In Haiti, where President Jean-Bertrand Aristide had been deposed in 1991, Clinton took a more consistent position, eventually ordering the first 'military intervention specifically to restore democracy at the request of a democratically elected government in exile'.[70] Even if also driven by humanitarian, immigration and political considerations, the intervention enabled Haiti's first handover of power from one democratically elected leader to another in the 1995 election. But otherwise the Clinton administration's assistance to Haiti was not matched by much democracy progress, perhaps not surprisingly given the considerable obstacles faced by the country. Elsewhere the United States can claim a small helping role in democratization in some countries, having engaged diplomatically at critical junctures in the Dominican Republic, Ecuador, El Salvador, Guatemala and Paraguay. But while Latin America made good democratization progress in the 1990s, American democracy promotion was not a major factor in this. For example, having adopted a low-profile stance and encouraged reforms behind the scene, it was not a direct influence in Mexico's transition from one-party rule.

In Africa the Clinton administration's actions did not match its words about making democracy a regional priority.[71] While there was significant progress across the continent, American democracy promotion was selective and reactive, over-ridden by economic interests or by security issues, especially in the Horn and Great Lakes regions. Washington maintained close relationships with 'soft authoritarian' rulers in Ethiopia, Rwanda and Uganda, which it needed to help maintain regional stability. Access to natural resources, especially oil, led to toleration of autocratic rulers in Angola, Equatorial Guinea, Gabon and Nigeria. The administration argued that its economic agenda, embodied in the African Growth and Opportunity Act, would assist democratization but it is not clear what impact this had. The United States did make a significant contribution to South Africa's transition in the run-up to the 1994 elections, and low-key assistance also helped transitions in countries such as Namibia and Mozambique. The administration also made a small contribution to Nigeria's transition from military dictatorship, but only after it was sparked by Sani Abacha's death in 1998. Elsewhere American efforts and their impact were negligible, particularly where democracy regressed as in Ivory Coast, Kenya and Zimbabwe.

Very little was done to promote democracy in Asia under Clinton. While the administration eventually engaged with Indonesia's transition, it did so very late.

Although American non-governmental organizations and some parts of the government engaged with Indonesian reform groups, the administration only changed its policy after President Suharto's fall in 1998. In Pakistan Washington did little to support democratization after the army coup in 1999. With China the administration backtracked quickly from attempting to leverage trade negotiations for progress on democracy and human rights. It abandoned any such rhetoric and spoke instead of strategic engagement and dialogue on the basis that economic interaction would help liberalization and human rights.[72] American officials later conceded that this had hardly any impact.[73] In the Middle East, there was a clear push-back against democracy promotion on strategic grounds in the State Department and other parts of the administration. Bilateral relations remained dominated by security and energy interests, and Clinton continued the policy of alliance with Egypt's military rulers and the theocratic monarchies of the Gulf States.

Legacies and lessons

Despite its shortcomings noted above, the Clinton administration left a positive legacy for American democracy promotion. It marked an important stage in its institutionalization, turning earlier disparate efforts into a broader approach. This, and the increased democracy rhetoric, influenced policy towards some countries, and there were attempts to incorporate democracy in nation-building in Bosnia, Haiti and Kosovo. The realignment of resources in AID and the State Department was consequential and there was an expansion of the cadre of democracy promotion experts. As a result, by 2000 a more developed institutional framework had taken shape to support democratization abroad, and the integration of diplomacy, development aid and democracy promotion was improving. That this 'upscaling' built on an inherited base does not diminish the Clinton administration's contribution. It might have happened under a re-elected Bush or another president in the same situation but perhaps not to the same extent. Clinton's presidency was also a period of trial and error during which the democracy promotion learning curve swung upwards. If their goals were highly ambitious, Clinton and his advisers were not alone in buying into the early 1990s' enthusiasm about democratization and what democracy promotion could achieve. That enthusiasm did not encourage rigorous strategizing, but inconsistency and haphazardness resulted also from bureaucratic factors, while international developments allowed little time for reflection. At first, American policy-makers operated on a basic understanding of democratization. Transitions everywhere appeared easy and country-specific problems of consolidation only gradually became apparent. The increase in democracy promotion was an iterative process that eventually produced feedback mechanisms to improve programmes. Having started with a simple template,[74] practitioners discerned more what democracy promotion required in practical terms, including a broader political economy approach that is still being developed today. In its later years, the Clinton administration also grew aware of needing to focus resources strategically, and that assistance had to be consistent and long term.

Democratic enlargement tried to articulate deep-rooted American ideas about political order, international relations and national interest in a cohesive and coherent strategy. With it, the Clinton administration made some progress in elevating democracy among foreign-policy considerations. Lake, Albright and others challenged, however inconsistently, the notion that promoting democracy in practice was incompatible with pursuing national-interest goals. This must be balanced with criticism, though. Enlargement was a global strategy in theory but not in application. Only in eastern Europe and Russia did it frame policy in a relatively comprehensive way. At the same time, security and economic interests exerted a greater influence than democracy in relations with many countries, problematically not least with Russia. The Clinton administration's challenge to the incompatibility between democratization and national interest was therefore more at the rhetorical level than the policy level. Democratic enlargement's architects gave insufficient consideration to what policies and instruments would be needed. When this combined with the usual policy-making competition in government, there was no fully integrated inter-agency approach to implementation, which was mostly left to officials willing and able to act as policy entrepreneurs. A fuller implementation of enlargement would have needed greater effort from a wider range of policy-makers, starting with the president.

As set out above, the Clinton administration's democracy promotion efforts had a small positive impact at some junctures in some countries by playing a supporting role to domestic factors. (This is supported by two global quantitative studies that find a small positive impact for AID's democracy assistance in the 1990s.)[75] But these efforts were also ineffective in many cases. Through the dawning realization that democracy promotion could do little more than support what was already happening abroad, the Clinton administration began to learn tentatively a broader lesson about the limits of the United States' ability to shape the political trajectory of other countries. In the 1990s, democratization made great strides worldwide and coincided with advances for American security and economic interests globally. In that respect, identifying the spread of democracy as beneficial for the United States was not mistaken. Setting this as a goal to be pursued proactively turned out to be problematic, however. That even a hegemon such as the United States in the 1990s could do little directly to drive democratization abroad, along with the complexity of the relationships between democratization and its presumed utilitarian consequences, undermines the core claim of enlargement about the instrumental value of democracy promotion.

Any enlargement-related strategic gains the Clinton administration made came in a much more diffuse way than a straight sequence of democracy promotion cause to democratization effect to utilitarian consequence.[76] Enlargement helped frame progress towards some national-security goals and build useful relationships with democratizing countries, particularly in eastern Europe but also in Latin America and Africa, bringing them into the American sphere of economic and diplomatic influence. The Cold War aftermath was managed peacefully in eastern Europe (except in the Balkans) with democratization assisting progress on security goals, especially in NATO expansion. Most of the region's countries were successfully integrated into the transatlantic community and became staunch American allies as well as economic partners. This was driven above all by their security bandwagoning with the United States against a resurgence of Russian power, but the enlargement framework played a facilitating role in this. The critical issue, though, is the impossibility to isolate a direct and independent role for American democracy promotion in helping produce these gains, compounding the problem regarding its impact on democratization. These gains happened within, and were contingent on, wider transformative developments in world politics and economics, and may well have done so had American policy been framed without reference to democracy. In the case of eastern Europe, for example, prospective membership of the European Union most likely played a greater role, at least in driving democratization.

Democratic enlargement becomes even more problematic where democracy promotion did not increase democratization and yet the United States made strategic gains. Russia is the ultimate example. The United States went some way towards integrating its former foe into the American-led international order and its institutions. While dealing with a frequently recalcitrant Russia, the Clinton administration met security goals in arms reductions and nuclear counter-proliferation, in building a new European security architecture, in Bosnia and in Kosovo. This was mostly due to the power imbalance between the two countries, but as with eastern Europe the enlargement framework smoothed the path.[77] The causal role of democracy promotion in this is doubtful, however, given the lack of democratization in Russia. It is only possible to see one by accepting the administration's questionable equation of democracy with Yeltsin. The partnership with Yeltsin often paid off for Clinton, but this was not the same thing as one with a democratic Russia. Another possible positive view of democratic enlargement and American democracy promotion in Russia depends on counterfactual propositions that Russia would have taken a worse path in their absence, that more and better democracy promotion would have made Russia more democratic, and that greater democracy would have led to a more cooperative Russia and more strategic gains for the United States. A case might be built for the first proposition, but less so for the other two.

Equally problematic for democratic enlargement are cases where lack of democratization (with no or barely any democracy promotion) matched strategic benefits for the United States. The Clinton administration made progress towards several goals in relations with Asian and Middle Eastern countries where there was no democratization and where democracy promotion was not a factor. Across the NIS there is no clear or consistent pattern between the limited American democracy promotion efforts, democratization trajectory and strategic gains. Other than in Georgia, Armenia and Azerbaijan, the region was more stable and peaceful than had been anticipated. It also became open to American diplomatic influence and business interests, with access to the energy resources of Central Asia and the Caucasus secured. Iranian influence did not spread and Russia struggled to hold on to its regional hegemony. These were good outcomes for the United States but they were not shaped by enlargement and democracy promotion. They were mostly explained by local and regional factors.[78] That substantial benefits can be had in the absence of democracy promotion as well as that of democratization raises a serious question about the instrumental utility of democracy promotion in foreign policy.

Conclusion

At the end of the Cold War, taking democratization as beneficial for the United States was part of a widespread mindset for policy-makers. Translating this into democracy promotion policies had begun before Bill Clinton took office and his administration must be placed in this context, as well as that of a propitious combination of international and domestic factors. The worldwide swell of democratization, the retreat of communism and the collapse of the Soviet Union created opportunities for American democracy promotion. On Clinton's watch, the United States had a historic chance to promote its interests worldwide in the absence of a significant rival in power or ideology while enjoying a domestic economic boom. The strategy of democratic enlargement and the expansion of democracy promotion did not come about only through the agency of policy-makers, therefore, but also because contemporary conditions made them possible and attractive, removing obstacles to the United States' liberal internationalist impulses. Clinton's United States was in a position to roll the dice on the proposition that it could pursue its national interest by promoting its political values abroad.

Despite furthering the institutionalization and operationalization of American democracy promotion, the Clinton administration did not come close to delivering all that democratic enlargement promised – but this owed even more to unrealistic goals than to insufficient effort. Where it could draw on previous democracy promotion experiences, the administration found some guidelines for implementing enlargement, but – as a whole – it ran into trouble in trying to harness directly the spread of democratization to American security and economic interests. Given its prescriptive weaknesses and its incomplete implementation, democratic enlargement can seem little more than the expression of a liberal internationalist wish for more democracies in the world and for the United States to support and profit from this rather than a strategy proper. However, it is more accurate to describe it as a strategic framework or orienting principle for foreign policy. And since it belongs in an American historical tradition, enlargement should not be judged as a radical attempt to reorient foreign policy but rather as its reframing to fit the times through greater emphasis on one of its established strands. In this respect, while the pursuit of enlargement through democracy promotion coincided and facilitated some strategic benefits to the United States in relations with some countries, these were more than matched by failures of execution and sins of omission. Therefore the record of the Clinton administration shows that, while elevating democracy among the goals of foreign policy was not detrimental to the United States, there was very limited justification for promoting it on short- or medium-term instrumental grounds.

Notes

1 Samuel P. Huntington, *Political Order in Changing Societies* (Yale University Press, 1968), p. 5.

2 Tony Smith, *America's Mission: The United States and the Worldwide Struggle for Democracy in the Twentieth Century* (Princeton, NJ: Princeton University Press, 1994), p. 286.

3 For overviews of Clinton's foreign policy, see for example Derek Chollet and James Goldgeier, *America between the Wars, 11/9 to 9/11: The Misunderstood Years between the Fall of the Berlin Wall and the Start of the War on Terror* (New York, NY: Public Affairs, 2008); Warren I. Cohen, *America's Failing Empire: U.S. Foreign Relations since the Cold War* (Oxford: Blackwell, 2005); John Dumbrell, *Clinton's Foreign Policy: Between the Bushes, 1992–2000* (Abingdon: Routledge, 2010); Emily O. Goldman and Larry Berman, 'Engaging the World: First Impressions of the Clinton Foreign Policy Legacy', in Colin Campbell and Bert A. Rockman (eds), *The Clinton Legacy* (New York: Chatham House, 2000), p. 249; Richard N. Haass, 'The Squandered Presidency', *Foreign Affairs*, Vol. 79, No. 3 (2000); P. Edward Haley, *Strategies of Dominance: The Misdirection of U.S. Foreign Policy* (Washington, DC: Woodrow Wilson Center Press, 2006); William G. Hyland, *Clinton's World: Remaking American Foreign Policy* (Westport, CT: Praeger Trade, 1999); Stephen M. Walt, 'Two Cheers for Clinton's Foreign Policy', *Foreign Affairs*, Vol. 79, No. 2 (2000).

4 See for example Zbigniew Brzezinski, *Second Chance: Three Presidents and the Crisis of American Superpower* (New York, NY: Basic Books, 2007), pp. 89–90.

5 Haass, 'The Squandered Presidency', p. 136.

6 John Dumbrell, 'Was There a Clinton Doctrine? President Clinton's Foreign Policy Reconsidered', *Diplomacy & Statecraft*, Vol. 13, No. 2 (2002), pp. 44–45.

7 Strobe Talbott, *The Russia Hand: A Memoir of Presidential Diplomacy* (New York: Random House, 2002), p. 133.

8 Dumbrell, *Clinton's Foreign Policy*, p. 41.

9 Walter Russell Mead, *Special Providence: American Foreign Policy and How it Changed the World* (London: Routledge, 2002), p. 285.

10 Stephen D. Krasner, 'An Orienting Principle for Foreign Policy', *Policy Review*, No. 163, October (2010).

11 Samuel R. Berger, 'Obama's National Security Strategy: A Little George Bush, Lots of Bill Clinton', *The New York Times*, 30 May 2010.

12 Michael Mandelbaum, 'Foreign Policy as Social Work', *Foreign Affairs*, Vol. 75, No. 1 (1996).

13 Chollet and Goldgeier, *America between the Wars*, pp. 35–36.

14 Bill Clinton, 'A New Covenant for American Security: Remarks to Students at Georgetown University', 12 December 1991.

15 Thomas Friedman, 'Foreign Policy: Turning His Sights Overseas, Clinton Sees a Problem at 1600 Pennsylvania Avenue', *The New York Times*, 2 April 1992.

16 'Excerpts from Interview with Clinton on Goals for Presidency', *The New York Times*, 28 June 1992.

17 Thomas L. Friedman, 'Excerpts From Speech By Clinton on U.S. Role', *The New York Times*, 2 October 1992.

18 Chollet and Goldgeier, *America Between the Wars*, p. 42.

19 John Lewis Gaddis, 'Toward the Post-Cold War World', *Foreign Affairs*, Vol. 70, No. 2 (1991), p. 121.

20 Samuel Berger, 'A Foreign Policy Agenda for the Second Term. Speech at Center for Strategic and International Studies, Washington, DC, 27 March 1997', (1997).

21 See for example, Tony Smith, *A Pact with the Devil: Washington's Bid for World Supremacy and the Betrayal of American Promise* (New York: Routledge, 2007).

22 Colin Dueck, *Reluctant Crusaders: Power, Culture, and Change in American Grand Strategy* (Princeton, NJ: Princeton University Press, 2006), p. 114.

23 See for example G. John Ikenberry, 'Liberal Hegemony or Empire? American Power in the Age of Unipolarity', in David Held and Mathias Koenig-Archibugi (eds), *American*

Power in the 21st Century (Cambridge: Polity, 2004) and 'America's Liberal Grand Strategy: Democracy and National Security in the Post-War Era', in M. Cox, G. J. Ikenberry and T. Inoguchi (eds), *American Democracy Promotion: Impulses, Strategies, and Impacts* (Oxford: Oxford University Press, 2000).

24 Smith, *Pact with the Devil*, pp. 26–29.

25 Clinton, *A New Covenant for American Security*.

26 Bill Clinton, 'American Leadership and Global Change: Address at the Centennial Celebration, American University, Washington, DC, 26 February 1993', *U.S. Department of State Dispatch*, Vol. 4, No. 9 (1993), p. 115.

27 Anthony Lake, 'From Containment to Enlargement: Address at the School of Advanced International Studies, Johns Hopkins University, Washington, DC, September 21, 1993', *U.S. Department of State Dispatch*, Vol. 4, No. 39 (1993).

28 Bill Clinton, 'Confronting the Challenges of a Broader World: Address to the UN General Assembly, New York, 27 September 1993', *U.S. Department of State Dispatch*, Vol. 4, No. 39 (1993).

29 *A National Security Strategy of Engagement and Enlargement* (Washington, DC: The White House, 1995), p. 22.

30 Anthony Lake, 'Laying the Foundations for a New American Century: Address at the Fletcher School of Law and Diplomacy, Tufts University, Medford, Massachusetts, April 25, 1996', *U.S. Department of State Dispatch*, Vol. 7, No. 18 (1996).

31 Bill Clinton, 'Inaugural Address, 20 January 1997' (Washington, DC: The White House, 1997).

32 Bill Clinton, 'Address Before a Joint Session of the Congress on the State of the Union, 4 February 1997' (Washington, DC: The White House, 1997).

33 Bill Clinton, 'Remarks by the President on Foreign Policy, Grand Hyatt Hotel, San Francisco, California, February 26, 1999' (Washington, DC: The White House, 1999).

34 Bill Clinton, 'Address Before a Joint Session of the Congress on the State of the Union, 27 January 2000' (Washington, DC: The White House, 2000).

35 Chollet and Goldgeier, *America between the Wars*, pp. 79–83.

36 David C. Hendrickson, 'The Democratist Crusade: Interventions, Economic Sanctions, and Engagement', *World Policy Journal*, Vol. 11, No. 4 (1994/1995), pp. 22–29. Alvin Z. Rubinstein, 'The new moralists on a road to hell', *Orbis*, Vol. 40, No. 2 (1996).

37 John C. Hulsman, *A Paradigm for the New World Order: A Schools-of-Thought Analysis of American Foreign Policy in the Post-Cold War Era* (London: Macmillan, 1997), p. 103.

38 Emily O. Goldman and Larry Berman, 'Engaging the World: First Impressions of the Clinton Foreign Policy Legacy', in Colin Campbell and Bert A. Rockman (eds), *The Clinton Legacy* (New York: Chatham House, 2000), p. 238.

39 Rick Travis, 'The Promotion of Democracy at the End of the Twentieth Century', in James M. Scott (ed.), *After the End: Making U.S. Foreign Policy in the Post-Cold War World* (Durham, NC: Duke University Press, 1998), pp. 262–65.

40 Clinton, 'Remarks by the President on Foreign Policy'.

41 Strobe Talbott, 'Democracy and the National Interest', *Foreign Affairs*, Vol. 75, No. 6 (1996), p. 52.

42 David F. Schmitz and Vanessa Walker, 'Jimmy Carter and the Foreign Policy of Human Rights: The Development of a Post-Cold War Foreign Policy', *Diplomatic History*, Vol. 28, No. 1, (2004).

43 Warren Christopher, 'Remaking American Diplomacy in the Post-Cold War World. Address at National Foreign Affairs Training Center, 13 October 1993', *U.S. Department of State Dispatch*, Vol. 4, No. 42 (1993), p. 719.

44 Thomas Carothers, 'Democracy Promotion Under Clinton', *The Washington Quarterly*, Vol. 18, No. 4 (1995), p. 19. Travis, 'The Promotion of Democracy', pp. 257–59.

45 Douglas Brinkley, 'Democratic Enlargement: The Clinton Doctrine', *Foreign Policy*, No. 106 (1997), p. 125.

46 Bill Clinton, *My Life* (New York: Alfred A. Knopf, 2004), p. 432.

47 I. M. Destler, 'Foreign Economic Policy Making Under Bill Clinton', in Scott, *After the End*, p. 94.

48 Thomas Carothers, *The Clinton Record on Democracy Promotion* (Washington, DC: Carnegie Endowment for International Peace, 2000), p. 4.

49 Sarah E. Mendelson, 'Democracy Assistance and Political Transition in Russia: Between Success and Failure', *International Security*, Vol. 25, No. 4 (2001), p. 70.

50 Calculated in constant 1995 dollars. All references to USAID democracy spending here are from Steven E. Finkel, Aníbal Pérez-Liñán and Mitchell E. Seligson, *Effects of U.S. Foreign Assistance on Democracy Building: Results of a Cross-National Quantitative Study* (Washington, DC: USAID, Vanderbilt University, University of Pittsburgh, 2006).

51 Travis, 'The Promotion of Democracy', pp. 259–60.

52 NED, *Annual Reports*.

53 Larry Diamond, *Promoting Democracy in the 1990s: Actors and Instruments, Issues and Imperatives.* (Washington, DC: Carnegie Commission on Preventing Deadly Conflict, 1995).

54 On overall evaluations of Clinton's democracy promotion, see Carothers, *The Clinton Record*; Michael Cox, 'Wilsonianism Resurgent? The Clinton Administration and the Promotion of Democracy', in Cox, Ikenberry and Inoguchi, *American Democracy Promotion*; David P. Forsythe and Barbara Ann J. Rieffer, 'US Foreign Policy and Enlarging the Democratic Community', *Human Rights Quarterly*, Vol. 22, No. 4 (2000); Barbara Ann J. Rieffer and Kristan Mercer, 'US Democracy Promotion: The Clinton and Bush Administrations', *Global Society*, Vol. 19, No. 4 (2005); and Travis, 'The Promotion of Democracy'.

55 Carothers, *The Clinton Record*, p. 2.

56 On Russia, see James M. Goldgeier and Michael McFaul, *Power and Purpose: U.S. Policy Toward Russia After the Cold War* (Washington, DC: Brookings Institution Press, 2003); Lee Marsden, *Lessons from Russia: Clinton and US Democracy Promotion* (Aldershot: Ashgate, 2005); Michael McFaul, 'American Efforts at Promoting Regime Change in the Soviet Union and then Russia: Lessons Learned' (CDDRL, Stanford Institute on International Studies, 2005); and Mendelson, 'Democracy Assistance and Political Transition'.

57 US Government Accountability Office, *Foreign Assistance: International Efforts to Aid Russia's Transition Have Had Mixed Results* (Washington, DC: 2000), p. 170.

58 ibid., p. 176.

59 Mendelson, 'Democracy Assistance and Political Transition'.

60 See for example Marsden, *Lessons from Russia*.

61 Janine R. Wedel, *Collision and Collusion: The Strange Case of Western Aid to Eastern Europe 1989–1998* (New York: St Martin's, 1998) and Stephen F. Cohen, *Failed Crusade: American and the Tragedy of Post-Communist Russia* (New York: W.W. Norton, 2000).

62 Archie Brown, 'From Democratization to "Guided Democracy"', *Journal of Democracy*, Vol. 12, No. 4 (2001); McFaul, 'American Efforts', p. 23; and Lilia Shevtsova, *Russia – Lost in Transition: The Yeltsin and Putin Legacies* (Washington, DC: Carnegie Endowment for International Peace, 2007).

63 Valerie Bunce and Sharon Wolchik, 'International Diffusion and Postcommunist Electoral Revolutions', *Communist and Postcommunist Studies*, Vol. 39, No. 3 (2006).

64 Thomas Carothers, 'Ousting Foreign Strongmen: Lessons from Serbia' (Carnegie Endowment for International Peace, 2001), pp. 3–5.

65 Rachel A. Epstein, 'Nato Enlargement and the Spread of Democracy: Evidence and Expectations', *Security Studies*, Vol. 14, No. 1 (2005) and James Goldgeier, 'NATO Expansion: The Anatomy of a Decision', *The Washington Quarterly*, Vol. 21, No. 1 (1998).

66 On the NIS, see Yury V. Bosin, 'Supporting Democracy in the Former Soviet Union: Why the Impact of US Assistance has been Below Expectations', *International Studies Quarterly*, Vol. 1 (2012); Neil MacFarlane, *Western Engagement in the Caucasus and Central Asia* (London: Royal Institute of International Affairs, 1999); Martha Brill Olcott, *Central Asia's Second Chance* (Washington, DC: Carnegie Endowment for International Peace, 2005); and Martha Brill Olcott, 'Democracy Promotion in Central Asia: From High

Expectations to Disillusionment', in Anna Kreikemeyer and Wolfgang Zellner (eds), *The Quandaries of Promoting Democracy in Central Asia: Experiences and Perspectives from Europe and the USA, Report of a Transatlantic Workshop at the Centre for OSCE Research in Hamburg* (2007).

67 MacFarlane, *Western Engagement*, pp. 62–63.

68 Thomas Carothers, 'Advancing Democracy: The Clinton Legacy', remarks at the Carnegie Endowment for International Peace, Washington, DC, 12 January' (2001).

69 On Latin America, see Carothers, *The Clinton Record*; Forsythe and Rieffer, 'US Foreign Policy'; and David Scott Palmer, *U.S. Relations with Latin America During the Clinton Years: Opportunities Lost or Opportunities Squandered?* (Gainesville, FL: University Press of Florida, 2006).

70 Morton H. Halperin and Michael Hochman Fuchs, *The Survival and the Success of Liberty: A Democracy Agenda for US Foreign Policy* (New York: Century Foundation Press, 2009), p. 191.

71 On Africa, see John F. Clark, 'The Clinton Administration and Africa: White House Involvement and the Foreign Affairs Bureaucracies', *Issue: A Journal of Opinion*, Vol. 26, No. 2 (1998); Brian J. Hesse, 'Celebrate or Hold Suspect? Bill Clinton and George W. Bush in Africa', *Journal of Contemporary African Studies*, Vol. 23, No. 3 (2005); Peter M. Lewis, 'Pursuing US Economic Interests in Africa'; Gwendolyn Mikell and Princeton N. Lyman, 'Critical US bilateral relations in Africa: Nigeria and South Africa', in J. Stephen Morrison and Jennifer G. Cooke (eds), *Africa Policy in the Clinton Years: Critical Choices for the Bush Administration* (Washington, DC: CSIS Press, 2001); and Peter J. Schraeder, 'Continuity and Change in US Foreign Policy Towards Southern Africa: Assessing the Clinton Administration', *Nordic Journal of African Studies*, Vol. 10, No. 2 (2001).

72 See, for example, Samuel R. Berger, 'Remarks at the Council on Foreign Relations, New York', 6 June 1997.

73 Harold Hongju Koh, 'A United States Human Rights Policy for the 21st Century', *Saint Louis University Law Journal*, Vol. 46 (2002), p. 298.

74 Thomas Carothers, *Aiding Democracy Abroad: The Learning Curve* (Washington, DC: Carnegie Endowment for International Peace, 1999), pp. 86–89.

75 Steven E. Finkel, Aníbal Pérez-Liñàn and Mitchell E. Seligson, 'The Effects of U.S. Foreign Assistance on Democracy Building, 1990–2003', *World Politics*, Vol. 59, No. 3 (2007); James M. Scott and Carrie A. Steele, 'Sponsoring Democracy: The United States and Democracy Aid to the Developing World, 1988–2001', *International Studies Quarterly*, Vol. 55 (2011).

76 Nicolas Bouchet, 'The Role of Democracy Promotion in US Foreign Policy: Evaluating Bill Clinton's Strategy of Democratic Enlargement', doctoral dissertation, University of London (2012).

77 Goldgeier and McFaul, *Power and Purpose*, pp. 355–62 and Stephen M. Walt, 'Two Cheers for Clinton's Foreign Policy', *Foreign Affairs* (2000), p. 71.

78 MacFarlane, *Western Engagement*, pp. 52–55.

10

GEORGE W. BUSH

Timothy J. Lynch

Despite assertions of a strong democracy promotion agenda – by both its proponents and detractors – the central character of George W. Bush's foreign policy remains the focus of intense debate. Did it fail because it promoted too much democracy or too little? Did it succeed because it embraced the universality of democracy or because it rejected it? During and after Bush's second term, it was clear to several commentators that the Arab Middle East – the central focus of Bush's 'freedom agenda' – had shown the least democratic improvement.[1] In 2011, however, Arab dictatorships began to fall. By February of that year, Barack Obama had joined a war to end the four-decade rule of Libya's Colonel Muammar Gaddafi. By August, regimes in Cairo, Tripoli and Tunis had been overthrown and the peoples of Bahrain and Syria were in open revolt. Gaddafi was pulled from a drain and summarily executed. By May 2012 Egypt had held the Arab world's first competitive presidential election and sentenced the ousted Hosni Mubarak to life in prison. This stunning and largely unpredicted revolutionary wave invites the question of how far Bush can be credited with its beginning, even as he seemingly lost faith with its inevitability later in his term.

This chapter assesses Bush's democracy promotion efforts in the Middle East (with some comparison of efforts elsewhere) and queries, first, how far his rhetoric was matched by an operable strategy and, second, how far that strategy can be credited with a catalytic role in the Arab Spring. In Chapter 7 of this book, John Dumbrell asks how far Jimmy Carter could be credited with the unravelling of Soviet communism. In this chapter, we ask a similar question about George W. Bush and the rupturing of Arab autocracy. The chapter's argument is that Bush's impact was neither as great as he would like to believe nor as negligible as his opponents insist. This analysis and attendant argument will also allow us to place Bush's democracy promotion alongside those of his predecessors – and of his successor.

This chapter offers a four-part typology of American democracy promotion from 2001 to 2009. The first type depicts Bush's democracy promotion agenda as both real and, at least in part, successful and appropriate: *promoter-positive*. The second type does not query the sincerity of his democracy promotion but claims it produced negative consequences: *promoter-negative*. The third type is of Bush as an insincere, merely rhetorically committed, democracy promoter but that on balance this was probably no bad thing: *non-promoter-positive*. The fourth type is of a president whose refusal to promote democracy had negative consequences: *non-promoter-negative*. I have chosen two particular case studies to illustrate the central features of each type.

An explicit rationale of Bush's democracy promotion strategy – insofar as it was defined in his public rhetoric – was to abandon stasis as the objective of American policy in the Arab world. 'For decades, American policy sought to achieve peace in the Middle East by promoting stability in the Middle East, yet these policies gave us neither', he declared in 2006.[2] This dismissal of the status quo, preferring revolutionary upheaval to autocratic constancy, argue his supporters, began a process that is now bearing fruit. When President Barack Obama told an Egyptian audience in 2009 that he would *not* impose democracy, he was met with an uncomfortable silence.[3] If the revolutionary agitation that overthrew Hosni Mubarak was not the direct consequence of Bush's rhetoric, Bush did articulate a discomfort with autocracy that many Egyptians seemingly shared. The process of democratization, perhaps because of the mixed signals American presidents have given about it, has not been smooth or linear. Its genesis is hotly contested. Its progress is irregular. As with the 'Springtime of Nations' in 1848, its end-point is far from clear. Even the existence of a 'process', by which people move from autocracy through revolution to democracy, is widely disputed. While this chapter does not claim to resolve these debates, it does attempt to locate Bush's place within them. Whether the process is seen as chaotic or ordered, accidental or purposeful, George W. Bush needs to be assessed within it – if only to better evaluate claims that his 'freedom agenda' was the key accelerant of the 2011–12 conflagration in the Arab world.

Bush, democracy promotion and the democratic peace

Bush's democracy promotion strategy – and the debate about it – is necessarily framed by a larger ideational and theoretical framework that neither American foreign policy nor those that study it have escaped – that of the democratic peace theory (or hypothesis) and the 'end of history' thesis.

The democratic peace theory holds that democratic states are highly unlikely – if not institutionally and/or normatively incapable – of going to war with each other.[4] Its logic was highly attractive to Western governments after communism's collapse. Bill Clinton explicitly predicated his early foreign policy on the theory.[5] In this new era, American security would be achieved less by confronting or containing an enemy than by enlarging the 'zone of democracies'. It was a causal connection that George W. Bush embraced wholeheartedly in the aftermath of 9/11.

While theories of a democratic peace framed much of the research agenda of Western international relations theorists in the 1990s, it was the thesis propounded by Francis Fukuyama that provided a popular version of it. In *The End of History and the Last Man,* he speculated that, with the demise of communism, mankind may have reached the end point of its ideological evolution.[6] Was liberal democracy, asked Fukuyama, perhaps 'the final form of human government'? He was pessimistic about this state of affairs – life at the end of history would be exceedingly dull. The policy prescriptions drawn from it, however, tended to be optimistic. Clinton and Bush each capitalized on a theory that reassured them not only that the spread of democracy would augment American security, but that it was inevitable.

Tony Smith, in Chapter 1 and elsewhere, has been highly critical of the impact of this theory on modern foreign policy, especially after 9/11. According to him, the democratic peace took on the attributes of a religious faith – 'liberal fundamentalist Jihadism'.[7] There is no doubting that Bush saw in democracy a cure for terrorism that a narrowly judicial response to 9/11 did not. Unlike the focused police response to the first attack on the World Trade Centre in 1993, Bush's solution to the second included the reformation of Arab politics. This chosen course was bold but also consistent with assumptions about the pacifying nature of democracy and its global inevitability rooted in a political science literature.

So in any assessment of democracy promotion as a foreign policy strategy we should remember its theoretical foundations. Democracy promotion, assuming we accept that is what Bush attempted, was not a recent aberration. It was grounded in a popular contemporary international relations theory. It drew on a tradition in American foreign relations that goes back at least as far as Woodrow Wilson, and arguably even further. Did Bush's version of it work? Is the Arab Spring, as yet highly imperfect and inconsistent, what Bush wrought?

I. Promoter: positive

The first type accepts that Bush's democracy agenda was pursued and that it achieved, or at least began, democratization in the polities made the subject of it. Bush doubtless would place himself in this category. His memoir, *Decision Points* (2010), affords a chapter to the 'freedom agenda' rather than to democracy promotion (a phrase he used rarely in office and not once in his book) though the conflation is warranted.[8] Cognitively, we have little reason to question that Bush believed that democracy in the Arab world, and further afield, was possible. Sources, sufficiently numerous and close to him, including his own speeches and writing, suggest he was personally convinced of the 'freedom agenda' and the theory on which it was built. In *Decision Points*, he writes that 'The transformative power of freedom had been proven in places like South Korea, Germany, and Eastern Europe', and marvelled how democracy had turned Japan from his father's Second World War enemy to his first post-9/11 ally (Prime Minister Junichiro Koizumi being one the first leaders to pledge assistance).[9]

In his second inaugural address, the president stated that

> one day this untamed fire of freedom will reach the darkest corners of our world [...] Eventually, the call of freedom comes to every mind and every soul [...] The best hope for peace in our world is the expansion of freedom in all the world [...] So it is the policy of the United States to seek and support the growth of democratic movements and institutions in every nation and culture, with the ultimate goal of ending tyranny in our world.[10]

A year later, speaking at Freedom House, Bush reiterated that 'the only path to lasting peace is the expansion of freedom and liberty [...] Free societies are peaceful societies'.[11] Echoing Fukuyama, he argued that

> freedom is taking root in places where liberty was unimaginable a couple of years ago. Just 25 years ago, at the start of the 1980s, there were only 45 democracies on the face of the Earth. Today, Freedom House reports there are 122 democracies, and more people now live in liberty than ever before.[12]

So, if the intent was sincere, what of the effect? USAID, the federal agency responsible for American spending in support of 'democratic governance' abroad, records a 2004 Bush spike. According to an independent academic study commissioned by the agency, this correlates with a measurable increase in democracy in the recipient countries:

> Specifically, the research concludes that, in any given year, $10 million of USAID DG funding produces about a five-fold increase in the amount of democratic change over what the average country would otherwise be expected to achieve.[13]

Of course, this only applies for USAID assistance funds and does not include what was spent via the State Department and through grants to the National Endowment for Democracy and other non-state institutions. But USAID spends much the larger share of funds and thus acts as a proxy for overall efforts (assuming the trends in USAID spending reflect overall effort, which they did under Bush). This, though, hardly produces an empirically robust measure of Bush's democracy efforts specifically since spending on such efforts tends to have a similarly and generally positive effect across administrations.

The promoter-positive position depends, therefore, on far more qualitative than quantitative arguments. Its conception of Bush as a successful promoter of democracy is defensible in at least two case studies: Iraq and Egypt. In the former, Bush changed the regime, giving way to civil war but eventually, if fitfully, to the first elections in Iraq's history. In the second, he articulated a notion of universal human freedom that framed a grievance common to many Egyptians in the revolutionary years of 2011–12.

Iraq

Freedom House Score in 2002 was 7; in 2012 was 5.5: classified as 'not free'.[14]

While the Iraq war was primarily defended by Bush as the more effective means of checking Saddam Hussein's weapons of mass destruction programme, military action was justified on several related levels. Not the least of these was the democratic-domino theory. Change this regime, argued Bush, and perhaps others would follow:

> The world has a clear interest in the spread of democratic values, because stable and free nations do not breed the ideologies of murder. They encourage the peaceful pursuit of a better life. And there are hopeful signs of a desire for freedom in the Middle East [...] A new regime in Iraq would serve as a dramatic and inspiring example of freedom for other nations in the region.[15]

As Gary C. Gambil notes, Bush's 'Freedom Agenda correctly identified the Middle East's dictatorships as the incubators of extremism'.[16] His one-time press secretary, in a memoir that otherwise excoriates much of the president's foreign policy, reminds us that Bush was sincere:

> Every President wants to achieve greatness but few do. As I have heard Bush say, only a wartime President is likely to achieve greatness, in part because the epochal upheavals of war provide the opportunity for transformative change of the kind Bush hoped to achieve [...] Intoxicated by the influence and power of America, Bush believed that a successful transformation of Iraq could be the linchpin for realizing his dream of a free Middle East.[17]

Assertions that Bush saw only material interests in the Middle East – most notably the capture of Arab oil – are the preserve of his political detractors. None of his aides afford oil significant explanatory weight. The symbolic value of democracy promotion in the minds of decision-makers is often elided or derided by economic determinists and rational choice theorists. But, as Thomas Carothers observes, 'U.S. debates over the appropriate role of democracy in U.S. foreign policy often take place at the level of symbols, myths, and other abstractions.'[18]

If Bush's sincerity is not in doubt, how should we estimate his actual democracy promotion efforts? Did he catalyse a democratic wave or merely attempt to ride it? Obviously, the small rise in Freedom House 'freedom ratings' in Iraq (7 to 5.5) and Afghanistan (7 to 6) are directly attributable to the American invasions and subsequent state-building efforts in those nations (at the estimated cost of between $3.2 and $4 trillion since 2001 – or $1.4 trillion per Freedom House point).[19] Toby Dodge, a consistent opponent of the invasion of Iraq, is not alone in asserting that this investment was not worth the return as Bush's 'success' was to swap one dictator (Saddam) for another (Nuri al-Maliki) using a nominally democratic process to achieve this new autocracy. Obama, says Dodge, was unable to block 'Iraq's road back to dictatorship'.[20]

Given the parlous state of Iraqi democracy it would be hard to credit Bush with major success in his signature foreign policy venture. However, this misses the importance of example and symbolism in Bush's actions. Despite their myriad failures, even a highly imperfect Iraqi democracy gave the lie to notions of the permanence of Arab autocracy. Saddam did not need to be replaced by a Mesopotamian Jefferson for his overthrow and subsequent execution (by a crude due process – but due process nonetheless) to carry enormous psychological import. Measuring that import is difficult; ignoring it, however, would be perverse.

In the absence of definitive evidence – though it remains unclear just what such evidence would look like – assertions of the power of example are just that, assertions that seem logical but remain beyond empirical verification. We can speculate on at least two levels, however. First, Saddam's fate was a revelation for other dictators. His demise was an object lesson in what might befall them if they resisted American pressure. Analogies with 1989, as we will argue shortly, are complicated (American pressure was essentially negligible in the earlier case, for example) but not invalid. When Tanzania's Julius Nyerere saw the overthrow of Romania's Nicolae Ceauşescu, he told a journalist: 'When you see your neighbour being shaved, you should wet your beard. Otherwise you could get a rough shave.'[21] Dictators do monitor the general climate of dictatorship globally. As Robert Kagan has argued, the modern-day autocracies of Russia and China – despite differences between themselves – have a default vested interest in the maintenance of autocracy in other lands.[22] They both remained barriers to regime change in Syria, for example, through 2012.

Second, the toppling of Saddam revealed to Arab populations just how tenuous their rulers' hold on power might actually be. The January 2005 elections that followed Saddam's overthrow, though hardly evidence of the entrenchment of democracy, were important both mechanically – it is impossible to imagine a democracy without elections – and symbolically. Even before the Arab Spring, regime change in Iraq presents itself as at least a tangential and symbolic cause of change elsewhere. In early 2005, the Saudi government held 178 municipal elections – the first since the 1960s. Egypt's Hosni Mubarak, perhaps with intimations of what would eventually befall him, declared he would run for re-election against a serious challenger (though winning by a landslide in September). The so-called 'Cedar revolution' of February 2005 in Lebanon deposed the pro-Syrian government, forcing Baathist Syria to remove its troops from that country (even as it allowed Hezbollah a role in its new government). Walid Jumblatt, the staunchly anti-American leader of the Lebanese Druze Muslims, credited much of this to the Iraqi elections of January 2005, which he said constituted 'the start of a new Arab world'.[23] As Amr Hamzawy and Nathan Brown, writing in the realist-leaning *National Interest*, observed in 2007:

> Dreams of democratic openings, competitive elections, the rule of law and wider political freedoms have captured the imagination of clear majorities in the Arab world. The dominance of the idea of democracy in the public space

has even forced authoritarian ruling establishments to cast about for new pro-reform language in order to communicate their policies to the populace. Even Islamist and leftist opposition movements have, at least rhetorically, dropped most of their skepticism about political rights, freedoms and pluralist mechanisms, developing a strategic commitment to gradual democratic reform.[24]

Despite a purported cooling of Bush's ardour for democracy promotion in this period, Walter Russell Mead argues his first term democracy promotion efforts achieved something as profound as they are unrecognized. His promotion of democracy in Iraq made the United States relevant to Middle Eastern politics in a way that the narrow pursuit of oil deals did not. For Mead, this was especially apparent in the wake of Gaddafi's fall in August 2011:

> there is one fact that needs to be pointed out because nobody really wants this to be true. That truth is that the United States has become more powerful in the Middle East today than at any time since the early 1950s. Perhaps not since President Eisenhower's CIA helped restore the Shah in Iran has the US loomed this large in the political calculations of Middle Eastern regimes.[25]

The machinations over access to oil, which conditioned much American strategy towards the Middle East in the twentieth century, actually reduced American influence on Arab civil society. If anything, petro-dollars cemented in place the regimes that after 9/11 Bush sought to destabilize. Bush brought a strategy to the region that previous administrations had lacked.[26] His promotion of democracy by force of arms and then by initially highly inconsistent and under-resourced nation-building effected more regime change in eight years (or 12 if we include the Arab Spring to date) than his predecessors had managed in 50.

Throughout the Cold War, balance-of-power realism had produced highly problematic American security gains. Not the least of these was the attempt to balance Iraq against Iran after the latter's Islamic revolution of 1979. American support for Baghdad emboldened its regime, a direct cause of its invasion of Iran in 1980, leading to nearly one million deaths, and suggested to Saddam Hussein that Washington would turn a blind eye to his further territorial ambitions. Ultimately, Saddam was defeated by George W. Bush's promotion of democracy in Iraq rather than by the realist-ordained containment of his regime by George H. W. Bush and Bill Clinton. Indeed, the example of Iraqi democracy did more to stir political protest (and thus promote democracy) in neighbouring Iran than did all the threats and blandishments inherent in the United States' policy towards Tehran after 1979. Examples, according to this interpretation of Bush's approach, count.

Egypt

Freedom House Score in 2002 was 6; in 2012 was 5.5: classified as 'not free'.

Bush's credentials as a positive promoter of democracy in Egypt rely on accepting two interrelated arguments. First, as argued above, the symbolic power of regime change in Iraq necessarily made an Egyptian version of it more likely. Seeing Saddam Hussein examining his American army-issue underwear in prison, for example, helped puncture the myth of invulnerability surrounding Arab autocrats. Second, Bush maintained democracy assistance to Egypt (increasing aid in support of legal reform, for example) and this meant that revolution when it came was, if not benign, certainly closer to American constitutional notions of peaceable assembly for the redress of grievances.[27] Across the region, popular trust in the judiciary is highest in Egypt and Saudi Arabia (though for many reasons but not excluding American support).[28] The absence of the penetration of American norms of protest is especially apparent, at the time of writing, in Syria, where a regime funded by Moscow has been far more brutal in its response to civil protest than was one funded by Washington.

As Gambil observes, even though American aid in support of democratic governance began to taper off after 2006, 'the U.S. Embassy in Cairo remained active behind the scenes encouraging and defending pro-democracy activists, as revealed in State Department cables released by WikiLeaks'.[29]

II. Promoter: negative

This assessment of Bush's democracy promotion efforts is sceptical that they achieved their desired objectives. The judgement is not that democracy promotion was never tried but that it was tried and did not work. For example, as already observed, nominal democracy scores have improved in Afghanistan and Iraq since the United States toppled their respective regimes. However, as Freedom House itself records, 'Iraq is not an electoral democracy. Although it has conducted meaningful elections, political participation and decision-making in the country remain seriously impaired by sectarian and insurgent violence, widespread corruption, and the influence of foreign powers.'[30]

The concept of Bush as an unsuccessful promoter of democracy is reaffirmed in at least two case studies: Afghanistan and Iran.

Afghanistan

Freedom House Score in 2002 was 7; in 2012 was 6: classified as 'not free'.

In 2011, according to Transparency International, Iraq and Afghanistan were the 175th and 180th most corrupt states in the world (out of 182). Only Myanmar, North Korea and Somalia were worse.[31] Bush's effort to democratize Afghanistan foundered for at least two reasons. First, the country has consistently shown itself highly resistant to successful foreign manipulation. The imposition of political order by outside powers – from the British in the late nineteenth century to the USSR in the 1980s and the United States after 2001 – has been a hard game, usually ending in its withdrawal. Second, even had Bush not been sidetracked by Iraq, there is little evidence to suggest democratization would have solved the enduring geostrategic problem Afghanistan symbolizes. Making the state a democracy – even if the capacity of the North Atlantic Treaty Organization (NATO) to do this was conceded – would not remove it from the national interest calculations of its neighbours. Pakistan, for example, has an interest in maintaining Afghanistan in a state of low-level conflict, because it guarantees continued American attention and aid (about $1 billion per year) for Islamabad, which in turn bolsters Pakistan's balancing of its traditional foe, India.[32]

It is also not clear why Iran would have an interest in an Afghan democracy unless it was able, as in Iraq, to exploit Kabul's nascent democratic politics to the advantage of pro-Iranian elements. Russia, similarly, in purely realist terms, has few long-term interests in the creation of a stable American ally in Afghanistan. Even the achievement of a nominally democratic Afghanistan would have only a marginal impact on the success of democracy elsewhere. This assessment has been the constant refrain of realists. John Mearsheimer, for example, derides a belief in the transformative power of democracy as 'hooey'.[33] Bush's deluded pursuit of democracy, according to this interpretation, sincere as it may have been, resulted in the diminution of American power and prestige. He attempted to promote democracy but it produced more negative (the longest war in American history, for example) than positive consequences.

Iran

Freedom House Score in 2002 was 6; in 2011 was 6: classified as 'not free'.

A similar argument informs the assessment of Bush democracy promotion efforts towards Iran. In this case, Bush-led intrigue in the domestic politics of the Islamic Republic did not weaken its regime. Instead, democracy promotion was a catalyst for an Iranian nuclear weapons programme. Bush's democracy promotion towards Iran was manifested in such bills as the 2003 Iran Democracy Act (which pledged 'to support transparent, full democracy in Iran') and the 2006 Iran Freedom Support Act (which determined 'to hold the current regime in Iran accountable for its threatening behavior and to support a transition to democracy in Iran').[34] Section 301 of the 2006 Act pledged '(1) to support efforts by the people of Iran to exercise self-determination over the form of government of their country; and (2) to support independent human rights and peaceful prodemocracy forces in Iran'. Such pressure by the United States may have stirred some democratic activism in Iran (cause and effect in this regard is difficult to measure). More likely, it convinced the Iranian government to seek a nuclear deterrent.

This logic was affirmed, albeit circuitously, in Libya. After 2003, Gaddafi abandoned his nuclear programme. This 'Libyan surrender', declared Charles Krauthammer, was the product of 'a clearly enunciated policy – now known as the Bush Doctrine – of targeting, by preemptive war if necessary, hostile regimes engaged in terror and/ or refusing to come clean on WMDs […] Hussein did not get the message and ended up in a hole. Qaddafi got the message.'[35] However, the obvious lesson for

Iran and North Korea after Gaddafi's demise in 2011 – he also ended up in a hole – was that a real weapon of mass destruction (WMD) capacity was the first and greatest deterrent to Western-sponsored regime change.

Marina Ottaway and Thomas Carothers advance the promoter-negative interpretation of Bush's democracy promotion efforts. For them, the failure was not in Bush's ambition to bring about democratic change but in the historical model through which this ambition was refracted.[36] The Middle East in 2003 was not eastern Europe in 1989.[37] The collapse of communism and its replacement with representative democracies in the space of months occurred with very little direct American democracy promotion and zero American military force. It remains one of the great ironies of the Cold War: an arms race ended without recourse to arms. After Bush changed regimes in Kabul and Baghdad, the Middle East represented the obverse situation where arms were central to calculations. Now, after its military power had deposed two despotic regimes, the United States was deeply enmeshed in the restoration of functioning government. The force of the American example may have motivated protestors in Prague and East Berlin at the end of the Cold War. In the Middle East, however, people and rulers felt the potential for actual American military penetration keenly. Hard American military power, rather than a spontaneous popular movement as in 1989, had been the sole cause of regime change in Afghanistan and Iraq. This convinced the Iranian government to resist American hard and soft power.

III. Non-promoter: positive

The conception of Bush's democracy promotion as a veneer for what was otherwise a sound strategy is made by prescriptive realists, i.e., those who prescribe national interest realism as the better guide to state behaviour. Rather than indict Bush, prescriptive realists acknowledge the necessity of a rhetorical commitment to an exportable liberalism while pursuing a traditional balance-of-power strategy that aims for American security before it worries about foreigner liberation. This assessment derives from the second Bush administration (2005–9) rather than from the first (2001–5). After the myriad failures of the Iraqi occupation, Bush adopted a more realistic, and minimal, foreign policy, in which democracy promotion played little to no part. Two case studies illustrate this switch: China and Russia.

China

Freedom House Score in 2000 was 6.5; in 2012 was 6.5: classified as 'not free'.

Occasionally, Bush included China in the target countries for democratization. China, he said, represented a 'big opportunity for democracy' and hoped that the People's Republic of China might embrace a free society as keenly as it had a free market: 'I happen to believe free markets eventually yield free societies [...] One of the most pure forms of democracy is the marketplace.'[38] However, very little actual policy attention was given over to catalysing political reform. Like his father, George W. Bush pursued a highly ambivalent diplomacy towards China. If his approach commands a label, it is 'realism' – an approach to international relations that sets very little store in democracy promotion. Realists, of course, divide on whether China's rise will be peaceful.[39] Bush seemed committed to the optimistic Fukuyamian argument that political freedom is an inescapable consequence of economic liberalization:

> Trade with China will promote freedom. The case for trade is not just monetary, but moral – not just a matter of commerce, but a matter of conviction. Economic freedom creates habits of liberty. And habits of liberty create expectations of democracy.[40]

Indeed, it was Ronald Reagan who had referred to trade as 'a forward strategy for peace and freedom'.[41] Trade with China, in Bush's articulation of the Reagan approach, was the surest way of promoting democracy. The China case study demonstrates a much more mobile and elastic conception of Bush's democracy promotion than a narrow focus on the Middle East would suggest. In both regions, Bush saw democracy as inevitable, part of the universal birthright of all people, and yet his pursuit of it could not have been more different.

Russia

Freedom House Score in 2002 was 5; in 2012 was 5.5: classified as 'not free'.

The same could be said for Bush's Russia policy. As Carothers argues in Chapter 11, Russian politics became 'steadily more authoritarian throughout the Bush years' and yet Bush remained wedded to the optimistic contention that the more Russia was locked into global capitalism the more democracy would become irresistible. It was an implicit democracy promotion strategy that he inherited from Bill Clinton: trade with them and it will all end happily. The actual amount of aid spent on 'democratic initiatives' in Russia pales against the hope of successive White Houses that Russian wealth will eventually translate into political freedom.[42]

Advocates of this passive form of democracy promotion – which does not rely on violent regime change nor the demonization of authoritarian capitalism as practised by Moscow and Beijing – argue that the gains to American interests and security were considerable, especially when set against the cost of aggressive democracy promotion in Afghanistan and Iraq. After 9/11, Bush placed a far greater emphasis on partnership with Vladimir Putin and Jiang Zemin. All three leaders, in the wake of al Qaeda's attack, saw the benefits of cooperative counter-terrorism. This was a time-limited opportunity, however. During the Bush (and then Obama) years, Moscow and Beijing became more reliable bastions of negation when it came to American democracy promotion, using the United Nations Security Council to compromise American-led interventions in Iraq and Libya.

The assessment of Bush by realists tends to be warmer towards his Chinese and Russian policy because it eschewed democracy promotion. Stephen Walt and John

Mearsheimer, however, indict powerfully the folly of democracy promotion in the Middle East – while simultaneously castigating American support for the region's first and oldest democracy, Israel.[43] While their manifold criticisms have some basis in the careless planning for post-invasion Iraq, realists have shown a refusal to acknowledge the realism underpinning Bush's democracy promotion and the rather limited reliance actually placed on democracy promotion in American national security strategy.

The National Security Strategy of 2002 had little to say about a renewed democracy promotion agenda. As Steven Hurst has argued persuasively, this was not a neoconservative document but a minimalist, conservative one.[44] Indeed, measured in terms of Bush administration personnel, there is more evidence of a dearth of democracy promotion advocates than a surfeit. The foreign policy principals were not democratic globalists in the Bill Clinton and Tony Blair mould. They were instead hard-nosed political realists, conservative nationalists whose faith in democracy was contingent not on its universalist character but its capacity to realize American security. Charles Krauthammer has called officials such as Vice-president Dick Cheney, Secretary of Defence Donald Rumsfeld and National Security Adviser Condoleezza Rice 'democratic realists' because they were prepared to advance the cause of democracy abroad only if it served explicit American national security objectives.[45] Bush was content to leave Zimbabwe alone, for example, because Robert Mugabe was a threat to his own people not to American security. He felt compelled to remove Saddam Hussein not because the Iraqi was any less democratic than the African dictator but because his regime was actively scheming against American interests and had previously attempted to assassinate the president's father. Being undemocratic did not make Saddam a target of American action; being engaged in nefarious plotting against the United States did.

Viewed from this perspective, the president's contingent understanding of democracy as a means to American security rather than an end in itself is a cause for both positive and negative assessments of his foreign policy. Its defenders claim that democracy promotion was used as a traditional means of entrenching victory in vanquished countries rather than justifying wars against them *per se*. The wars in Afghanistan and Iraq, like those against Germany and Japan, were waged not to make their citizens free but to make Americans safer. Democracy promotion after 2001, as after 1945, was considered the more reliable means of keeping the newly constituted regimes in the American camp. Making foreigners free was the means to realize American security. Democracy promotion was, by this understanding, an expression of an essentially realist strategy – despite the many realist indictments of its botched implementation in the Middle East.

IV. Non-promoter: negative

The opponents of the Bush approach claim that the reconstruction of Afghanistan and Iraq was such a disaster because, unlike in Germany and Japan, the United States did not take democracy promotion seriously in its post-war planning.

Instead, the Bush administration relied on hopeful assertions that democracy would spread like a benevolent virus when history suggested it required entrenched American military occupation and sustained economic subvention over decades. As some research (and historically informed common sense) suggests, 'higher force levels for longer time periods promote successful nation-building'.[46] Bush's problem was not his bad faith in democracy but his inability to pursue its promotion with appropriate resources. According to this type, Bush talked the democracy promotion talk but did not walk its walk. His strategy, claims Marina Ottaway, was 'never clearly defined, long on rhetoric, short on strategy, and fitfully implemented'.[47] The conception of Bush's democracy promotion as a rhetorical cloak for an essentially half-hearted strategy is given credence in at least two case studies: Saudi Arabia and Georgia.

Saudi Arabia

Freedom House Score in 2002 was 7; in 2012 was 7: classified as 'not free'.

According to James Harkin, Saudi Arabia remains 'so democratically backward as to make the Syrian government look like a hippie commune'.[48] The irony, of course, is that George W. Bush enjoyed few warmer relationships in the Middle East than that with Riyadh. The kingdom is as rich in oil reserves as it is poor in personal freedoms. It combined both in response to the Arab Spring: increasing social welfare *and* repression in areas of unrest.[49] The ironies are manifold. Osama bin Laden, whose 9/11 plot was the inspiration for Bush's promotion of democracy, was a Saudi national, as were 15 of the 19 hijackers. And yet their state survived Bush's tenure relatively untouched by democratic pressures.

While oil – and the Bush–Saud family intimacy built around it – is a necessarily important explanation for Bush's quietude on the home of Wahhabism – a version of Islam that has inspired significant numbers of Jihadi terrorists – his approach was not obviously hypocritical.[50] Throughout the Cold War, the United States was prepared to ally with some unsavoury regimes in order to advance the larger cause of communist containment. Josip Broz Tito of Yugoslavia, Nicolae Ceauşescu of Romania, Francisco Franco of Spain, Antonio Salazar of Portugal and Syngman Rhee of South Korea (to name only a few) were supported by Washington for reasons of geostrategy – and in most cases gave way, if imperfectly, to democratic forms of government. It would have been perhaps more ironic had Bush facilitated bin Laden's first objective and brought down the House of Saud.

Georgia

Freedom House Score in 2002 was 4; in 2011 was 3.5: classified as 'partly free'.[51]

One of the reasons eastern Europe after 1989 has been touted as the model for the Middle East after 2011 – aside from the fact that in both cases no regional experts predicted such changes in even general terms – is the rapidity with which autocracies were overthrown and replaced with pro-American democracies.[52] The newly liberated states of the Soviet buffer rushed to join NATO for fear of a renewal of Russian aggression. European Union membership took second place to this quest for American-provided security. In 1999 the Czech Republic, Hungary and Poland joined NATO. In 2004, Bulgaria, Romania, Slovakia, Slovenia and the Baltic republics followed suit. The logic in Tbilisi was that Georgia, having waited in line, and feeling even more vulnerable to Russian penetration, would be one of the next. This miscalculation set the stage for the 2008 war with Russia. On the pretext that Georgia was violating the rights of Russians in two disputed enclaves within Georgian territory (South Ossetia and Abkhazia), the Kremlin ordered their protection by force.

Bush faced a pristine but highly risky test of his democracy promotion strategy. Should he come to Georgia's aid and protect its democratic government from being overthrown by Russian autocrats or abandon this new democracy to its geographic destiny within a Russian sphere of influence? Accepting the geostrategic realities, Bush took the second option. Georgia was not re-colonized by Russia but its ambitions to join NATO were placed on permanent hold. The episode reflected for many liberal hawks and neoconservatives the bad faith of much of Bush's democracy promotion rhetoric. Without the complicating factors of oil and Islam, which might have provided some excuse for inaction towards Middle Eastern states such as Saudi Arabia, Georgia represented a clear case of a fledgling democracy facing possible extinction by a traditional great power American rival.

Bush had made Tbilisi the target of democracy aid but this was difficult to defend as much more than a token gesture when the White House sat on its hands as Russian tanks rolled towards the Georgian capital. This final interpretation of Bush as a flexible friend of democracy promotion – using it partially and inconsistently – with generally negative consequences is one often made by those depicting a decisive break between Bush's first and second term democracy promotion efforts. Senator John McCain, for example, was highly critical of Bush's pusillanimity in the face of Russia aggression.[53] Tellingly, however, it was a cautious approach supported and essentially sustained by Bush's successor.

From Bush to Obama

Without wishing to pre-empt the chapter on Barack Obama in this volume, a potential method of ranking the accuracy of the foregoing types would be ask which one – if any – has endured after Bush. On balance, let me argue that the first type – *promoter-positive* – captures the centralities of the Bush approach more than the other three and that, thus far, Obama has continued this approach more than he has rejected it or embraced the alternatives. When it comes to democracy promotion, there are both superficial and substantial continuities across both administrations. Those seeing a decisive break with Bush insist Obama has jettisoned a democracy agenda, especially in the Arab world.[54] His first major speech in the region was in Cairo in 2009. While he rejected notions that democracy could be imposed on an unwilling people, he did not offer moral relativism in its place: 'no system of government can or should be imposed upon one nation by any other [...] That does not lessen my commitment, however, to governments that reflect the will of the people'.[55] Consistent with this statement has been a democratic governance funding commitment that at least rivals that of his predecessor.

Obama's dismissal of Bush's Middle East strategy has not led him to disengage with the region nor abandon entirely the democracy agenda. The Arab Spring has made realist prescriptions to leave well alone seem impolitic. Obama, like Bush (and like Clinton and Bush Sr.) has found himself at war in defence of a Muslim population, this time in Libya, albeit in a smaller international coalition than that which fought in Iraq in 1991 and 2003.

Again, the parallels are striking. Dwight Eisenhower inherited a discredited containment strategy from Harry Truman. He shifted his rhetorical emphasis and reduced defence spending. The effect was to render more competent and further embed the strategy of his predecessor. The same can be argued about Obama's adaptation of the Bush Doctrine. Rather than jettison it, Obama recalibrated it for a more global audience. He has not been shy in the use of force – from killing bin Laden to complicity in regime change in Libya – but he has committed this aggression in synchronization with 'the international community'. Bush was unable to achieve this, despite a far more explicit democracy promotion agenda. As Mead argues:

> The most irritating argument anyone could make in American politics is that President Obama, precisely because he seems so liberal, so vacillating, so nice, is a more effective neoconservative than President Bush. As is often the case, the argument is so irritating partly because it is so true [...] In many ways we are living through George W. Bush's third term in the Middle East, and neither President Obama's friends nor his enemies want to admit it [...] well over half way through President Obama's tenure in office, we can see that regime change and democracy promotion remain the basis of American strategy in the Middle East – and that force is not excluded when it comes to achieving American aims.[56]

Conclusion

Despite a strong rhetorical commitment to democracy promotion, President Bush left office with only four countries in the world freer than at its beginning (85 in 1999 vs. 89 in 2009).[57] This simple metric is difficult to dissociate from his wider 'freedom agenda'. Its failure is easier to quantify than its success. In assessing how far Bush's approach created the conditions for the ongoing revolutions in the Arab world we thus face the problem of measurement. How can we tell? Even Jimmy Carter could plausibly maintain, as John Dumbrell argues in this book, that his promotion of human rights, despite the meagre short-term return, was in some way connected with the demise of Soviet communism and the rise of democracies in South America throughout the 1980s and 1990s.

A more robust argument – though still prey to charges that it is empirically dubious – relies on connecting the fate of the Taliban in Afghanistan and of Saddam Hussein in Iraq to the revolutionary fervour of 2011–12. Men and women saw that dictators could be overthrown and democracies, of a sort, could be countenanced in a region seemingly inimical to them. Lacking reliable opinion poll data of protesters in the Arab Spring, we should treat with caution – though not disdain – assertions that Bush's strategy of regime change was a substantial inspiration.

It might be that Bush's greatest contribution, despite an initially poor return on American investments (of both blood and treasure) was to make democracy a conceivable project in the Arab world. Obama has not been so 'unBush' that he avoided war in that theatre on behalf of an oppressed Muslim population (in Libya). Obama, by his actions, did not fundamentally reject Bush's diagnosis of the Arab problem as one of too little democracy, and of too little American effort to promote it.

Presidential failure is now a basic feature of American politics. Expectations for the office and its holder are not synchronized with its institutional capacities. This is particularly the case in foreign policy. Most presidents fail, especially when it comes to promoting democracy. Woodrow Wilson did not lead the world into a new democratic age. Franklin Roosevelt established the parameters of a Cold War with Soviet communism. Truman left office with the world less free than when he found it. John F. Kennedy and Lyndon B. Johnson waged wars for democracy that produced the obverse in south-east Asia. George W. Bush's failure puts him in good company.

Notes

1 See Thomas Carothers, *US Democracy Promotion During and After Bush* (Washington, DC: Carnegie Endowment for International Peace, 2007), pp. 13–14; Larry Diamond, 'The Democratic Rollback', *Foreign Affairs*, March/April 2008; and James Traub, 'A Funny Thing Happened on the Way to the Forum', *Foreign Policy*, 14 January 2011.
2 George W. Bush, Radio Address, 29 July 2006.
3 Barack Obama, Speech at Cairo University, 4 June 2009.
4 See Michael E. Brown, S. M. Lynn-Jones and S. E. Miller, eds., *Debating the Democratic Peace: An International Security Reader* (Cambridge, MA: MIT Press, 1996).
5 See Anthony Lake, 'From Containment to Enlargement', Address at the School of Advanced International Studies, Johns Hopkins University, Washington, DC, 21 September 1993, in *U.S. Department of State Dispatch*, Vol. 4, No. 39, 1993; Douglas Brinkley, 'Democratic Enlargement: The Clinton Doctrine', *Foreign Policy*, No. 106, Spring 1997; and John Dumbrell, 'Was There a Clinton Doctrine? President Clinton's Foreign Policy Reconsidered', *Diplomacy & Statecraft*, Vol. 13, No. 2, 2002.
6 Francis Fukuyama, *The End of History and the Last Man* (New York: Free Press, 1992).
7 Tony Smith, *A Pact with the Devil: Washington's Bid for World Supremacy and the Betrayal of the American Promise* (New York and London: Routledge, 2007), pp. 195–236.
8 George W. Bush, *Decision Points* (New York: Crown Publishers, 2010), pp. 394–438.
9 Bush, *Decision Points*, p. 397.
10 George W. Bush, Second Inaugural Address, 20 January 2005.
11 George W. Bush, President Discusses Democracy in Iraq with Freedom House, 29 March 2006.

12 Bush, Freedom House. In *The End of History*, Fukuyama offers a table making the same point, pp. 49–50.

13 'Deepening our understanding of the Effects of US Foreign Assistance on Democracy Building Final Report', USAID, 28 January 2008, http://www.usaid.gov/our_work/democracy_and_governance/publications/pdfs/SORA_FinalReport_June08_508c.pdf.

14 Freedom House Scores ('freedom ratings' specifically) for 2002 and 2011 or 2012 are given for each case study in this chapter. The lower the score, the greater the freedom. Denmark, for example, scores 1 (in all yearly reports), North Korea 7 (the lowest possible rating). See http://www.freedomhouse.org/reports. Similar scoring is provided by the Economist Intelligence Unit, *Democracy Index 2011* at http://www.eiumedia.com/index.php/component/k2/item/301-democracy-index-2011.

15 Bush, Speech to the American Enterprise Institute, 27 February 2003.

16 Gary C. Gambil, 'Bush was Right', *Foreign Policy*, 9 April 2012.

17 Scott McClellan, *What Happened* (New York: PublicAffairs, 2008), p. 131.

18 Thomas Carothers, *U.S. Democracy Promotion During and After Bush* (Washington, DC: Carnegie Endowment for International Peace, 2007), p. 1.

19 See Brown University, *Costs of War Report* (2011), http://costsofwar.org/article/did-wars-bring-democracy-afghanistan-and-iraq#_edn3. If we accept that together both wars cost in the region of $3.6 trillion and delivered a 2.5 improvement in Freedom House democracy scores, this means that each point costs about $1.4 trillion.

20 Toby Dodge, 'Iraq's Road Back to Dictatorship', *Survival*, Vol. 54, No. 3, 2012, pp. 147–68.

21 Quoted in Colleen Lowe Morna, 'Tanzania: Nyerere's Turnabout', *Africa Report*, September–October 1990, p. 24, in Lucan Way, 'The lessons of 1989', *Journal of Democracy*, Vol. 22, No. 4, 2011, pp. 17–27.

22 Robert Kagan, *The Return of History and the End of Dreams* (New York: Knopf, 2008).

23 David Ignatius, 'Beirut's Berlin Wall', *Washington Post*, 23 February 2005, A19.

24 Amr Hamzawy and Nathan Brown, 'Arab Spring Fever', *National Interest Online*, 29 August 2007, http://www.carnegieendowment.org/2007/08/29/arab-spring-fever/tqj.

25 Walter Russell Mead, 'W gets a third term in the Middle East', *American Interest* blog, 22 August 2011, http://blogs.the-american-interest.com/wrm/2011/08/22/w-gets-a-third-term-in-the-middle-east/.

26 See Steve A. Yetiv, *The Absence of Grand Strategy: the United States in the Persian Gulf, 1972–2005* (Baltimore, MD: Johns Hopkins University Press, 2008).

27 See the 1st Amendment to the US Constitution. American aid to Egypt in support of democratic governance is detailed at http://egypt.usaid.gov/en/Programs/Pages/democracyandgovernance.aspx.

28 See Anthony H. Cordesman and Nicholas S. Yarosh, 'The Underlying Causes of Stability and Unrest in the Middle East and North Africa: An Analytic Survey', CSIS, 21 May 2012, fig. 63; http://csis.org/files/publication/120514_MENA_Stability.pdf.

29 Gambil, 'Bush was Right'.

30 Brown University, *Costs of War*. See also Dodge, 'Iraq's Road Back to Dictatorship'.

31 Transparency International, *Corruption Perceptions Index 2011*, http://www.transparency.org/whatwedo/pub/corruption_perceptions_index_2011

32 David E. Sanger and David Rohde, 'U.S. Pays Pakistan to Fight Terror, but Patrols Ebb', *New York Times*, 20 May 2007, and Christophe Jaffrelot, 'The Indian-Pakistani Divide: Why India Is Democratic and Pakistan Is Not', *Foreign Affairs*, 90, 2 (March/April 2011).

33 John Mearsheimer, 'Hans Morgenthau and the Iraq war: realism vs. neo-conservatism', Open Democracy, 21 April 2005, http://www.opendemocracy.net/content/articles/PDF/2522.pdf, p. 4.

34 S. 1082 (108th): Iran Democracy Act (19 May 2003), www.Gpo.Gov/Fdsys/Pkg/Bills-108s1082is/Pdf/Bills-108s1082is.Pdf and H.R. 6198, (109th): Iran Freedom Support Act (30 September 2006), www.Gpo.Gov/Fdsys/Pkg/Bills-109hr6198eh/Pdf/Bills-109hr6198eh.Pdf.

35 Charles Krauthammer, 'The Doggedness of War', *Washington Post*, 26 December 2003, A35.

36 Marina Ottaway and Thomas Carothers, 'Getting to the Core', in Ottaway and Carothers, eds., *Uncharted Journey: Promoting Democracy in the Middle East* (Washington, DC: Carnegie Endowment for International Peace: Brookings Institution Press, 2005), pp. 251–67.

37 This point is also argued by Katerina Dalacoura, 'The 2011 Uprisings in the Arab Middle East: Political Change and Geopolitical Implications', *International Affairs*, Vol. 88, No. 1, 2012, pp. 63–79.

38 Bush, Freedom House.

39 See Aaron Friedberg, 'The Future of U.S.-China Relations: Is Conflict Inevitable?', *International Security*, Vol. 30, No. 2, 2005.

40 George W. Bush, Speech at Boeing Plant, 17 May 2000.

41 See Ronald Reagan, Address before the Town Hall of California in Los Angeles, 26 August 1987, and John Arquilla, 'Ronald Reagan', in Timothy J. Lynch, ed., *The Oxford Encyclopedia of US Military and Diplomatic History* (New York: Oxford University Press, 2013).

42 USAID to Russia is detailed at http://russia.usaid.gov/documents/1622/DI+fact+sheet_Eng+A4.pdf.

43 John J. Mearsheimer and Stephen M. Walt, *The Israel Lobby and US Foreign Policy* (New York: Allen Lane, 2007).

44 Steven Hurst, 'Myths of Neoconservatism: Bush's Neocon Foreign Policy Revisited', *International Politics*, Vol. 42, 2005.

45 Charles Krauthammer, *Democratic Realism* (Washington, DC: AEI Press, 2004).

46 James Dobbins, 'Nation-Building: The Inescapable Responsibility of the World's Only Superpower', *RAND Review*, Vol. 27, No. 2, 2003, p. 23. Staying, Dobbins argues, does not guarantee success, leaving guarantees failure. No effort at democratization, he concludes, has taken less than seven years.

47 Marina Ottaway, *Democracy Promotion in the Middle East: Restoring Credibility*, Policy Brief 60 (Washington, DC: Carnegie Endowment for International Peace, May 2008), p. 1.

48 James Harkin, 'Who Broke Syria?', *Foreign Policy*, 17 April 2012.

49 Dalacoura, 'The 2011 Uprisings in the Arab World', p. 66.

50 See Craig Unger, *House of Bush, House of Saud: The Secret Relationship Between the World's Two Most Powerful Dynasties* (New York: Scribner, 2004).

51 This does not include South Ossetia or Abkhazia.

52 Lucan Way, 'The lessons of 1989', *Journal of Democracy*, Vol. 22, No. 4, 2011.

53 See Elisabeth Bumiller and Michael Falcone, 'Candidates' Reactions to Georgia Conflict Offer Hints at Style on Foreign Affairs', *New York Times*, Top of Form, 9 August 2008.

54 Jackson Diehl, 'South Sudan Shows What Obama Can Do When he Leads', *Washington Post*, 4 July 2011.

55 Obama, speech at Cairo University, 4 June 2009.

56 Mead, 'W gets a third term in the Middle East'.

57 According to Freedom House, the number of electoral democracies fell from 121 in 2002, to 119 in 2009 and to 115 in 2011, http://www.freedomhouse.org/sites/default/files/inline_images/ElectoralDemocracyNumbersFIW1989–2011.pdf.

11

BARACK OBAMA

Thomas Carothers[1]

Introduction

Upon taking office, President Barack Obama faced a daunting array of inherited foreign policy challenges – a war of course in Afghanistan, a diminishing but still difficult military engagement in Iraq, a moribund Israeli–Palestinian peace process, a collision course with Iran over that country's nuclear programme, a broken relationship with Russia, a dysfunctional counter-terrorism partnership with Pakistan, and blocked negotiations with a belligerent and nuclear armed North Korea. Complicating this picture was a severe economic crisis, both at home and abroad, the harshest since the Great Depression.

If this troubling international policy landscape was not enough, a further foreign policy problem also awaited the new president – the seriously damaged legitimacy and credibility of American democracy promotion. President George W. Bush raised greatly the profile of American democracy promotion. He tarnished that profile badly, however, by closely associating democracy promotion with the American-led invasion of Iraq and forcible regime change more generally. The Bush administration also hurt the United States' standing as a global symbol of democracy and rights through its serious abuses of human rights associated with its war on terrorism. The negative consequences were manifold: an international backlash against democracy assistance in many regions, with suspicion about democracy promotion especially high in the Arab world; efforts by European and other international democracy supporters to disassociate themselves from American democracy policies and programmes; and a marked decline in support from the American public for democracy promotion as a priority of their country's foreign policy.[2]

The sobering state of democracy in the world further darkened the landscape of democracy promotion for the incoming Obama administration. The momentum and sense of optimism that defined the first decade of the post-Cold War world was largely gone by the time Obama became president. The number of democracies in the world had plateaued during the first decade of the new century and some analysts were warning of an emergent 'democratic recession'.[3] Many new democracies born in the 'Third Wave' of democracy from the mid-1970s to the mid-1990s were struggling, unable to turn democratic forms into working democratic substance and to show their citizens that democracy could deliver a better life. China, Russia and other authoritarian challengers were gaining strength and self-confidence, prompting some observers to lament that the once hoped-for 'end of history' had been eclipsed by its return.[4]

In this context of damaged American pro-democratic credibility and uncertain global democratic prospects, President Obama and his senior foreign policy team perceived a clear need to recalibrate American democracy policy and acted accordingly. A basic question therefore in assessing American democracy promotion under Obama is what this attempted recalibration consists of and whether it has succeeded in reversing the damage wrought by the previous administration.

This question connects naturally to a second, broader question that this chapter also seeks to answer: what has been distinctive about Obama's approach to supporting democracy abroad compared to the longer pattern of American democracy promotion? Despite some sharp differences in the personal style of the different presidents of the past 30 years, significant lines of continuity have marked the evolution of American democracy policy over this period. These include:

- Expansive pro-democracy rhetoric, significantly exceeding the actual commitment to supporting democracy.
- A tendency by incoming presidents to get pulled into democracy promotion by major international developments despite originally not intending to devote significant time to the topic.
- Considerable development of democracy promotion at the 'low policy' level through a steady expansion of democracy assistance, quiet pro-democracy diplomatic engagement in countries facing political junctures, and efforts to institutionalize democracy concerns in multilateral organizations and other international fora.
- Substantial attention to democracy promotion in countries where the United States has no significant countervailing economic and security interests, but a tendency to downplay democracy in places where such interests exist.
- An assumption that the United States has a central role to play in international democracy promotion, based both on its status as a global symbol of democracy and the idea of the country as an exceptional, transformative global power.

Although the Obama presidency is still unfolding currently, enough time has passed to assess the success of his attempted recalibration and the extent to which his approach represents a continuation or a divergence from the larger path of American democracy promotion.

Stepping back

President Obama set out a changed rhetorical line on democracy support right from the start. He did not mention promoting democracy abroad in his Inaugural Address – a sharp contrast to the previous presidential Inaugural Address in which President Bush delivered a soaring statement proclaiming a global freedom agenda for the United States. Similarly, Hillary Clinton said little about democracy promotion in her confirmation hearings for the position of secretary of state. Her formulation of 'the three Ds' – diplomacy, defence and development – as a framework for American international engagement conspicuously omitted the potential fourth 'D' of democracy.

When President Obama and Secretary Clinton did begin to talk publicly about democracy promotion, as for example in Obama's widely noted speech in Cairo in June 2009, they emphasized a set of messages to distinguish their intended approach from that of the Bush administration. Using less lofty, more measured terms, they stressed that they would not seek to impose democracy on other countries by force, that they would not promote American-style democracy but instead emphasize universal rights and principles, and that democracy was not just about freedom and elections but also about the rule of law, justice, dignity and other values.

The Obama team applied this lowered rhetorical emphasis on democracy to the American military engagements in Afghanistan and Iraq. They stopped holding these countries out as democratizing missions or democratic success stories, instead focusing on the more limited goal of stability and openly acknowledging the limitations of what the military endeavours had achieved so far. When Afghanistan's elections in the summer of 2009 went badly – flawed by significant irregularities – the administration reacted with only subdued expressions of concern, accepting the necessity of working closely with President Hamid Karzai despite his serious political shortcomings. The ambassador to Iraq, Christopher Hill, captured this anti-triumphalist line when asked in 2010 about whether Iraq could be a beacon of democracy in the Middle East. He replied:

> I think if Iraq can get its own house in order, if they can sort of sort through these political issues which involve a lot of shoving and pushing between their political leaders, you know, they'll be okay. As for being some shiny city on the hill that is a beacon of freedom to others, I think maybe we'll leave that to pundits to describe.[5]

President Obama also sought to recalibrate American democracy policy by repairing America's own standing as a symbol of democracy. As one of his first acts as president he issued orders to close the Guantánamo detention facility, end the Central Intelligence Agency's (CIA's) secret detention programme and prohibit the 'enhanced' interrogation practices authorized by the Bush administration. The Obama team also hoped that other domestic political reforms, such as an initiative to increase governmental transparency, would contribute to an improved American image. Perhaps even more significantly, the administration counted on Obama's popularity around the world and what it saw as the stirring democratic story of his rise to power to help repair the United States' global image.

As a further element of his larger effort to chart a new foreign policy line, Obama advanced the view that patient diplomatic engagement was a better way to further American interests *vis-à-vis* a range of hostile or at least semi-hostile states than a cold shoulder or confrontation. He made Russia a leading example of this new outlook. In February 2009 he launched a 'reset' of Russia policy aimed at moving beyond accumulated tensions over Georgia, North Atlantic Treaty Organization (NATO) expansion and other issues to achieve a friendlier relationship with the Russian government, with the hope that greater cooperation on various security matters of mutual interest would follow. Obama also tried to break the thick ice of American–Iranian relations, sending two personal letters to Iran's Supreme Leader Ayatollah Khamenei that made clear his interest in dialogue. He sent signals of possible openness to engagement to other leaders frozen out by past administrations including Venezuela's Hugo Chávez, Syria's Bashar al-Assad, Cuba's Fidel Castro and the Burmese military junta.

President Obama and his team did not intend their emphasis on diplomatic engagement as a retreat from concern over democracy in such countries. Obama officials argued in private that the cold shoulder of the past had not produced any noticeable gains for democracy in Russia, Iran, Syria or elsewhere. Russian politics, for example, had become steadily more authoritarian throughout the Bush years. If the United States was able to open a line of direct communication with such leaders, they speculated, it might gain greater receptivity for messages on democracy and human rights. Nevertheless, the new emphasis on engagement did mean publicly trying to get along with various non-democratic governments and toning down overt criticisms of their political shortcomings. As a result, it was perceived by some as a backing down on democracy.

Tension between engagement and democracy support made itself acutely felt very quickly on Iran. After Iran's problematic elections in June 2009 provoked large-scale protests under the banner of the Green Movement and harsh repression by the Iranian regime, the Obama administration faced a quandary: should it avoid pointed public criticisms of the elections so as not to jeopardize incipient engagement with the Iranian leadership or speak out forcefully in the hope of bolstering the protesters?

As would prove to be a pattern in other contexts where the administration confronted a choice of how quickly to shift gears and support pro-democracy protesters, the administration initially leaned towards a minimalist line on democracy. When the facts shifted (greater repression and stronger criticism of the Iranian government by other Western powers) it tilted towards a tougher rhetorical line over the ensuing weeks and months. Obama officials justified the administration's initially circumspect stance as reflecting the president's desire not to hurt the protesters' domestic image by associating the American government too openly with them. Yet worries over harming the chances for engagement on the broader strategic agenda clearly inhibited the Obama response.

With Russia, the administration tried to mitigate the tension between engagement and democracy through a two-track approach. Alongside the primary track of engagement and cooperation on matters of mutual interest, the administration pursued a second track focused on democracy and human rights. During Obama's first presidential visit to Russia in July 2009, for example, he took time away from his meetings with Russian officials to give a speech at the New Economic School on the value of democracy and to meet with a group of independent civic activists. This attention to civil society was formalized through a working group on the issue within the newly created United States–Russia Bilateral Presidential Commission.

This initial stepping back on democracy promotion reflected not just the 'anything but Bush' outlook of the incoming Obama team (typical for a new administration replacing one of the opposing party). It also appeared to embody some important core instincts of the new president and his top foreign policy advisers. As evidenced in his own political campaign and in early speeches when he did address international democracy issues, including his 2009 Cairo speech, President Obama clearly resonated with the inspirational power of democracy and its centrality to the American place in the world. Yet that outlook was mixed with strong pragmatic instincts – a wariness of overstatement, a disinclination to lead with ideology and a desire to solve specific problems by building consensus rather than fostering confrontation. And Obama appeared to be especially disinclined to put the United States in the position of imposing itself politically on other societies, telling others what to do or assuming that it has all the answers. Applied to foreign policy, this pragmatism and wariness about imposition appeared to some observers simply as realism. But at least for Obama it was less about the discounting of the importance of democracy ideals *vis-à-vis* other interests than about finding a different, more effective way to pursue them, a distinction the president seemed to struggle to articulate and put into practice.

Obama's initial three top foreign policy advisers – Secretary of State Clinton, Secretary of Defence Robert Gates, and National Security Adviser General James Jones – inclined more noticeably towards traditional realism, although Clinton was clearly well-versed in democracy and rights issues, and interested in ensuring a real place for them in the foreign policy agenda. Thus, unlike in the Bush and Clinton administrations, democracy promotion had no top-level champion in the Obama team (such as National Security Adviser Anthony Lake and Secretary of State Madeleine Albright during the Clinton years or George W. Bush himself during his administration).

The initial stepping back was not intended as, and did not constitute, a major shift in the place of democracy support within American foreign policy. It was primarily a change of tone and messages, a prelude to putting into place a more considered approach over time. Yet some observers, especially on the conservative side of the aisle, took it as a dramatic downgrading of democracy and sounded the alarm. Writing in the summer of 2009, for example, Joshua Muravchik lambasted Obama's 'abandonment of democracy'.[6] On Fox News, Doug Schoen lamented that 'one of the core principles of American policy [democracy promotion] that has guided presidents of both parties over the past 50 years, has been largely reversed'.[7] The *Wall Street Journal* regretted that, in its view, Obama had 'changed the focus entirely' of American foreign policy away from democracy concerns.[8]

This harsh view of Obama's initial recalibration on democracy promotion rested on interpreting some relatively minor things as major steps. For example, critics made much of a comment by Hillary Clinton to reporters before her first trip to China in February 2009 that pressing China on human rights 'can't interfere with the global economic crisis, the global climate change crisis and the security crisis'.[9] In fact, she was just acknowledging a reality of American United States–China policy that has prevailed for decades. Critics also made much of Obama's decision in October 2009 not to meet with the Dalai Lama, contrasting it to Bush's willingness to meet with him in 2001. Yet while presidential meetings with the Dalai Lama have some symbolic importance, they have never counted for much against the broader American willingness to maintain positive ties with China despite the country's continued anti-democratic posture.

A decision by the Obama administration early in 2009 to reduce one part of the democracy aid programme in Egypt elicited especially vociferous criticism among some American observers. This decision did signal the Obama team's inclination to prioritize friendly relations with President Hosni Mubarak above democracy concerns there. But the Bush administration had followed the same overall policy line after it backed away in late 2005 from its tentative efforts to push Mubarak on democratic reform. The democracy aid that the Obama team reduced was only a small part of the overall United States–Egyptian aid relationship, which in turn was itself only one part of the deep American ties to the Egyptian establishment. Even if it had been fully funded, this would not have amounted to much given the larger American accommodation of Mubarak.

Critics of the new president's approach to democracy promotion often proceeded from a mythical view of Bush's. They quoted the lofty promise of Bush's second Inaugural Address that 'all who live in tyranny and hopelessness can know: the United States will not ignore your oppression, or excuse your oppressors' as though it was an accurate description of Bush policy in actual practice. They then held Obama to account for anything that fell short of this illusory ideal. They glossed over the utterly realist nature of the bulk of Bush foreign policy – the cooperative, continually forgiving relationship with a Chinese government moving steadily backwards on political liberalization; the ardent embrace of Pakistan's military dictator Pervez Musharraf as an invaluable ally; the effort to look into President Vladimir Putin's soul, see a democrat and try to build a friendly relationship with him; the warm ties with Saudi Arabia and the other Gulf monarchies; the wide-ranging support for other Arab autocrats in Egypt, Jordan, Tunisia, Morocco and elsewhere; the diligent pursuit of useful friendships with dictators in Kazakhstan, Uzbekistan and elsewhere in Central Asia; the cosy ties with various undemocratic African governments useful to the United States on oil and counter-terrorism, and much else.

Stepping up

After this initial cooling-off period, President Obama and his team began to engage more actively on the subject, staking out their approach to the issue across the rest of 2009 and in 2010 as one part of the larger rolling out of Obama's overall foreign policy. It was not a sharp shift away from the initial cautious line, but nevertheless did constitute a stepping up, driven by at least three factors.

First, the Obama team moved towards a more public, active engagement on democracy issues as a response to the minor firestorm of criticism that their initial stepping back set off in the Washington policy community. Although it is difficult to assess the relative sensitivity of different administrations to criticism from policy peers in the Beltway circuit, Obama's political appointees in the foreign policy bureaucracy were as sensitive as any of their predecessors, if not more so. The Obama team was surprised that what they had intended as a cooling off and rethinking of democracy promotion was being interpreted as a major downgrading or abandonment of the issue.

They pushed back by looking for ways to publicly highlight their commitment to supporting democracy abroad. They made sure, for example, that democracy promotion featured repeatedly in the 2010 National Security Strategy of the United States, which stated that 'America's commitment to democracy, human rights, and the rule of law are essential sources of our strength and influence in the world'.[10] After initially downplaying democracy promotion in major speeches, both Obama and Clinton spoke repeatedly on the subject. At the United Nations General Assembly in 2009, Obama added a fifth pillar of democracy to what initially was going to be a four-pillar policy framework focused on other issues. The following year at the General Assembly he went further, speaking at length about democracy and urging other nations to stand up for human rights and open government around the world. Clinton spoke forcefully about American support for democracy and human rights, particularly the importance of civil society and Internet freedom, in multiple speeches, including at Georgetown University in 2009, at the Newseum in Washington, DC in January 2010 and in Krakow, Poland in July 2010.

Second, as has been the case in every administration over the past several decades, political events in the world, especially democratic crises or democratic break-throughs, pulled the administration into democracy-supporting endeavours. New administrations start with the idea of setting out clear lines of policy according to well-planned frameworks but end up devoting large portions of time scrambling to react to unexpected breaking events. Whatever their intended approach on democracy issues, when a coup occurs somewhere in the world they usually find themselves hurrying to help reverse it. And when a sudden breakthrough occurs, like the collapse of the dictator, they find themselves scrambling to provide at least some support for the incipient democratic transition.

Thus, for example, when a coup occurred in Honduras in June 2009, the administration plunged into the regional diplomatic process aimed at restoring civilian rule. After Haiti's devastating earthquake in January 2010 the Obama administration found itself immersed not just in an intensive humanitarian relief effort but also a combined diplomatic and assistance undertaking to help Haiti get through the national elections later that year. As Kenya tried to make a power-sharing government work (one formed after the harsh violence that followed the 2007 elections) and moved ahead with long awaited constitutional reform, the administration lent substantial diplomatic support (including visits to Kenya by Secretary Clinton and Vice-president Joe Biden in which they both talked at length about democracy) and technical assistance to the process. The administration joined an array of other international actors in helping the political opposition in Cote d'Ivoire oust President Laurent Gbagbo after he ignored the results of the 2010 elections that did not go his way. As South Sudan moved to independence, the administration built on efforts by the Bush administration by providing sizeable volumes of assistance and important diplomatic elbow grease to support the holding of the referendum on independence and then the establishment of the basic institutions of a democratic state.

To help ensure it had adequate assistance tools to support these diplomatic endeavours on the democracy front, the administration maintained or slightly increased the high levels of American spending on democracy programmes that the Bush administration had reached. Overall American assistance spending on democracy, governance and human rights increased from $2.24 billion in 2008 to $2.48 billion in 2010.[11] As part of a broader set of reforms intended to revitalize the United States Agency for International Development (USAID), the largest source of American democracy assistance, the Obama team upgraded the place of democracy and governance within the agency's bureaucratic structures.

Third, when its early efforts at engagement hit walls in various places, the Obama team gave greater public attention to the political shortcomings of some potential engagement partners. This was especially true towards Iran, where engagement proved especially fruitless. As the Iranian regime continued to defy the international community over its nuclear programme and stepped up repression at home, the administration adopted stronger rhetoric and actions in support of human rights. President Obama's 2011 Nowruz address to the Iranian people was significantly more critical of the Islamic Republic than his initial 2009 remarks urging engagement, saying that the regime 'cares far more about preserving its own power than respecting the rights of the Iranian people'.[12] The Obama team also imposed several rounds of targeted sanctions on Iranian officials accused of human rights abuses.

Faced with continual push-back from China on politics and rights issues, the administration adopted a somewhat tougher line on these issues within the larger framework of its efforts to get along with the Chinese government, clearly feeling the country's growing international heft. Secretary Clinton's January 2010 speech on internet freedom specifically criticized increased Chinese censorship and called for an investigation into allegations that China hacked the email accounts of human rights activists. Clinton delivered an even stronger critique in a major speech in

January 2011, pointing to specific Chinese rights abuses and defending the United States' right to speak out on these issues.[13] President Obama met with the Dalai Lama twice, in February 2010 and July 2011, and called publicly for China to release Nobel Peace Prize winner Liu Xiaobo.[14]

The long game

As the Obama administration engaged more actively on democracy issues, some American officials in positions of responsibility for democracy supporting policies began talking about the importance of also developing what they called 'the long game'. They acknowledged the importance of effective engagement in the day-to-day cut and thrust of pro-democratic diplomacy – timely statements from White House and State Department briefers criticizing democratic backsliders, diplomatic engagement on important upcoming political junctures, signals sent by ambassadors to key counterparts on democracy and rights issues, and so forth. But they believed that the United States could and should do more to bolster the long-term place of democracy support in the normative and institutional frameworks that undergird both American diplomacy and the transnational diplomatic domain. Greater attention to 'the long game' on democracy would, in their view, reinforce the defining values of Obama's foreign policy, such as multilateralism and consensus-building, more generally. With an emphasis on indirect, quieter measures rather than high-profile gestures, the long game would align with the heightened sensitivities in many parts of the world about democracy promotion as political interventionism. And in its emphasis on partnerships it would match the changing realities regarding the diffusion of power in the world.

The long game did not take shape as a formalized policy line or package – it emerged piece by piece as a loose collection of undertakings or initiatives.

A greater democracy support role for rising democracies

In recognition of the growing international weight of emerging democratic powers such as Brazil, India and Turkey, the Obama administration has sought to stimulate the interest and involvement of such countries in supporting democracy in their own regions and globally. In his 2010 United Nations (UN) speech Obama told rising democracies 'we need your voices to speak out', reminding them that 'part of the price of our own freedom is standing up for the freedom of others'. In visits to Brasilia, Delhi, Jakarta and elsewhere Obama emphasized to his counterparts the value of engaging in international democracy support.[15]

Promoting international consensus on and commitment to open government

Dialogue on open government is a central part of the administration's attempt to engage new actors in democracy support. Obama announced cooperation on open government initiatives with India and Brazil during his trips there, and in September 2011 his administration launched the multilateral Open Government Partnership. This initiative, co-chaired with Brazil, asks member countries to make concrete, verifiable, commitments to improve transparency and empower citizens, and is intended to serve as a platform to share innovative tools and strategies on making government more open.

Advancing transnational work on anti-corruption norms

In addition to its open government initiatives, the Obama administration is engaged in a broader effort to strengthen international anti-corruption efforts. President Obama and Secretary Clinton have spoken frequently about the costs of corruption and the administration played a leading role in pushing the G20 to adopt a specific action plan to combat corruption. The United States was one of the first countries to submit to a peer review under the UN Convention Against Corruption and it has urged others to do the same. The administration has also supported initiatives to help recover stolen public funds and to require American mining and energy corporations to report payments to foreign governments.

Establishing civil society dialogues

The State Department has made civil society engagement a cornerstone of its democracy policy. Secretary Clinton has delivered several major speeches on the subject and consistently met with civil society groups during her trips abroad. The State Department formalized this outreach in February 2011 with the launch of a Strategic Dialogue with Civil Society. This initiative includes five working groups, chaired by senior State Department officials, examining governance and accountability, democracy and human rights, women's empowerment, religion and foreign policy, and labour.

Linking democracy and development support

Some administration officials believe that democracy support can gain greater international purchase and access to greater funding if it is more closely associated with socio-economic development assistance. President Obama and Secretary Clinton have publicly emphasized the connection between democracy and development. USAID is seeking to integrate democracy and governance more extensively into its assistance in socio-economic areas such as health, agriculture and education.

The larger picture

By the end of 2010, the primary elements of the Obama administration's approach to supporting democracy abroad were fairly clear:

- Repeated high-level declarations of commitment to democracy support, emphasizing universalism and consensual principles.
- Multiple efforts in countries around the world to support shaky democratic transitions and push back against coups and other types of democratic back-sliding, using pro-democratic diplomatic engagement, democracy assistance, and economic carrots and sticks.
- A series of longer-term efforts to support international norms and multilateral action relating to democracy, governance and rights.

Taken together, these activities constituted an important engagement on democracy support. But in the larger perspective of the administration's overall foreign policy, they constituted only a secondary policy emphasis. The Obama team dedicated the vast majority of its foreign policy time, energy and political capital to a complex set of pressing strategic concerns: the interconnected military engagements in Afghanistan and Pakistan, the conflict in Iraq, relations with a rising China, the reset of relations with Russia, the Israeli–Palestinian peace process, Iran and counter-terrorism efforts against Al-Qaeda. Concerns about democracy turned up at the edges of some of these endeavours – such as the effort to maintain a second pro-democracy track in the improved American relationship with Russia. On the whole, however, democracy support was not central to any of the major areas of attention and effort in Obama's foreign policy.

Additionally, the imperatives of American economic and security interests impelled the Obama team to downplay their stated commitment to democracy and rights in a number of countries for the sake of useful friendships with autocratic governments. These included the familiar cases of China and Saudi Arabia. But they also included many others less in the limelight, like Kyrgyzstan, for the sake of maintaining the American military base there; Ethiopia, for the sake of cooperation in maintaining regional security; and Equatorial Guinea and Angola, for the sake of oil.

This larger realist framework, with its mix of policies, some emphasizing democracy and some contradicting it, is hardly unique to the Obama administration. It has been the pattern of American foreign policy for decades. Despite their sweeping statements of global support for democracy, Presidents Reagan, Bush Sr., Clinton and Bush Jr. all pursued decidedly mixed policies, whether it was warm ties with helpful anti-Communist dictators in places like Zaire, Indonesia, Nigeria and Pakistan during the Reagan years, or cooperation with autocrats in Kazakhstan, the Gulf states, Indonesia and elsewhere during the Clinton years. Every American administration of the past 30 years has talked nobly of fusing America's foreign policy ideals and interests, and then lived with the reality of frequent disjunctions between them.

What was different in the first two years of Obama's presidency was that his administration, unlike previous ones, was not engaged in a major way with democracy support in at least one region central to its overall foreign policy concerns. Reagan had framed his policy toward the Soviet Union as a struggle over democracy. George H. W. Bush, despite his clearly realist inclinations, embraced democracy promotion in central and eastern Europe as a defining issue of his presidency. For Bill Clinton, democracy in Russia was a prominent preoccupation. George W. Bush took up the cause of democracy in the Middle East, however unevenly and controversially.

Some observers hoped that President Obama might make Middle East democracy a major cause of his presidency, to build on and reconfigure the Bush opening on that issue. But after his June 2009 Cairo speech, the issue languished through 2010, pushed aside both by the administration's preoccupation with other issues and its lack of interest or desire to go against the familiar comfort of supporting Arab autocrats in return for help on oil, Israeli security and counter-terrorism. When, for example, President Mubarak stayed true to his authoritarian mode by manipulating and undermining Egypt's 2010 parliamentary elections, the Obama administration protested only softly.

Thus, when the Arab Spring hit the region in early 2011, the administration had yet to stake a strong position on democracy in the Middle East. The regional uprisings posed a defining question for the Obama administration: would it now put democracy at the core of its policy in one major region of the world?

The Arab Spring

The dramatic, historic outbreak of political change in the Arab world in 2011 presented the Obama administration with a complicated set of policy challenges and opportunities. Events moved fast. The fall of Tunisian President Zine El Abidine Ben Ali was expected by almost no one and occurred just one month after protests erupted there. President Mubarak left the scene even more quickly, with his 30-year rule evaporating just 18 days after protests broke out in Cairo. Events also continually defied expectations. After Ben Ali fell many observers wrongly predicted Egypt would likely stay calm. After Mubarak fell they doubted Syria would experience significant protests. Events also proceeded along uncertain paths. In every case where protests emerged and governments fell it was unclear what shape successor systems would take. Although some optimistic observers rushed to herald the event as a democratic wave-washing over the Arab world, the possibility that some Arab countries would descend into chaos, civil war or state collapse was keenly felt.

The implications of this political turmoil and transformation for American interests in the region were unusually complicated and unclear. In outbreaks of authoritarian collapse and incipient democratization in other regions during recent decades, a broad American interest in democratization was usually powerfully evident. In central and eastern Europe after the fall of the Berlin Wall, for example, the United States saw successful democratization as a clear plus or even a pressing imperative for American strategic interests. By contrast, every one of the main American economic and security interests in the Arab world – including reliable access to Gulf oil, close cooperation on counter-terrorism and moderate policies towards Israel – was at least arguably as likely to be jeopardized as strengthened by the arrival to power of genuinely democratic Arab governments.

The response by President Obama and his team during the first intense half-year of the Arab Spring was a cautious, incremental and moderate embrace of change:

- The administration broke with Mubarak only when it became clear that his days were numbered and made clear its preference for an orderly transition that would be led by the military.
- The administration urged the Bahraini government to take a peaceful approach to the wave of protests of March–April 2011 in Manama but did not break with it when the government carried out a harsh crackdown and stonewalled any significant political reforms.
- In Yemen, American efforts to encourage President Ali Abdullah Saleh to leave power in the face of mass protests stopped short of cutting off aid and imposing sanctions despite protracted intransigence from Saleh.
- When popular protests hit Syrian President Bashir al-Assad and he responded with brutal repression, the administration only evolved slowly towards a hard line against him, apparently worried about how a successor government might stand *vis-à-vis* various matters of importance to the United States.
- The administration praised the leaders of Morocco and Jordan for their rather mild reform efforts in response to domestic protests, staying well short of any serious proactive efforts to push for more significant democratizing steps.

In the parts of the Gulf not experiencing protest movements – Saudi Arabia, the United Arab Emirates, Oman and Kuwait – the administration largely carried on business as usual with its autocratic allies.

Only in Libya did Obama take more decisive action, joining Britain and France to strike militarily against the regime of Muammar Qaddafi when it appeared that the Libyan tyrant was on the verge of crushing the rebels fighting against him. The Obama team initially sought to limit the scope of its intervention, insisting publicly that it was aiming only at avoiding a humanitarian disaster, not fostering political change, and keeping American military participation within tight bounds, even when it appeared for some time that the rebels were failing to gain ground. But the administration and its NATO allies stayed with the intervention as the rebels eventually gained ground, playing a significant role in the eventual collapse of Qaddafi.

The administration's strong inclination in most of the region to avoid getting out in front of the roiling wave of Arab political change reflected a combination of factors: (1) its uncertainty about the value of political change for underlying American interests in the region; (2) a desire to avoid situations where the United States would break all ties with a leader buffeted by protests but then have to get along with him if he survived in power; and (3) the instinctive belief on the part of President Obama himself that the United States should avoid putting itself at the centre of potential political change in other countries, out of concern over discrediting those pushing for change and assuming a level of responsibility for the change that the United States might be unable to fulfil.

Where countries succeeded in moving from political upheaval into attempted democratic transitions, the administration's response was modestly supportive. In both Tunisia and Egypt, senior American officials weighed in with counterparts, cajoling and advising them on how to ensure successful transitions to new constitutions and elections. The administration tried to put together a special economic aid package for Egypt to help it get through the transition, featuring investment guarantees and debt relief, but it had little success getting it approved by Congress. It also ramped up democracy aid for both Tunisia and Egypt, supporting the near-term challenges of elections, political party development, civil society strengthening and civic education. But where Arab autocrats did not face significant pressure for political change, such as in most of the Gulf, the administration was content to remain supportive of such governments, appreciating their useful role on matters of common economic and security concern.

In short, despite its various diplomatic and assistance efforts to support Arab political change, the administration fell short of fully backing a historic opportunity for democracy in the Arab world. The administration's arguments for not moving too fast and shifting the American stance towards the various Arab leaders suddenly facing mass-based political protests made some sense case by case. Yet the overall net impression was of an American administration consistently behind the curve, soft on autocratic friends and not keeping up with the tide of new political thinking and expression among ordinary Arabs. When President Obama did step above the events in specific countries and set forward an overall affirmation of support for the Arab Spring – in a speech at the State Department on 19 May 2011 – it failed to gain much attention in either the Arab world or the West. The speech lacked both the compelling narrative of the sort that had captured Arab attention in the Cairo speech of June 2009 and a weighty list of actual policy deliverables. The aid measures that Obama announced in that speech, such as the investment credit and debt relief for Egypt, were notable mostly for their modesty compared to the hopes of many Egyptians and Tunisians and the aid promises already made by Saudi Arabia. They also did not compare favourably with the aid response that the United States put together for post-communist countries after the collapse of the Soviet Union.

This mixed American approach that was set out in the tumultuous first six months of 2011 continued as the Arab Spring unfolded in increasingly complex ways during the rest of that year and into 2012. The administration did keep trying to support political change where it was occurring, by increasing aid to Tunisia, looking for meaningful ways to support the Syrian opposition and encouraging the Egyptian military to carry through its transition promises. But the limits of American policy were often more apparent than the areas of positive engagement. After the government of Egypt arrested some Americans and Europeans engaged in democracy assistance programmes in Egypt, the administration ended up continuing large-scale assistance to the Egyptian military. Despite a complete lack of interest on the part of Saudi Arabia and other major Gulf oil producers, the United States continued to embrace these governments, announcing an enormous arms sale to Saudi Arabia at the end of 2011.

Conclusion

Obama's approach to supporting democracy abroad will undoubtedly continue to evolve throughout his presidency. It is, however, sufficiently elaborated that answers to the two basic questions framing this chapter are possible. First, has Obama's recalibration of democracy policy succeeded in overcoming the negative legacy of the Bush period – have the credibility and legitimacy of American democracy promotion been restored? The answer here is mixed. Obama has succeeded in ending the close association of American democracy promotion with the Iraq war and with American unilateral geostrategic interventionism more generally. The United States is of course still present militarily in both Iraq and Afghanistan, but given that the man who started both wars is no longer in office and the focus now being clearly on stability and the United States' exit, many fewer people in the Muslim world devote substantial time to denouncing the evils of American democracy promotion. The American participation in the NATO intervention in Libya did not appear to rekindle that negative association. The fact that this intervention operated under a UN resolution, came in response to a call by the Arab League for outside intervention, was not led by the United States, and did not involve Western troops on the ground helped avoid inflaming old wounds.

Many Arabs are still certainly angry about American foreign policy and Obama's reputation in the Arab world on the whole is not good. But the issue of American democracy promotion is no longer among their top concerns – American policy toward Israel and the Palestinians once again dominates their outlook. In fact, in some Arab countries that are attempting democratic change, frustration exists in some quarters that the United States has not done more to help democracy. The previous hostility in European policy circles towards American democracy policy has also faded considerably, as part of a greatly lessened concern about American military interventionism. European foreign ministries and aid agencies engaged in democracy support efforts no longer try to steer clear of American democracy policies and programmes. Within the United States, debates over democracy promotion have shifted away from the angry arguments about Iraq and are focused again more on how to make American democracy promotion effective rather than whether to pursue the goal at all.

Yet the repair is only partial. The harshly negative view of democracy promotion that crystallized in Russia, China and a number of other undemocratic places in the middle years of the last decade has not changed much. The paranoia that all outbreaks of public protest are manifestations of a sinister American hand wrapped in the deceptive cloak of 'democracy assistance' continues to hold wide sway among non-democratic governments. And the trend over the last decade towards highly restrictive laws on international support for civil society continues. Although the backlash against democracy promotion may have arisen in response to various events of the last decade, it appears to have put down lasting roots and is unlikely to go away anytime soon.

In addition, Obama's attempted restoration of the United States' standing as a symbol of democracy and rights in the world has made less progress than initially hoped. Although the Obama administration has taken some corrective actions with regard to American respect for law and rights in its counter-terrorism policies, Obama has not accomplished his signature goal of closing Guantánamo and, bowing to congressional pressure, reversed an earlier decision to hold civilian trials in New York for five detainees accused of planning the 9/11 attacks.[16] The Obama administration has also been criticized by human rights advocates for failing to hold anyone accountable for past abuses and instead adopting many of the Bush administration's legal positions in order to block lawsuits by former detainees seeking redress for illegal detention, rendition and torture.[17]

On top of that, the fractious domestic politics that has characterized Obama's time in office has hit hard at the United States' international image and reputation. The titanic efforts put into trying to enact healthcare reform by the administration and Democrats in Congress astonished many foreign observers, both for the amount of time and energy required for the American political system to tackle a potential major reform, and for the deep divisions that this revealed within the American political system and society as a whole. The semi-paralysis of governance that prevailed after the Republicans gained a majority in the House of Representatives in the 2010 congressional elections – especially the crisis in the summer of 2011 over raising the national debt ceiling – caused many foreign observers to ask whether American democracy is capable of dealing effectively with the multiple serious challenges facing the country. With many commentators both within the United States and abroad asking what has gone wrong with the American political system, the idea of American democracy as a way to solve problems is less appealing to citizens in China, Russia or in many other non-democratic countries than even just a few years ago.

Second, to what extent is Obama's approach on international democracy support a departure from the broader lines of American policy on this topic established over the last 30 years? Certainly, there are important common elements. Like their predecessors, Obama and his senior advisers have engaged in expansive pro-democracy rhetoric, often somewhat grander in aspiration than reflected in actual policies on the ground. Obama has found himself pulled into the subject by events in the world, as was George H. W. Bush by the fall of the Berlin Wall and the collapse of the Soviet Union, Bill Clinton by Haiti and the Balkans and George W. Bush by the terrorist attacks of 11 September 2001. The Obama administration has devoted important time to continuing or even expanding democracy promotion at the 'low policy' level. It gives much more attention to democracy promotion in places where few competing interests exist, such as Haiti, Cote d'Ivoire and Zimbabwe, than in places where they do, such as Ethiopia, Angola, Equatorial Guinea and Kazakhstan.

At the same time, however, some important differences can be identified. As discussed above, the administration has not yet made democracy promotion a truly central concern in any major region that is at the heart of the American geostrategic agenda, even despite the outbreak of democratic change in the Arab world. It seeks to support democracy in some Arab countries, such as Egypt and Tunisia, but is relatively comfortable resting on friendships with autocratic allies in many other countries in the region, such as the Gulf states, Jordan, Morocco and others. It appears that American economic and security interests in the region still pull as much towards continuity as change with respect to the traditional American support for Arab autocracies. And the administration's modest response also reflects its unwillingness or inability to try to find significant new assistance resources for the region – illuminating American power in an age of fiscal austerity.

This partial line towards Arab political change reflects a broader outlook on the role of the United States with regard to democratic change abroad that distinguishes Obama from his recent predecessors. This outlook is defined by (1) significant doubt about the ability of the United States to be a transformative actor in the current international context; (2) concern that if the United States pushes itself too directly or forcefully into sensitive political contexts it may discredit local democratic actors or otherwise distort a locally driven process of change; (3) a feeling that the United States will get a better hearing abroad on democracy if it approaches the issue through related, less politically sensitive issues such as justice, governance and development; (4) a willingness to see other countries take the lead and for the United States to be more in a supporting role in efforts to resist democratic backsliding or advance shaky transitions.

President Obama and his foreign policy team hold that this outlook represents not a turning away on democracy promotion but rather a tailoring of it to new international realities, such as the diminished weight of American power in an increasingly multipolar world and the increasing demand by citizens all over to see that democracy delivers tangible benefits. In the administration's view, insisting on democracy promotion based on older assumptions of the United States as a transformational power, the value of pointed ideological confrontation and the need for the United States to act first or alone would ultimately diminish rather than bolster its contribution on this topic. It is yet unclear whether their view will carry over the longer term in an American policy community and society long used to different assumptions about how the United States should stand and act with regard to advancing democracy in the world.

Notes

1 I would like to thank Alexandra Blackman and Diane de Gramont for their valuable research assistance. The arguments made in this chapter are elaborated further in Thomas Carothers, 'Democracy Policy Under Obama: Revitalization or Retreat?', Carnegie Endowment for International Peace, January 2012.

2 Thomas Carothers, 'U.S. Democracy Promotion During and After Bush' (Washington, DC: Carnegie Endowment for International Peace), 2007.

3 Larry Diamond, 'The Democratic Rollback', *Foreign Affairs*, March/April 2008.

4 Robert Kagan, *The Return of History and the End of Dreams* (New York: Vintage Books, 2008).

5 Christopher Hill, Interview with The Daily Rundown, MSNBC, 'End of U.S.-Combat Mission in Iraq', 31 August 2010.

6 Joshua Muravchik, 'The Abandonment of Democracy', *Commentary*, July 2009.

7 Douglas Schoen, 'Obama's Foreign Policy: Abandon Democracy', FOXNews.com, 1 September 2007.

8 'Democracy's Wane', *Wall Street Journal*, 12 January 2010.

9 'Clinton softens her tone on China', *The New York Times*, 20 February 2009.

10 Barack Obama, *National Security Strategy* (The White House, May 2010), p. 2, http://www.whitehouse.gov/sites/default/files/rss_viewer/national_security_strategy.pdf.

11 See www.foreignassistance.org

12 Barack Obama, 'Remarks of President Obama Marking Nowruz', The White House, 20 March 2011, and 'Remarks by the President in Celebration of Nowruz', The White House, 20 March 2009.

13 Hillary Clinton, 'Inaugural Richard C. Holbrooke Lecture on a Broad Vision of U.S.-China Relations in the 21st Century', Washington, DC, 14 January 2011.

14 For further discussion see Michael Swaine, *America's Challenge: Engaging a Rising China in the Twenty-First Century* (Washington, DC: Carnegie Endowment for International Peace, 2011), pp. 286–88.

15 Thomas Carothers and Richard Youngs, 'Looking for Help: Will Rising Democracies Become International Democracy Supporters?' (Washington, DC: Carnegie Endowment for International Peace), July 2011.

16 'US: Military Commission Trials for 9/11 Suspects a Blow to Justice', Human Rights Watch, New York, 4 April 2011.

17 See John Schwartz, 'Obama Backs Off a Reversal on Secrets', *The New York Times*, 9 February 2009; Adam Liptak, 'Justices Appear to Back U.S. on Material Witness Law', *The New York Times*, 2 March 2011; Michael Tarm, 'Rumsfeld Torture Lawsuit Moves Forward', *The Christian Science Monitor*, 10 August 2011.

BIBLIOGRAPHY

Borgward, Elizabeth, *A New Deal for the World: America's Vision for Human Rights* (Harvard University Press, 2005).

Carothers, Thomas, *Aiding Democracy Abroad* (Washington, DC: Carnegie Endowment for International Peace, 1999).

——, *The Clinton Record on Democracy Promotion* (Carnegie Endowment for International Peace, 2000).

——, *US Democracy Promotion During and After Bush* (Carnegie Endowment for International Peace, 2007).

——, *Democracy Policy Under Obama: Revitalization or Retreat?* (Carnegie Endowment for International Peace, 2012).

Chollet, Derek and Goldgeier, James, *America Between the Wars: From 9/11 to 11/9* (Public Affairs, 2008).

Cox, Michael, Ikenberry, G. John and Imoguchi, Takashi (eds.), *American Democracy Promotion: Impulses, Strategies, and Impacts* (Oxford University Press, 2000).

Diamond, Larry, *Promoting Democracy in the 1990s: Actors and Instruments, Issues and Imperatives* (Carnegie Commission on Preventing Deadly Conflict, 1995).

Dobbins, James *et al.*, *After The War: Nation-Building from FDR to George W. Bush* (RAND Corporation, 2008).

Dueck, Colin, *Reluctant Crusaders: Power, Culture, and Change in American Grand Strategy* (Princeton University Press, 2006).

Hunt, Michael H., *Ideology and U.S. Foreign Policy* (Yale University Press, 1987).

Ikenberry, G. John, *After Victory: Institutions, Strategic Restraint, and the Rebuilding of Order after Major Wars* (Princeton University Press, 2001).

——, *Liberal Leviathan: The Origins, Crisis and Transformation of the American World Order* (Princeton University Press, 2011).

Ikenberry, G. John *et al.*, *The Crisis of American Foreign Policy: Wilsonianism in the Twenty-first Century* (Princeton University Press, 2009).

Kagan, Robert, *Dangerous Nation: America's Place in the World from its Earliest Days to the Dawn of the Twentieth Century* (Alfred A. Knopf, 2006).

Lennon, Alexander T. J. (ed.), *Democracy in US Security Strategy: From Promotion to Support* (Center for Strategic and International Studies, 2009).

Lowenthal, Abraham (ed.), *Exporting Democracy: The United States and Latin America* (Johns Hopkins University Press, 1991).

Marsden, Lee, *Lessons from Russia: Clinton and US Democracy Promotion* (Ashgate, 2005).

McFaul, Michael, *American Efforts at Promoting Regime Change in the Soviet Union and then Russia: Lessons Learned* (CDDRL, Stanford Institute on International Studies, 2005).

——, *Advancing Democracy Abroad: Why We Should and How We Can* (Hoover Institution, 2010).

Mead, Walter Russell, *Special Providence: American Foreign Policy and How it Changed the World* (Routledge, 2002).

Muravchik, Joshua, *Exporting Democracy: Fulfilling America's Destiny* (AEI Press, 1991).

Nau, Henry, *At Home Abroad: Identity and Power in American Foreign Policy* (Cornell University Press, 2002).

Peceny, Mark, *Democracy at the Point of Bayonets* (Pennsylvania State University Press, 1999).

Quinn, Adam, *US Foreign Policy in Context: National Ideology from the Founders to the Bush Doctrine* (Routledge, 2010).

Robinson, William I., *Promoting Polyarchy: Globalization, US Intervention, and Hegemony* (Cambridge University Press, 1996).

Schwartzberg, Steven, *Democracy and U.S. Policy in Latin America During the Truman Years* (University Press of Florida, 2003).

Smith, Gaddis, *Morality, Reason and Power: American Diplomacy in the Carter Years* (Hill and Wang, 1986).

Smith, Tony, *A Pact with the Devil: Washington's Bid for International Supremacy and the Betrayal of the American Promise* (Routledge, 2007).

——, *America's Mission: The United States and the Worldwide Struggle for Democracy* (second edn., Princeton University Press, 2012).

Traub, James, *The Freedom Agenda: Why America Must Spread Democracy (Just Not the Way George Bush Did)* (Farrar, Straus and Giroux, 2008).

Williams, William Appleman, *The Tragedy of American Diplomacy* (revised edn., Norton, 1972).

Zakaria, Fareed, *The Future of Freedom: Illiberal Democracy at Home and Abroad* (W.W. Norton, 2004).

INDEX